The Creation of Value by Living Labour

A Normative and Empirical Study

Canut International Publishers

Berlin London Istanbul Santiago

Cheng Enfu   Wang Guijin   Zhu Kui

The Creation of Value by Living Labour
A Normative and Empirical Study

VOL. I

Translating Editor Alan Freeman   Sun Yexia

"B&R Book Program"
The Creation of Value by Living Labour: A Normative and Empirical Study
Volume I
by Cheng Enfu, Wang Guijin and Zhu Kui
Hui Lui and Sun Yexia, translators
 Alan Freeman and Sun Yexia, translating editors
Originally published (in Chinese) by Shanghai University of Finance and
Economics Press
Original Chinese Copyright © 2005
1st Chinese Edition (ISBN: 978-7-81098-525-3)

Canut International Publishers
Canut Turkey, Batı Mh. Karanfil Sk.. 10, Istanbul, Turkey
Canut Germany, Heerstr. 266, D-47053, Duisburg, Germany
Canut UK, 12a Guernsay Road, London E11 4BJ, England
Tel: +49-216-499-75-09
www.canutbooks.com / info@canutbooks.com

Paperback Edition
ISBN: 978-605-4923-25-0

About the Authors

Cheng Enfu, born in July 1950, is the Director of the Academy of Marxist Philosophy and director of Western Economic Studies Center of CASS, and the President of WAPE (World Association of Political Economy). Besides, Cheng Enfu is the chief editor of the journals *International Critical Thought* and *World Review of Political Economics* (World Association of Political Economics) published by Routledge and Pluto Press, respectively. His academic expertise is in theoretical economics. His other works include:

Enfu Cheng, Xin Xiangyang. "Fundamental elements of the China model", *International Critical Thought.* Volume 1, 2011 - Issue 1;

Enfu Cheng, "Four Theoretical Hypotheses of Modern Marxist Political Economy", *Social Sciences in China*, Autumn 2007, 3-17;

Enfu Cheng, Xiaoqin Ding. "A Theory of China's 'Miracle': Eight Principles of Contemporary Chinese Political Economy", *Monthly Review*, Jan 01, 2017;

Enfu Cheng, Yexia Sun. "Israeli Kibbutz: A Successful Example of Collective Economy", *World Review of Political Economy*, Vol. 6, No. 2 (Summer 2015), pp. 160-175;

Enfu Cheng, Jiankun Gao. "Comments on and Prospects for China's Current Macroeconomic Development: Ten Measures to Guide the Economic New Normal", *World Review of Political Economy*, 2016, 7;

Enfu Cheng, Zhongbao Wang. "Enriching and Developing Marxism in the Twenty-First Century in Various Aspects: Six Definitions of Marxism", *International Critical Thought,* 2018, 2;

Enfu Cheng. "Marxism and Its Sinicized Theory as the Guidance of the Chinese Model: The 'Two Economic Miracles' of the New China", *World Review of Political Economy,* Vol. 9, No. 3, Fall 2018;

Enfu Cheng. "La interdependencia económica y comercial como posible amortiguador del conflicto", *Vanguardia Dossier,* Vol.70, No. 4, 2018.

Wang Guijin, born in 1965, Doctor of economics, Shanghai University of Finance and Economics, currently works in the finance bureau of Huangshan city, Anhui Province.

Zhu Kui, born in 1974, Doctor of economics, is a tutor in Huazhong Agricultural University.

Figures and tables

Figures

Tables

Explanatory note

The research findings of this book are based on key research projects of the Ministries of Education of China and Shanghai led by Professor Cheng Enfu, president of the Academy of Marxist Philosophy and director of Western Economic Studies Center of CASS.

This is the first of two volumes, containing the first 11 of 18 chapters.

Professor Cheng was responsible for designing the structure and framework of this book. He also helped finalize the ideas in the first part of this book and made final revisions for the whole book. Professor Cheng contributed the first chapter. Wang Guijin, Professor Cheng's doctoral student, contributed Chapters 3–11. Zhu Kui, another doctoral student of Prof Cheng, contributed Chapters 12–18, which will be published in Volume II. Prof. Qi Guangying contributed Chapter 2.

The English translation was edited by Alan Freeman by the diligent aid of Sun Yexia.

Considering the complexity of the research projects, the authors of this book welcome criticisms should any inappropriateness occurs. The authors of this book may be reached at 65344718@vip.163.com.

Acronyms used in the text

GDP   gross domestic product

GNP   gross national product

MELT   monetary expression of labor time

OCC   organic composition of capital

R&D   research and development

S&T   science and technology/scientific and technological

Contents

Chapter 3

After Marx: research into the labor theory of value   65

Chapter 4

Main theoretical positions on productive labor   87

References

Foreword
Sound policy, sound theory, sound facts: A breath of fresh air from China

The world of Chinese Marxism is little known to Western Marxist scholars, let alone the general Anglophone reading public. This book is therefore of double importance. First, it serves as an introduction to Chinese economic thinking, for anyone wanting to study, with an open mind, China's economic successes and the principles that underlie them. Second, it will introduce Western Marxists to Chinese Marxist thinking.

Marxist economic analysis is integral to the policies underlying China's success. This may not be apparent to readers whose contact with Chinese economics is confined to university departments where the neoclassical canon prevails. However, Western "standard economics" is by no means the basis of Chinese political decision-making. Marxist thinking plays a major role in Chinese policy, and debates initiated by Marxists are at the forefront of the choices facing policy-makers, as this fascinating book shows.

For this very reason, the book is highly practical. In order to confront the complexity and uniqueness of China's economic miracle, the authors have developed Marxism in exciting and innovative ways.

The book thus provides an unparalleled introduction to the dynamism and breadth of the issues facing Chinese Marxists and Chinese economists in general. It extends the boundaries of Marxist political economy in creative and productive directions which are of world-wide importance, not in China alone.

Labor and technology: the worldwide significance of Chinese Marxism

This world-wide importance needs to be understood. Chinese scholars in general describe China's economy as "socialism with Chinese characteristics," which although a legitimate description, can lead to the misapprehension that China's achievements are unique to China and cannot be reproduced elsewhere.

However, though the new developments contributing to China's growth come together in a unique way in China, as in every nation, they are in and of themselves universal, and indeed are at the forefront of many Western controversies. The book's extensive discussion of creative labor, of scientific and technological labor, of research and development, managerial labor, and service labor in general, is applicable to any economy in the world today.

This highlights the book's timeliness. At its core is a detailed theoretical analysis of the nature and function of labor. This is in one sense as it should be, because labor is, and remains, the most universal resource of every economy.

But it is also the correct place to start studying the modern economy. When it tries to understand technology, Western "guru discourse" is apt to speak as if labor plays no role in it. Its focus is on the machinery – microchips, cellphones, nanotech, bioscience, new materials, and not least robotics.

However, those who take this perspective are looking in the wrong place. It is reminiscent of the joke about the drunk who has lost his keys at night. A passer-by asks him why he is only looking under the streetlamp. "Because that's where the light is," replies the drunk. The "light" of Western economic thinking surrounds the world of machines and the brilliance of their ever-expanding capabilities. Drunk with wonderment, it forgets to shed light on the humans that use the machines.

Radhika Desai and I (Desai and Freeman 2011; Freeman 2014b) call this the 'Machinocratic' outlook, by analogy with the Physiocrats who mistakenly thought that value came originally from nature. The Machinocratic outlook attributes to machinery the magical power to create value, which disables the capacity to understand the distinct role of labor.

The resulting discourses, especially those surrounding so-called "post-industrial society," omit from consideration a vital consequence of the increasing replacement of labor by machinery; labor is not vanishing from production, but is taking new forms. Specifically, as the mechanical, or "drudge," functions of labor are steadily replaced by machinery, research shows that successful producers do not simply discard labor, but specialize in new types of labor for which machines cannot substitute. Indeed, the rustbelt is, precisely, the site of those companies that have failed to keep up with what Moretti (2012) terms the "smart" revolution, and those short-sighted administrations that have failed to cultivate their labor force.

In short, machines do not eliminate labor; they transform it – in general, but not uniquely, into higher forms. The function of machinery is not to replace humans, but to allow them to become truly human.

The types of labor that come to the fore, through this process, are various. In some cases, labor is simply employed in preference to machinery because consumers prefer to interact with humans. Thus, robot football players are certainly technically possible, but not likely to draw large crowds. Equally, current social preferences are for human actors and human caregivers; robot childcare does not currently find a large market.

In other cases, labor performs tasks that machines are not suited for – notably functions such as creative and cultural production, research, and management. These categories can often overlap, which is why for example handmade goods are more highly prized than mass-produced ones. They are typically, but not exclusively, found in areas of production in which services are either central to the production process, or indeed constitute the product. This includes service delivery through media, such as the internet, in which the physical form of the medium takes second place to the "content" of what is enjoyed, and constitutes a use-value, for the consumer.

The critical point is that such production is conducted by humans because it is for consumption by humans, a feature of labor to which neoclassical economics is coldly indifferent. If, and when, humans were to find the company of robots preferable to that of their fellows, they would not be abolished by robots but would *become* robots, or create with robots some kind of joint society, as science-fiction writers such as Ian Banks have imagined, in which humans and robots form a continuum.

All this is yet fantasy, but it serves to illustrate the fundamental error of the neoclassical approach. As the authors show, with convincing empirical demonstrations drawn both from Chinese and world experience, in the here and now the key technological revolutions shaping the economy of the future are taking place not in the realm of machinery, but in the use that labor makes of it.

This work is thus first and foremost a book about labor – but, as a Star Trek fan might say, not as we know it. In focusing squarely on the modern transformation of labor, it exhibits the sophistication and originality of Chinese Marxism in a pathbreaking contribution to both Marxism, and Western knowledge of economics, innovation, and creativity.

The superiority of Marxism for the study of new technology

Marxism is eminently suited to this task. Labor is Marxism's most fundamental category, and Marxism is arguably the school of economic thought that both pays the most attention to labor, and understands it best.

This is not to say that labor receives no attention in the neoclassical tradition, and the authors make substantial reference to, and use of, non-Marxist studies and approaches where relevant. However, the neoclassical tradition also creates its own obstacles to the study of these new types of labor, which the book explains clearly. Foremost among these is its preoccupation with "things," with physical objects, which it mistakes for the social relations that allow these things to be bought and sold in the market.

Because of this confusion, which Marx termed "commodity fetishism," neoclassical economics further misunderstands production itself. Whereas for Marx, the concept of production requires a clear distinction between labor itself, and the objects that labor transforms – raw materials and means of production – neoclassical economics places the machinery and labor on an equal footing, calling them "factors of production." It views labor and machinery as completely interchangeable, assigning labor no special status.

The machinocratic view is an extension of this general commodity fetishism which also fetishizes *capital*, which it also misunderstands, viewing it as a simple conglomeration of productive assets rather than, as Marx put it, self-expanding value – value that can grow in the hands of private owners, thanks to the specific property relations of capitalism which confer on these owners the (theoretically) unrestricted right to everything their employees produce.

The "Midas touch" which converts lifeless machinery into self-expanding value is the work not of a king but of his subjects; capital expands only because it sets humans to work to transform nature with the use of the machines.

The misconception that capital expands on its own produces the phenomenon I have termed *capital worship* (Freeman 2014c), sadly as common among Western Marxists as among neoclassicals. Capital worship emphasizes only the revolutionary, transformative characteristics that capital exhibits during its feverish "long booms" in which innovation is fully harnessed by capital to bring about stunning technological revolutions: the Victorian industrial age, the "Golden epoch" of the *fin-de-siècle,* and not least, the postwar boom of modern times.

This wild optimism forgets one of Marx's most fundamental discoveries – that capitalism generates, from within itself, contradictions that it cannot resolve. Its "long booms" alternate with extended periods of "Great Depression" during which all the tensions and problems of an economy dominated by capital multiply, seemingly without end, eventually bursting out in tumultuous political transformations including wars, revolutions, and also times of great barbarity such as fascism.

The words "Great Depression" were first applied to the depression of 1870–93, which culminated in the new imperialism and eventually produced the Great War and the Russian revolution. The "Great Depression" of 1929–42 brought German and Japanese fascism, a new war, and the Chinese revolution. Currently, we are clearly not living in a phase of expansive capitalism, and many scholars now rightly speak of a third "Great Depression." Indeed, the current depression which, truth be told, dates back to the 1970s, is the deepest and longest that capitalism has ever known.

All the more reason, therefore, that those countries enduring the consequences of the stagnation, including rising poverty amidst obscene wealth, gross inequality, and increasingly repressive governments, need to learn from countries, notably China, that have so far escaped it.

Labor, property, and the creation and distribution of wealth

In contrast to the machinocratic approach, the authors meticulously analyze the role of distinct forms of labor, especially labor services, in which labor activities are directly consumed, either in production, as with scientific research or management consultancy services acquired from specialized companies and research centers, or in consumption, as with performance, health, hospitality, and caregiving.

The book draws on Professor Cheng's "New Four Theory" on value, wealth, and distribution, among which the "new living labor value theory" is particularly creative. Its basic idea is as follows. According to Marx, all labor that directly produces physical and mental or cultural goods for exchange in the markets, or direct services for the production and reproduction of labor goods, including internal management labor and scientific and technical labor, falls in the category of value-creating labor or labor of production. The theory precisely follows Marx's train of thought in his analysis of material production, and extends it to all social and economic sectors.

A second obstacle to understanding the specific role of labor in emergent labor-intensive technologies is the exclusive focus of neoclassical economics on private production. The underlying assumption is that of an ideal system of production conducted by entirely distinct legal entities, each producing only for the market and interacting with others only through the market.

But the results of mental productive activities such as scientific labor, creative labor, and even management, increasingly take the form a general acquisition for society, which is therefore inherently social. Marx referred to this as "general social labor." Private labor, within an enterprise, draws both on this general social labor and on the inputs that it acquires through the market. The same also applies to much cultural labor, which forms part of the process through which labor power itself is reproduced, not least shaping its productive powers. The most obvious example of this is education, which even neoclassicals have to recognize, up to a point, as a "public good."

China's economy, as the authors point out, involves a combination of ownership forms – public, private, and co-operative. Moreover, these ownership forms, under the definite and distinct conditions of Chinese society, are not necessarily the same as their formally identical equivalents in Western society, in exactly the same way that land ownership in 18th-century England, though formally the same as that prevailing in the French *ancien* régime of the same date, had already assumed capitalist characteristics far removed from those swept away in the revolution of 1789.

Even completely private capital operates under significantly greater and even qualitatively different public constraints in China than those found in fully capitalist economies, and is able to call on public resources that are not found in the same form. It is of course true that public constraints and resources exist in all societies, even those that proudly proclaim their capitalist character.

However much neoclassical economics ignores this fact, and speaks as if all production were as private as the monads of Leibnitz. As a result, it has to deploy elaborate circumlocutions to deny the obvious fact that government, education, health, caregiving, and countless other public activities not only contribute to the value and wealth of society, but form an indispensable mental infrastructure without which private production could not even take place, any more than it could subsist without air, water, or sunshine. Western theory does not even grant government, let alone the public realm, the status of a factor of production. No wonder it cannot account for China's growth.

A national policy that optimizes the general use of labor must take into account the contribution of each type of labor, not just to the enterprise that employs it, but to the general level of productiveness of the workforce, and the general well-being of society. In consequence, it cannot study the creation of wealth, or value, independent of its distribution. If any branch of labor is rewarded disproportionately to the actual contribution it makes to value, whether paid too much or too little, then this is clearly going to result in an inefficient allocation of labor types, because the laborers who create the value that society needs will either if underpaid fail to reproduce their kind, as with artists, or, if overpaid reproduce in parasitic numbers, as with financiers.

This is such an obvious principle that it is astonishing that economic theory has had to wait until now for principles governing the optimum distribution of revenue, articulated in terms of labor contribution, to be clearly enunciated and theoretically grounded.

The best example of the principle is the book's innovative treatment of the question that neoclassical economics studiously avoids: what is the appropriate reward for an owner of capital? Since neoclassical economics takes capitalism, and private ownership, for granted, it assumes without proof that the owner of any capital to which value accrues – which may be a productive enterprise, land, patent rights, or just a monetary instrument such as an equity – should be entitled to a revenue proportional to the size of the capital.

All the optimality theories with which the neoclassical student is bombarded, such as the Pareto theorem which "proves" that the market allocation of resources is optimal, take it for granted that no other system for the allocation of revenue might apply.

An alternative, socialist principle is that owners should be rewarded in proportion to their contribution to wealth – ultimately, their labor. This is the concept that the book develops, based on the "Gong theory of distribution."

How much value does labor create?

But what exactly does an owner contribute to production? The book shows that, historically as well as actually, capitalist ownership involves the *management* of capital. Marx himself studied the separation of profit into "labor of superintendence" – a wage paid to managers appointed by the owner – and "profit of enterprise" – the remainder, exploitatively expropriated by the owner in consequence of legal rights conferred by capitalism.

However, this separation is not as complete as modern management theory would have us believe. In small and medium enterprises, the owner frequently doubles as manager, and indeed, the "hard-working owner" is the Weberian ideal explanation for capitalism's success. On the other hand, as Piketty (2014) shows, modern corporate managers, above a certain level in the hierarchy, are paid enormous salaries far above their actual contribution to value. They are receiving a share of the profits, not a wage. Effectively they are integrated into the capital of the company, as is clear from institutions such as bonuses directly awarded in the form of share capital.

When this has been said, it is easy, but wrong, to dismiss all managerial salaries as bribes or disguised profit. Management is also a necessary function, and part of the collective social labor of the enterprise. Moreover, as the authors demonstrate with empirical examples, good management can and does make a considerable difference to the value realized by the enterprise. This is not just because managers help their enterprises to compete with each other in some kind of zero-sum game, but because they genuinely organize production, and tailor it to consumer needs and trends, in ways that optimize the creation and realization of value both for the enterprise and across the whole of society.

The task of Marxist analysis is therefore actually to measure this contribution effectively, thus providing workable instruments of policy. To this end the authors develop, and apply, Marx's concept of labor *complexity* and *intensity*.

Marx does not at all exclude, from the fundamental principle that labor is the sole source of value, the possibility and indeed the reality that different types of labor, or even the same labor organized in different ways, add different amounts of value in the same time. Labor is more *intense* if it creates more use-values in the same time as less intense labor by virtue of working harder, better, with less down time or by means of more effective cooperation. Labor is more *complex* if it creates more value by virtue of its product. Thus, for example, an artist whose work is valued highly in the market does not simply profit from a high reputation, but also supplies labor of a higher general quality – as the socialist art critic Ruskin noted well before his time – which is why creative labor is proving a major and growing source of value-added in both fully capitalist economies and the Chinese economy.

In Western Marxist literature on labor complexity, which is scant and tends towards superficiality, the distinction between complex and simple labor is widely confused with the distinction between concrete and abstract labor. Complex labor is not distinguished from simple or undifferentiated labor in the same sense that, for example, the labor of dancers is different from the labor of carpenters. It does not create a particular product, nor accomplish a particular function in production. It is labor that, as a result of being more skilled, or by fulfilling a higher social function, creates more value in the *same* branch of production as less complex labor. A carpenter who has passed through seven years of training is simply a better carpenter than an apprentice. An inspiring ballet dancer who has devoted her life to the rigorous demands of the conservatory is normally a better dancer than a novice. They therefore produce more value.

The labor of the modern manager, the authors demonstrate, is not only necessary but complex, and makes a measurable contribution to the value of the product and also to the wealth of society. Of course, a bad manager contributes less than a good one – as is true of any labor. Nevertheless, it is possible on a scientific basis to measure management's contribution and reward it accordingly.

At first sight, this seems no different from the neoclassical principle of reward according to marginal productivity – until we realize that it is proposed not merely as a means to calculate appropriate management remuneration, but an alternative to rewarding capital according to its size. This is a radical, not a minor difference. Applied systematically, it would deprive capital of most, if not all, of its privileges. It constitutes, without question, what Marx and Engels in the *Communist Manifesto* termed a "despotic inroad into property."

But the issue of labor complexity, and the appropriate reward to labor in different branches of the economy, surfaces in many other places. It is, indeed, a perfectly general issue because mental and service labor, which dominate the new technologies, are inherently social. Once a new theorem or formula exists, or a new song is released, any human being and any enterprise has a call on it. Indeed, the attempt to restrict access to knowledge and culture by means of copyright and patent legislation is a major expression of the limits of the commodity form. When Trump thunders against China for "stealing" US technology, apart from ignoring America's own "theft" of knowledge from scientists the world over, he forgets the most fundamental characteristic of mental acquisitions, which is that they perform best when made available to all.

This is evident for scientific labor, everywhere acknowledge as a driver of innovation and productivity growth. Neoclassical economics has never fully mastered the understanding of its role in national and enterprise development, even though neoclassical economists who specialize in the issue have contributed to our knowledge of the interrelations involved, especially between innovation and research and development (R&D) (see for example

Freeman 2015). The underlying theoretical issue, addressed in this book, is a proper analysis of the specific characteristics of the labor of research.

This need is equally evident in relation to the most dynamic driver of modern economic growth, namely creative labor. Its role in the production of value is such a mystery to neoclassical thinkers that it is almost universally branded, especially by conservative administrations, as a luxury and a drain on the public purse, and made the first target of austerity. Apart from the moral crime of such policies, they are also profoundly economically ignorant, because they seek to curtail the growth of one of the most dynamic growth sectors of modern society by restricting the general conditions of its existence.

Theory, debate, and policy

Finally, the third misconception that this book abolishes is the myth, assiduously cultivated by Western propagandists and redoubled in the wake of Trump's trade war offensive, that China consists of an authoritarian regime in which there are no debates and in which dissent is impossible.

These myths serve the principal purpose of providing a justification for unfair and warlike measures. They have, however, a collateral – and perhaps not altogether unintended – effect. They give rise to the illusion, or pretense, that since the reason for China's success is a "dictatorial" and suppressive state system, dictatorship is required in the West. Western capital is seeking a solution, however far removed from the both its myths and the reality of China, which grants it powers it does not presently possess. Sections of Western capital, at present thankfully in a minority, are in short groping towards fascism.

How long until Trump supporters start telling ordinary Americans that in order to compete with China, America must ruthlessly suppress not merely immigrants and racialized minorities, but "foreign-inspired" internal opposition, "un-American" civil organizations and "disruptive" trade unionists?

The myth ignores a vital fact: Communist China is the site of passionate, dynamic debates whose consequences have included, throughout its history, profound and important changes of policy. This book is evidence of that fact: authored by senior figures and experts, it does not simply celebrate what is now happening in China, but argues for change. Its proposals include many that are hotly contested. However, these debates are not conducted over the president's twitter-feed but by means of serious, respectful, scientific engagement.

Policy in China is in short *contested*; the debates addressed in this book are therefore not matters of dry academic interest, but deal with profound theoretical issues, backed by solid empirical study, with enormous practical significance.

No better recommendation can be found.

A note on translation

My contact with this work began when I was asked to write an introduction to the English translation. I accepted readily but soon realized that to ensure the work could be accessible to a Western audience, a significant amount of editing was needed. In the course of editing the work, I undertook to work also on the translation. In its original form this was technically of a high standard, and in particular, at pains to be as faithful as possible to the original. However, Chinese grammatical forms are significantly different from English, to such an extent that a technically correct translation can be far from readable. In addition, because the authors are at the forefront of new topics, they have on occasions constructed new terms that are critical to understanding the meaning, but which are not always best rendered by a simple dictionary translation.

My knowledge of Chinese being extremely limited, I worked for several years with helpful scholars, most especially Sun Yexia, without whose indefatigable processing of my insistent questions, I doubt the book would have appeared.

It is perfectly possible, even likely, that the final version, produced in this way, may fail, even in critically important respects, to render correctly the scientific insights and discoveries of the authors. For all such failings, I am personally responsible.

Alan Freeman
Geopolitical Economy Research Group, University of Manitoba

1
Introduction

Why this book?

As a new epoch dawns, the role of labor is becoming ever greater, and ever more diverse, confronting the Marxist theory of labor and value with bewildering new problems and challenges.

Mechanization and automation have gradually displaced manual labor in production, resulting from the rapid development of science and technology (S&T). In developed countries around the world, up to 95% of formerly manual activities have been automated. By the early 1990s, there were more than 400,000 robots in the world, bringing about a tremendous change in the way labor functions. The number of front-line workers had dwindled away, leading to a sharp decrease in living labor in material production. As early as 1977, mental laborers had become 50.1% of the US workforce. According to estimates made in 2008, the percentage of frontline workers in the United States had by that year dipped to less than 20%. This figure was forecast to fall to 10% by 2010. Moreover, working hours were reducing. These were forecast to fall in the developed countries to an average of 35 hours per week by 2010.

How can we apply Marx's theory of value to explain the new issues arising from such scientific and technological (S&T) progress? For instance, if living labor turns out to be a declining input, would that mean it had ceased to be the sole factor in social value creation? Could other productive factors be sources of value creation? Since the percentage of mental labor has become dominant in economic production, do S&T mental laborers also create value? If the answer is yes, what are the similarities and differences in the value created by mental and manual laborers?

The advance of S&T, and the resulting improvement of the means of production, have contributed to a significant growth of labor activity in the economy. In most countries around the world, the structure of the national economy has undergone dramatic change, as evidenced by the shrinking volume of material production, typically manifested in the declining share of agriculture and industry in the economy as a whole. As a result, labor engaged in these two sectors has shrunk, while labor in the service sector has risen, as a proportion of the economy. As a consequence, the proportion of mental labor input in the economy, typically in service industries, has increased progressively, while that of manual labor, typically engaged in the material goods sector, has dwindled. Currently, the share of the agricultural sector in the economy the developed countries is well under 5%, while that of the service sector is above 60%. In 2001, the proportion of China's service industry reached 33.6%. The theoretical issues that arise from these phenomena are as follows. Is it plausible that value-creating labor is strictly limited to material goods production when the service sector occupies such a large share of the economy? Can labor in the service sector be treated as productive of value? Does labor engaged in education and cultural production also create value?

A third challenge is that, with the increase in productivity, elements of production such as commodities, capital, technologies, and information, as well as human talents, are moving rapidly between countries on a larger and larger scale. This allows resources to be allocated in the most efficient way. As the economies of each region become more and more interdependent, the pace of world economic integration accelerates at an unprecedented rate. Let's take world trade in tangible goods and service to illustrate this point. At the end of the Second World War, world trade totaled $60 billion; by 2000, it had risen to $7.8 trillion. The World Trade Organization (WTO) then predicted that by 2005, the total volume of trade would reach $10 trillion.

The driving forces of this near complete economic global integration are the multinational corporations. According to the United Nations (UN), by the end of 1999, there were about 63,000 multinational corporations with more than 700,000 subsidiaries and affiliated enterprises scattered around the world, forming a huge production and distribution system. It is estimated that multinational corporations monopolized one-third of world production, 90% of foreign direct investment (FDI), two-thirds of total trade volume and 70% of the world's patent and technology transfers. The volume of sales generated by some multinational corporations even surpassed the gross national product (GNP) of some small countries. To ensure smooth development, these behemoths need high-level expert management teams. This is where the theoretical problems arise: if the management of a modern enterprise is so important, what is the role of the labor in management? Can the labor of management create value? How does it differ from the labor of production in other fields?

Finally, China is still in the primary stage of socialism and has adapted by developing a socialist market economy. Since China's overall productivity and level of general management remains low, we should expect that its relations of production will have some unique characteristics. China needs to uphold and improve the basic economic system of socialism in which public ownership dominates, side by side with other economic sectors. China unswervingly encourages, supports, and guides the development of the non-public sector; however, the public sector still depends on state capital. Therefore, there is every reason for other types of capital to operate, while the leading role of labor has yet to be established.

For this reason, production based on independent (autonomous) labor cannot be dominant in the whole society. Laborers have to enter the job market and find employment. By combining their labor with means of production, they can engage in social production and the market can allocate labor resources and other productive factors. Under the socialist market system, a product cannot be a social product in a real sense unless it is publicly traded on the market. This differs dramatically from what Karl Marx envisaged, according to which neither value nor trade would exist in a socialist society, and the means of production would be collectively owned. Production would be based on autonomously united labor, and products and services would be distributed proportionally to the labor that each individual supplies as an input. But in a market economy, most products trade through an intermediary: the market. The real value of a socially produced good will therefore manifest itself through trade in the market.

Since the characteristics of China's current relations of production differ from those of socialism as envisaged by the classical theorists of Marxism, a detailed theoretical study of these issues is required. Specifically, we seek to answer the following questions. In China's current phase of social development, what relations hold between value creation and value distribution? Is labor value theory[1] a basis for distributing goods according to labor input? In privately owned enterprises, does management labor still have a dual function, part creative of value and part unproductive? How should we view such concepts as the "labor of capitalists," and what is their relation to exploitation? The new circumstances present new challenges to the validity of Marx's theory of value, and demand from us a scientific interpretation of this theory as it applies in these new circumstances.

Since Marx's labor value theory forms the basis of Marxist political economy, it should be the starting point in revising socialist political economy. Faced with its academic prominence and political importance, even capitalist economists and politicians accept that the theoretical constructs of Marxist political economy and communism cannot simply be overturned unless Marx's labor value theory is shown to be fundamentally flawed.

In our opinion, with the new developments in society, previous theories either claiming to be based on or inspired by Marx's ideas, or to present valid interpretations of Marx's own theory, have failed to address the issues discussed above. Various theoretically fuzzy constructs have emerged as a result. Although these theories have been crowned with many different titles, they can generally be divided into two categories: living labor theories of value, and theories of the value of productive factors. We argue that if we are determined to remain within the boundaries of Marx's labor value theory, we must adhere to the notion that value is created by living labor. We should, while adhering to this core concept, continue to perfect and develop the theory, providing a scientific interpretation of classical theory while taking new circumstances into account.

Abundant research into the labor value theory has emerged both in China and abroad. However, many issues remain unresolved. Some current

1   Editor's note: in this book, the terms "labor theory of value" and "labor value theory" are used interchangeably.

16

research, while addressing some issues raised by the current economic situation, neither adheres to the core concepts of Marx's theory nor develops it. Other research adheres to these core concepts but fails to address one or more issues relating to the real world of today. Still others claim to adhere to and develop the theory, but lead to radically opposed conclusions. We argue that it is imperative to deepen research into Marxist and labor theories of value. The purpose is to extend the boundaries of this body of theory, and apply it when analyzing economic issues or guiding economic development.

In terms of current practice, the development of China's socialist market economy also needs appropriate theoretical guidance. Yet research into socialist economic theory has lagged far behind practice. Since the contribution of those laborers who do not directly manage production operation is rising, we have to find an effective way to generate enthusiasm among mental laborers, laborers employed in enriching people's spiritual life or providing services for society, S&T laborers and management laborers. All these laborers are the engine of China's economic growth. We therefore believe that all concerned should deepen their understanding of labor and of the labor value theory. Furthermore, an effective mechanism providing both incentives and limits, tailored to business leaders and the backbone of China's S&T corps, has to be created and perfected. Finally, because of the significance of the Chinese experience for the theory and practice of development as a whole, our research findings have practical implications for many other societies in different stages of development.

Questions, methods, and origins

Theoretical and practical issues concerning value creation by new living labor

With the increasing role of S&T, with economic globalization, as the uses of labor becomes wider and more diverse, and as the development of China's socialist market economy throws up new issues, a range of labor theories of value have begun to compete for validity in explaining the new phenomena. This obliges us to provide a scientific explanation of the implications for labor under these new circumstances. On the basis of the social development of the capitalist countries of their time, scientific labor value theory was formulated by theorists who had critically assimilated the essentials of classical economics. Since social conditions have dramatically changed, Marxist economists need to evaluate whether and how Marx's labor value theory applies under the new circumstances, whether its central concepts can be applied to explain current social situations, and how to use and develop it. For this reason, theoretical and practical issues concerning value creation by living labor are central to this book.

As noted, due to rising labor productivity and scientific and technological advance, the extent and variety of the uses of labor have grown. Value creation by productive labor is no longer limited to the production of material goods, and has indeed extended to spiritual service provision and services in general. Likewise, productive labor is no longer confined to manual labor. The mental labor of innovation, management, and so on plays an increasing role. Although automation has reached a high level, value is still created by living labor. The materialized labor arising from the application of S&T, knowledge, and many other non-labor productive factors does not *per se* create value. But since labor is used in ways that have changed dramatically, it should be expected that it will create value in ways that exhibit special features not seen in previous decades.

How this book approaches the problem

We combine abstract with concrete analysis. It is to be expected that abstract analysis will play a special role when researching social and economic situations. This is particularly relevant to value creation by living labor. Unless we eliminate less important factors, we risk missing the regularities hidden behind the veil of complex real life. We can then identify key variables, conduct in-depth research into the issues raised within each specific sector of economy where labor creates value, and deepen our understanding of the different ways it operates.

We combine dynamic with static analysis, with dynamic analysis dominating. Comparative static analysis aims to study how value is created, and how material is converted into product, without considering time or the process of production. Dynamic analysis, in contrast, introduces the time factor and seeks to analyze the creation of value of a product at one or several points of time. It also aims to find out which is the determining factor.

We combine empirical with theoretical analysis, with empirical analysis dominating: we investigate whether labor creates value in each new sector, and how the magnitude of this value is determined, by starting from empirical analysis and developing the theoretical conclusions.

Dialectical materialism is our essential research method. However, quantitative and qualitative research methods will also be incorporated. By analyzing how labor creates value in management and innovation historically as well as economically, our aim is to identify the determining factors that influence value creation. We used some econometric models for quantitative analysis.

We employ comparative analytical methods: in studying the different sectors where value is created we used a cross-sectional method, comparing the contribution of labor in these sectors in China with some of the most important developed countries.

A new unitary theory of the value contribution of living labor and a new value transformation thesis, with the "four new principles" as base

This book seeks a scientific interpretation of the interconnections between essence and phenomenon belonging to value, wealth, and wealth distribution. To this end it elaborates four new principles on which the argument rests: the living labor value theory, meaning the value created by productive labor; the total factor theory of wealth, meaning all social wealth and use-values of commodities realized by total factor productivity and the total factor economy; the multi-ownership theory of distribution, meaning the multiple forms of wealth distribution based on capital factors or labor input dictated by various types of ownership; and the theory of form and essence, applied to wealth distribution based on factor contribution. In form, the distribution of wealth is based on the value and wealth created by the owners of productive factors, but in essence, the distribution of wealth is based on the ownership of productive factors.

The authors hope that based on the four new principles, this book will give an overview of a unitary theory of living labor. We hope its findings transcend and develop the original unitary theory of living labor theory which was developed by Marx, facilitating a clear distinction between this new unitary theory and various other theories of value.

This is a comprehensive work. Presenting in-depth research into value-creating labor in material goods production, cultural goods production, and the service industries in general, as well as in scientific innovation and management, it covers most areas of social life in terms of value creation by labor in the current stage of social development. Most previous research into this issue covered only one or some of these areas.

A notable feature of this book is its emphasis on the empirical or quantitative method. To estimate the value created by labor in each area considered, we adopt a variety of econometric models. This leads to sounder research and more accurate estimates. Abundant quantitative analyses and numerous case studies further strengthen the accuracy of the theoretical logic inherent in our approach. This contrasts with the great majority of research into the labor value theory which is limited to abstract theoretical analysis, empirical or quantitative studies being few and far between.

The book includes new findings. It delves into the changed role of labor by drawing on research into Marxist labor value theory conducted by economists both at home and abroad. Some novel ideas result. For example, in our theoretical analysis of the conversion of complex to simple labor, we found it to be path dependent; this conversion was achieved by tracing the evolution of complex labor rather than skipping over its lower levels. Another example is that in investigating the value contribution of scientific labor, we found it to be different from that in material goods production in the conventional sense. We believe the law that determines the value of labor in science has changed to some extent. Specifically, the value created by labor is subject not solely to the influence of socially necessary labor time, but also to that of individual labor time, which is widely believed to be the factor that produces scientific and technical goods.

This book transcends traditional comparative static analysis and in so doing, casts further doubt on the thesis that labor productivity bears little relation to value creation by labor. The authors hope this will deepen the readers' understanding of labor and the labor value theory. In affirming the thesis that advances in S&T will lead to the increase in labor productivity,

20

this book also argues that such advances must lead to an increase in labor's complexity, dexterity, and capacity to coordinate. We elaborate the concept of labor intensity time, and make it a tool to test the theoretical validity of the proposition that complex labor creates greater value. We hypothesize that this can increase not only the amount of use-value, but the amount of value created per unit of time. Therefore, a dynamic analysis of labor value theory helps us understand that the value of commodities is not necessarily negatively related to labor productivity. Under certain circumstances, they can be positively related to each other.

Combining logic and history, this book treats the process of transformation of value into price of production by splitting it into two phases: static transformation and dynamic transformation. Consequently, two econometric models are created. These are not intended as fully developed models but as a means to conduct a historical analysis of the essential relationship between these variables at different stages of capitalist economic development, after converting constant and variable capital to value and price of production based on Marx's methodology. In doing so, the authors hope to reveal new characteristics of the static transformation model. Our research suggests that a proper understanding of Marx's labor value theory is the key to an understanding of value transformation. The transformation of value into price of production exists in history, and conforms to logic. Karl Marx was therefore right in his analysis of value transformation in Volume III of *Capital*. The only thing that matters is that he dealt with this issue in his own way.

Framework and contents

As noted, the authors see it as imperative that contemporary Marxist scholars adhere to Marx's labor value theory and make this the premise of their research. Marxist scholars should also combine theory with practice, employing both quantitative and qualitative research methods. We argue that these goals should be achieved by examining the socialist market economy and theories of it, distilling Marxist value theory as well as creating scientific economic models.

In consequence, the main topic of this book is the development of the labor form, starting from its widening use and diversity. We consider labor value theory as it applies to material production, cultural production, and the service industries from the standpoint of its widening use. We consider the role of simple and complex labor, mental labor, and physical labor, as well as labor in management and S&T, from the standpoint of the diversity of its forms.

Key viewpoints and conclusions

Marx's theory of value has what we call a "three in one" character: its construction is based on the critique of capitalist economics, the starting point of political economy. Therefore, the theory reflects both its scientific and class character. Meaningful research is required to eliminate misinterpretation and misunderstanding of Marx's theory, such as the idea that "Labor only creates value in material production."

Marx held that only products created by living labor for the purpose of trade in the market possess value, whereas the simple transformation of the form of the product's value does not create value. The authors argue that labor engaged in producing material goods or making cultural commodities for trade in the market, or that provides service inputs to the production or reproduction of material goods and cultural products, or that is engaged in management and innovation, is value-creating: that is to say, productive labor. This thesis does not contradict the core idea of Marxist philosophy, and follows the way that Marx studies value creation in the area of material goods production. However, the new thesis extends the implications of Marx's thoughts to virtually all areas of economic production, arguing that value is created by labor that produces tangible goods, intangible goods, and cultural goods; in services; and indirectly by the unproductive labor involved in the production and reproduction of the labor force.

The book articulates a total factor theory of wealth: that is, use value. Living labor is the only source of value but in the labor process, it is not the only factor required to create value. Other productive factors are required for laborers to engage in meaningful production, to provide real services, or in general to provide the many types of use value that people need. These

22

productive factors include land, capital, technology, and information, as well as natural resources and the ecological environment. Wealth is directly created by all relevant productive factors. The total factor theory of wealth simply recognizes that in modern societies, value creation requires an efficient combination of an abundant, well-educated labor force and the most advanced means of production, combined with efficient management which fulfills the functions of organization, scientific research, education which imparts knowledge to laborers, information which connects laborers from different scattered locations, and the environmental factor which acts as a constraint on production. To meet the growing and diverse material and cultural needs of the people, we should develop the potential of all those productive factors which contribute to the creation of wealth.

The book articulates a multi-ownership theory of distribution. Currently, China pursues an income distribution system under which labor input is dominant, but a variety of modes of distribution coexist. The combination of this unique distribution system with productive factors forms the bedrock of the income distribution system of the socialist market economy. Broadly speaking, the distribution of income to productive factors subsumes the distribution of income based on the dominant factor – labor power. This becomes particularly clear when we understand how this differs from labor. Labor is an independent productive factor, but work-based income distribution when governed by the market mechanism does not distinguish it from other productive factors, so that it is labor power that participates in the distribution of income, being entitled to receive value or money in accordance with its contribution to output. We, however, seek a logic for distributing income in accordance with labor input *per se*, separate from other productive factors.

We consequently develop the notion of "distributing income in accordance with the contribution of each productive factor." This notion is usually presented as being based on the *size* of the productive factors engaged in wealth or value creation. We argue however that when living labor is recognized as the source of value, income should be distributed in accordance with the contribution of the *owners* of these factors.

Constrained by its class nature, Western capitalist economics mistakes the form of this concept for its essence. The Shanghai school of economic theory, which informs the authors of this book, is committed to a notion of its essence informed by the "Three Represents."[2] It thus not only acknowledges the validity of the notion, but also reveals its economic characteristics. The notion can best be understood and applied by integrating its form and its essence. The logic and the interpretation of the Shanghai school of this notion of income distribution is fundamentally different from that offered by Western economic theorists.

We highlight the notion of high-intensity labor in S&T as well as in management. The improvement in labor's complexity, coordination capacity, and intensity is highly indicative of its increasing contribution to value. It is generally believed that labor in S&T is highly innovative and complex by its very nature, and characterized by intense mental activities. Therefore, the value created by labor in S&T is in principle very large. It is largely determined by the individual labor time required to make the commodity first, before productivity has improved.

As a result, the law that the amount of a commodity value is determined by socially necessary labor time diverges somewhat from its normal logic. Wealth distribution should be biased toward those supposed to have made the largest contribution to innovation and its management. Clearly, this arises from a market-oriented type of wealth distribution based on labor input. We argue that both complex and simple labor are abstract by nature,

2 The Shanghai school is a school of Marxist economics in China, founded in 2004 by Professor Cheng Enfu. The "Three Represents" is a theory enunciated by China's former leader Jiang Zemin to describe what the Communist Party stands for. According to the Baidu encyclopedia he expressed this in February 2000 as follows: "the Party has always represented the developmental needs of China's advanced production capacity, represented the progressive direction of China's advanced culture, and represented the fundamental interests of the broad majority; in establishing the development of the correct lines, principles and policies, the Party has untiringly struggled to realize the Nation and People's fundamental interests. Humanity has come again into a new century and a new millennium. In these new historical conditions, how our Party can best dispatch these 'Three represents' is an important issue that all comrades, especially the Party's senior cadres, need to consider deeply."

but that complex labor is an aggregate of simple labors. The reason is that the intensity time-period of complex labor is greater than that of simple labor. The evolution of complex labor generally follows a path from simple to complex labor and then to even more complex labor. This is determined by the market mechanism behind the backs of the laborers.

We develop the notion that the labor of production-related management on the part of capitalists may also create value: although international capital and China's private capital may have an exploitative aspect, it is subject to restriction and regulation to some extent by socialist countries like China, and will continue to exist and develop within a scope circumscribed by the state authorities. However, this situation is largely determined by current productive forces and relations of production. If the capitalists assume the responsibility of managing productions, we argue that part of the capitalists' labor may also create value (excluding such practices as making laborers work overtime or falling into arrears on laborers' payments). Although the form taken by wealth distribution based on the possession of capital has a strong exploitative coloration, it can be empirically proved that labor of this type in management does create value, and enables an enterprise to gain an edge over its competitors by driving down production costs.

We articulate a new thesis regarding changes in labor productivity and the magnitude of value. The fact that labor productivity is inversely related to the magnitude of value rests on a series of rigorous assumptions. Since the increase in labor productivity will inevitably coincide with an increase in labor intensity, and the intensity time-period of labor will diverge from the natural time-period, it is reasonable to suppose that an increase in labor productivity has the potential to increase the magnitude of value of commodities. Therefore, labor productivity can, under certain circumstances, be positively related to the magnitude of value.

We establish a dynamic analytical framework for the study of value transformation, arguing that a meaningful study of transformation must combine mathematical logic with historical and real logic, and then conduct a dynamic analysis of the transformation process from value to production cost. This approach also views social reproduction as a continuous process. It suggests that the relationship between overall production costs and overall value at any point in time must affect production costs and the value of the input factors in the next cycle of reproduction. This should be expected to affect overall production costs and overall value. The two "invariance" equations then surface in a complex way.

Structure of the book

This book contains an introduction, a main body, and a reference section, and is divided into two parts.

In this Introduction, we have outlined the research background and formulated the primary research questions, namely the theoretical and practical issues concerning value creation by labor in the new historical circumstances in which we find ourselves. We have outlined the research method we will adopt and explained what is new about our ideas. We complete this overview with a summary of the contents of the remaining chapters.

Chapter 2 reviews the foundational literature on the labor value theory. Structurally, the book devotes much space to elaborating on the key points of Marx's theory of value. He developed this theory after critically absorbing the central ideas of classical economics. For this reason, this book briefly introduces the labor theories of value proposed by such classical economists as William Petty, Adam Smith, and David Ricardo.

Chapter 3 then examines the reactions of Western and Chinese economists, their findings, and the debates that have animated their discussions.

Chapter 4 outlines the main theses of the productive labor value theory. We examine the way that patterns of labor have been transformed, from the standpoint of its extent and diversity. Despite these transformation, we find that living labor, contributed by laborers, remains the only factor that creates value. Together with other productive factors, it can create wealth – that is, use value. Materialized labor does not create value. In the debate on the labor value theory, we argue that the conversion of complex to simple labor is one of the most difficult issues. After a review of the relevant literature, this chapter sets out a distinct perspective on this question.

Chapter 5 deals with value creation by labor in material goods production, in relation to which many of the basic theoretical issues appear. This chapter first deals with value creation by labor in the context of automation. It then focuses on the relationship between the amount of value and labor productivity. It explains why labor productivity is not necessarily inversely related to the magnitude of value, as conventional wisdom suggests. The chapter then deals with productive and non-productive labor. Finally, it examines exploitation in the light of the theory of surplus value.

Chapter 6 deals with value creation in cultural production. After a close examination of culture, cultural products, and their characteristics, we explore both the way value is created and the demand for, and supply of, labor in this sector. The chapter includes an empirical study of value creation by labor in the cultural industry, and concludes with a comparative study of value creation in a number of different countries.

Chapter 7 deals with value creation in the service industries. We briefly review Marx's concept of service as well as that developed by Western scholars. We then analyze the classification and scope of the service industries, focusing primarily on the mechanism of value creation before proceeding to examine the particular nature of labor productivity in the service industries. A linear regression model is used to analyze value creation by labor in the Chinese and American service sectors.

Chapter 8 focuses on value creation in S&T. Employing the same method as Chapter 6, we first classify the labor engaged in S&T and analyze its characteristics. We then propose a quantitative and qualitative theoretical framework for studying value creation by scientific and technological labor, before conducting an evaluative study of value creation using Zhongguancun Hi-Tech Park as an example. We finally undertake a comparative study of value creation by labor in S&T across the world.

Chapter 9 deals with value creation by labor in management. After examining the concept in depth, we look at the dual nature of labor in this area, and analyze laborers' qualifications and ability. The central feature of this chapter is the presentation of the authors' views on the "labor of capitalists." A "dependence theory" is elaborated which determines the exact amount of value of labor in management. We then test this with what we term the "second-cost" model, and conclude with an empirical study of value creation using the Handan Steel Corporation as an example.

The second volume, which is in preparation, will deal with the theoretical issue of the transformation of values into prices, a critical pivot of Marx's labor value theory.

2
The history of value theory

The next two chapters summarize the literature on value theory that will be drawn on in this work. The current chapter is a historical survey of value theory from ancient times until the marginal revolution. The next chapter deals specifically with modern reaction to labor value theory after Marx.

Early value theories

Theories in Ancient Greece

The concept of value is the most fundamental in economics. As the most abstract category of the commodity economy, its emergence and development are closely related to the latter's.

Ancient Greek culture bred modern western civilization, and ancient Greek economic thinking laid the foundation of modern economic theory. We can reasonably say that value theory starts in Ancient Greece.

From the 8th to the 6th century BC, Ancient Greece gradually developed from a clan society to an association of slave city-states. Though the natural economy predominated, a commodity economy emerged. Currency was widely used; commerce developed, especially foreign trade, and both merchant and usurer's capital came into being. The city states were in different stages of economic development. Athens was the most prosperous thanks to its favorable geographical location. By the 6th century BC, it had already become the center of handicraft industry, and its harbor Piraeus developed into the trade center of the Mediterranean region in the 5th century BC. From the 5th to the 4th century BC, currency exchange between city states, currency management, and usury became the prevailing commercial activities. This economic environment nurtured many outstanding philosophers: the economic theories of Xenophon, Plato, and Aristotle, whose ideas on value we now review, exerted great influence on subsequent generations.

Xenophon

Xenophon (around 430–355 BC), a student of Socrates, was well known for two works: *Economics* (2014) and *De Vectigalibus* (2014). *Economics* was the first monograph on economics in ancient Greece. He noticed that commodities had two functions, use and exchange. In economics, he took as example a flute, which could either be played or sold. It was a treasure to the person who sold it: he didn't know how to play it, but did know how to use the currency obtained from the sale. This was arguably the first discussion in the history of value theory of the two aspects of the commodity.

Xenophon noticed that the fluctuation of supply and demand influenced the price of commodities, and that the price further influenced the distribution of social labor. In *De Vectigalibus,* he mentioned that if copper was over-produced, its price would fall, and the producers would go bankrupt. If the price of agricultural products fell, producers would abandon agriculture and change to other industries where they could make more profits. In this initial stage, people were thus trying to understand market mechanisms, including supply and demand, and the factors affecting production.

Plato

Plato (430–347 BC) was also a student of Socrates. His thoughts were mainly reflected in *The Republic* (1986) and *Laws* (2001).

Plato was the first to propose the concept of value, in his *Laws*. Value, he argued, was an objective quality or inherent attribute of the product. The price of a product should accord with its value; otherwise, it was against the principle of equity. "When a person makes a product, the law requires both the person and the seller not to increase the price at will, but to ask for the price that is equal to its value; for a crafter definitely knows the value of the product." Aristotle held similar opinions.

Aristotle

The economic thought of Aristotle (384–322 BC), based on previous ancient Greek thinking, is mainly reflected in the *Politics* (2007) and the *Nicomachean Ethics* (2003).

30

Aristotle pointed out that each article has two properties: use and exchange. He took shoes as an example. Some people make shoes to wear, and others make shoes to exchange for money or food. He thought that *use* was the inherent or essential property of an article, while *exchange* was not an inherent property, for in early history the article was not produced for exchange.

Aristotle was the first to analyze the form of commodity value, in the *Nicomachean Ethics*. In his discussion of equity, he introduces the ethical principle of reward according to proportion, to which exchange must conform. Since the two parties exchange different articles, the amount of each article must be equivalent proportionally. A standard is therefore required to compare the exchanged articles in accordance with the principles of equivalence and equity. He thought this standard was supplied by the demand of each party for the exchanged articles, which was the connection between exchanges. How should this be expressed? He thought that in real life or by custom, currency was the universal expression of demand, so that it could express the equality of the exchanged articles. For example, suppose three people, A, B, and C, exchange with each other. A has a house, B has 10 minas,[1] and C has a bed. If we take a, b, and v to be the magnitudes that each brings to the exchange, and if $a = b/2$ and $c = b/10$, and if C exchanges the bed for A's house, then 5 beds = 1 house, so that 5 beds equals some quantity of currency, and 1 house equals the same quantity of currency. The equivalence of the bed and the house was reflected in their mutual equivalence to the currency. Aristotle thus identified the form of value –currency.

The definition of fair price

Fair price subsequently exerted great influence. It was initially proposed in Ancient Rome, where during the prosperous period of the slave system, jurists delved into relationships of commodity exchange. They explained *fair price* or *real price* as a price not influenced by the state of market at any particular time, which could be regarded as an exchange standard. This was also, therefore, called the *common judgment.*

---

1   A monetary unit of his time.

In this period, the early Christian theologian Aurelius Augustinus (353–430), more generally known as St Augustine or Augustine of Hippo, first advanced the concept of *fair price* in his discussion of commodity exchange. He said that sometimes the buyer of a manuscript would give the seller its fair price even though the seller did not know its value. However, he offered no further explanation of fair price or its determinants.

Fair price in Ancient Rome was actually an average price, which was designated the value of a given commodity. Since philosophers at that time looked down upon manual labor, they could neither reasonably relate fair price and value to labor consumption, nor penetrate any deeper into the true nature of value. It was not until the Middle Ages that this concept was fully elaborated.

The natural economy dominated Western European feudal society until the commodity economy boomed in the 15th century. The economic ideas of the time were dominated by early mediaeval Christian Scholasticism, represented by 13th-century Italian theologian St Thomas Aquinas (1225–1274). The *Summa Theologica* (Aquinas 2017), his master work, sought to subject the commodity economy to the guidance of the church, judging the legality of economic relationships or actions according to common principles.

Aquinas, following his teacher Magnus, argued that fair price was given by labor consumption. Articles could only be exchanged fairly in proportion to the labor they consumed, and different jobs existed because of the equivalent exchange of labor. For example, if a shoemaker exchanged a pair of shoes for a house, he should pay the housemaker more because the latter used more labor and currency to build the house. Fair price was also related to the seller's circumstances, which in feudal society were closely related to their social status. A price was still *fair* if it diverged from labor proportions because of the sellers' different social status. Fair price was, thirdly, determined by utility. It was unfair to sell an article at a price more expensive than its value, but if the buyer was in urgent need of this article or if the seller would lose interest by selling it, then it was fair for the seller to ask for a relatively high price. Finally, fair price reflected supply and demand. If a seller took his wheat somewhere where prices were higher, and wheat prices then decreased because lots of sellers went there, both prices were nevertheless fair.

Aquinas's various concepts of fair price reflect different perspectives. From the perspective of labor consumption, Christianity held that God loved labor, which was therefore necessary; moreover, the feudal lord of the time opposed business profits obtained by buying low and selling high since these contained surplus value that the feudal lord could get from the serf. Aquinas's definition represented the interests of church and feudal lord; it also reflected the rigid feudal hierarchical system of the time. His other definitions stressed further factors bearing on fair price such as utility, which meant that subjective factors were also involved. His fourth definition recognized that market price fluctuated with supply and demand. Though Aquinas could not unify these definitions, he had made huge progress, since his ideas reflected real phenomena in the commodity economy. He also popularized the concept of fair price and made it the dominant economic theory of the time.

Calculating value added

From the 15th century on, the expansion of the commodity economy speeded up the emergence of capitalist production relations in the feudal society of Western Europe. The primitive accumulation of capital, the discovery of the New World, and the development of commercial capital all inaugurated the transition from a system of feudal principalities and dynasties to one of capitalist nations in various stages of development. The *mercantilist* system, representing the interests of the rising commercial bourgeoisie, is the term generally used to describe the rationale given to protectionist systems that arose during this great era of transition. Departing from previous research into static equivalence in fair trade, mercantilism studied how to achieve growth and calculate increases in wealth dynamically.

Under mercantilism, people regarded currency as gold and silver, or treasure. Besides making profits by exploiting gold and silver mines, people could also make money in foreign trade. If a country wanted to accumulate treasures, it should therefore maximize exports and set the best price. It should monopolize the market and determine the price most beneficial for exports. Policies should protect and promote exports, expand colonies and the country's sphere of influence, eradicate competitors, and monopolize pricing. Enterprises should set competitive prices for export, ensuring these will not increase at the expense of a falling volume of sales.

Mercantilism, by enquiring into the causes of the growth of wealth, created a new field of research into value. But in limiting itself to the difference between buying and selling prices, it confined itself to the external form of the commodity, and did not study the commodity economy in depth.

Theoretical thoughts on value

In the mid-17th century the capitalist economy, particularly capitalist handicraft workshops, witnessed significant development. As capitalist primitive accumulation evolved into capitalist accumulation, industrial capital took the place of commercial capital. Mainstream economics shifted its focus away from circulation and trade to production. Reflecting those changes, a new theoretical system emerged, which came to be known as classical political economy. Its representative figures included William Petty, Adam Smith, and David Ricardo from Great Britain, and Boisguillebert, Francois Quesnay, and Jean Sismondi from France. These masters joined up the dots of earlier thinking to build a systematic theory.

Rational taxation

William Petty (1623–1687) was the founder of British classical political economics, and completed works such as *A Treatise on Taxes and Contributions* (1662), *Verbum Sapienti* (finished 1664, printed 1691), *Political Anatomy of Ireland* (1672), *Political Arithmetic* (1672), and *Quantulumcunque Concerning Money* (1682). His interrelated economic ideas appear in different books, not as a general or systematic theory.

His economic enquiries begin with taxation. *A Treatise on Taxes and Contributions* argues that if a rational fiscal system is to adapt to a changeable society, taxation should be determined by its sources but not in isolation. The incomes of all social classes are sources of taxes and are acquired through the distribution of wealth. Hence, taxation is directly related to wealth.

His dictum that "labor is the Father and active principle of wealth, as lands are the Mother" signifies that wealth originates in land (nature) and labor: wages are what the laborer deserves, the surplus labor going to the landowner as interest and land price, so that wages, rent, interest, and land price are all components of wealth. Rent, the main source of tax income, is inversely related to wages.

Petty's studies of taxation led him to seek a unified system; its basis was the creation of wealth and value though labor. He was thus moving toward the labor theory of value, which was further articulated by Adam Smith (1723–1790) and David Ricardo (1772–1823), the founders of British classical political economy, whose thoughts were elaborated in *An Inquiry into the Nature and Causes of the Wealth of Nations* ([1776] 2007) and *On the Principles of Political Economy and Taxation* ([1817] 2004) respectively. The labor theory of value, a central concept of classical economics, had reached maturity after a century's evolution.

Basic definitions

Political price and natural price

The classical economists defined and improved the basic definitions of value theory. Thus, Petty for the first time distinguished political price – referring to market price – from natural price. He offered an analogy for natural price, rather than a clear definition. Suppose a laborer could transport an ounce of silver from a mine in Peru in the time needed to produce a bushel of wheat, then an ounce of silver is the natural price of a bushel of wheat. Natural price, thus determined by the consumption of labor, serves as a standard around which market price fluctuated. It is safe to take "natural price" here as a reference to the value of a good.

Value in use and exchange value

Adam Smith was the first to distinguish value in use from exchange value, and explained the interrelation between them. Value in use is the utility of a certain item, while exchange value is the purchasing power acquired by owning something. Some things of significant value in use often have small or even no exchange value, while others, of great exchange value, often have little value in use. For instance, water is an essential of daily life, but cannot be used to buy things. Diamonds lack practical value but are very expensive.

Smith concluded that value in use was not a determinant of exchange value.

Ricardo agreed on these definitions, but proposed a widely accepted correction concerning their interrelation. He held that value in use, though not a measure of exchange value, is indispensable for it. If an item is useless in all respects, meeting no needs, it cannot possess exchange value no matter how scarce it is or how much labor is required to produce it.

Natural and market price

Adam Smith also distinguished natural price from market price, and analyzed their interaction. Market price is the actual price in the market, while natural price is, roughly, the average of wages, profits, and rents. Market price is determined by conditions of supply and demand, and could be higher or lower than natural price depending on their relation. But it always fluctuates around and tends to equate to natural price, because of its effect on productive inputs. If demand exceeds supply, market price will be higher than natural price, attracting producers to make more goods. Productive inputs will also flow to sectors where market prices are higher, yielding higher profits; market price will then fall towards natural price. Conversely if demand falls short, this mechanism will reverse, and market price will rise towards natural price. Only when supply is equal to effective demand will the market price of a good be equal to its natural price.

Under special circumstances, such as accidents, natural reasons, or policies, market price can stay above natural price for a long term. Under normal circumstance (free and perfect competition), market price will fluctuate constantly around natural price. This analysis of the market mechanism was highly spoken of by subsequent scholars.

The measurement of exchange value (value)

Petty's primitive idea

When explaining price Petty, as we have noted, basically believed that labor determined value. An ounce of silver is the natural price of a bushel of wheat because their production consumes the same amount of labor, measured in working time. Although two different forms of labor are employed, they can be compared in terms of quantity. This indicates that Petty had

grasped the existence of general labor, the common property of these different forms. This forms the basis for all exchanges, whose proportion depends
on working time. Petty also recognizes here that the value of silver is not inherent but is determined by the amount of labor to produce it and transport
it, say from Peru to London.

Labor productivity thus affects the quantity of value in goods. Petty even
said that if the number of farmers involved in production increases from 100
to 200, the natural price of their products should increase correspondingly.
The division of labor would however enhance labor productivity and lower
the quantity of value in goods. If, when production moved to a new mine,
the labor formerly needed to produce two ounces of silver could now only
produce one, then Petty inferred that with other factors remaining the same,
the price of wheat would double. He thus in fact suggests that the value in
goods is in inverse proportion to labor productivity of the goods, but in proportion to the labor productivity of currency (silver).

Petty thus went beyond ancient thinking on fair and equal exchange, but
his ideas still needed improvement.

Adam Smith's two measurements: labor consumed and labor purchased

Adam Smith approached the determination of exchange value through
his concept of the division of labor. Each individual worker makes only a
limited contribution to the goods he needs, most of which comes from the
labor of others. If a person is willing to exchange some of his possessions,
their value will equal the amount of labor he could thus afford or control.

He also argued, however, that the real price of any item is the effort required to acquire it. Its real value in exchange is the effort it could save the
buyer. This is the labor consumed in its production.

He held that the labor consumed is equal to the labor purchased, because
labor is the fount of national wealth. People use currency or goods to purchase other goods, but are actually using labor, so the exchange of goods is in
fact an exchange of labor. In equal exchange, labor commanded in exchange
is equal to labor contributed. He concluded that labor is the real measure of
the exchange values of all goods.

He thus treated the external and internal measures of value as one thing. Labor consumed in production is the internal measure, and labor commands the external measure, of the value of a commodity. The former is its content and the latter its form.

Ricardo's unitary conclusion

Ricardo, following in Smith's footsteps, arrived at a conclusion he considered very important to political economy, and that we designate the *unitary* conclusion, that exchange value is determined by the labor consumed in production. This applies to goods whose quantity can be expanded without limit by manual effort, and under circumstances of free competition, as with industrial and agricultural products.

Ricardo criticized Smith, pointing out that labor consumed, and labor purchased or possessed, are not the same in quantity. For instance, due to improvements in machinery, the labor consumed in producing workers' shoes and clothes was only a quarter of that needed in the past. But the amount of living labor purchased by the same amount of shoes and clothes would not change much, because the real wage is equal to the value of the necessities of life in a given period. The labor bought or commanded should not be confused with the labor consumed in production, and cannot serve as the measure of value.

This analysis was clearly restricted in scope because he considered only the purchase of living labor (the wage) and did not enquire more deeply into the distinction between the two kinds of labor in the general exchange between commodities.

What kind of labor serves as the determinant of value?

The classical economists also analyzed the nature of labor. Adam Smith distinguished simple from complex labor. Labor of varying complexity creates different amounts of value: one hour of a difficult job contains more labor than one hour of a simple job. One hour of work requiring ten years' training might contain more labor than a month of ordinary work.

Based on Smith's analysis, Ricardo defined direct labor, indirect labor, individual labor, and necessary labor. Direct labor, also living labor, is that directly engaged in the production of goods. Indirect labor is that invested in tools, equipment, plant, and buildings. He held that direct labor and indirect labor play different roles in the determination of value. Direct labor creates value, but indirect labor transfers value from the means of production into the goods they are used to create. The more value is thus consumed, the more is transferred to these goods. The longer the production materials and equipment last, the less the value transferred.

Individual labor is the actual labor consumed by every worker in production. Necessary labor is that required even in the most adverse conditions. Ricardo believed that necessary, not individual, labor determines the value of goods.

The French scholar Sismondi, Ricardo's contemporary, added his own views on this matter. He emphasized the social character of the labor that creates value. With the emergence of commercial society, people worked for others and to sell in the market, rather than for themselves. Exchanges had become a social phenomenon and there was a proportional relation among production, consumption, and demand. Since people worked to bring goods to market, they needed to know the scale of demand, which expresses the relation between labor and social need. Only labor that is socially needed can create exchange value. Socially necessary labor then boils down to the relation between society's demand and the labor required to meet it. The value contribution of labor is that required to satisfy social need. Ricardo thus explained necessary labor from the perspective of production, Sismondi from the perspective of need.

Deficiencies of the classical economists

Flaws in economic definitions

The achievement of the classical economists was to formulate a systematic labor theory of value for the first time in history. However, their theoretical flaws left some deficiencies. Though they developed many basic definitions, such as use value and exchange value, and natural and market price, even Ricardo did not distinguish value from exchange value scientifically. When studying the quantitative relations of exchange, Ricardo noticed that the value of one good would be reflected in another, and the proportions in which they exchanged would be influenced by the labor consumed in producing each. He had thus implicitly distinguished value from exchange value, but his terminology was not clear-cut. For example, he described value using terms like value, real value, and absolute value, while he spoke of exchange value as relative value, exchange value, or comparative value. Because the classical economists studied value in the form of exchange value, it was harder for them to understand its true nature.

Classical departures from a unitary theory of value

Though the classical economists mapped out the basic argument that labor determines value, they did not reach agreement. Petty recognized that, though labor consumed is the basis of comparisons, most countries use currency (gold and silver) to measure value. But the values of these materials are not stable, so their own prices fluctuate, and their quality and weight are not consistent. He held that natural price is determined by working time, but value is determined by two natural units: labor and land. If these are translated into a common unit – the ration for an adult a day – the value of a commodity can then be determined by this ration. Since Petty could not clearly distinguish the external from the internal measure of value, this theory fell apart.

Adam Smith offered a dual value theory. To explain the coexistence of labor and income determinations he resorted to a primitive society, before private ownership and capitalist accumulation, when all products belonged to laborers and commodity exchange was equal to labor exchange. The labor consumed in producing any good is then equal to the labor it can be exchanged for, and value is therefore determined by the former. That is why the value of goods produced in two days is double that produced in one.

But in civilized society, with private land ownership and capitalist accumulation, products no longer belonged just to the laborers. The capitalists employed workers and shared the products. They wanted profits from the wages they paid and the material they provided. As the laborers ploughed, sowed, or mined, they had to give up some of their products to the land owners as rent. The price or exchange value of goods now consisted of three parts: wages, profit, and rent, the sources of all exchangeable value. Smith's observation of the social phenomenon of capitalist and commercial society thus moved him away from labor determination towards the income determination of value.

Although Ricardo persisted in the unitary view that the labor consumed in production determines value, he could not distinguish value from production price, and found it difficult to understand how changes in wages would affect the relative value of goods, eventually declaring that a correction was required. If capital composition (for Ricardo, turnover time) differed from one production sector to another, he found that the relative value of goods varied inversely with the wage according to the longevity of the fixed assets, while the relative value of goods produced mainly by labor varied in proportion to the wage. This result conflicted with his proposition that the wage would not affect relative value, but only profit. He concluded that his own view needed to be corrected.

Such deficiencies mirrored two aspects of the challenges that classical economics faced. Its inability to apply labor value theory to explain the source of profit, and the reasons why equal capitals yield equal profits, eventually led to the collapse of the Ricardian school. Different attempts to solve these problems foreshadowed the different directions in which economics was to develop after that.

Value theories of the opponents of classical economics

Since the early 19th century, the British industrial revolution had been in full swing, giving rise to a great era of large-scale industrial machinery in Western Europe. These countries enjoyed significant development in social productivity and economic competitiveness, raising questions such as, what role does capital (for example machinery) play in the determination of value? How does increasing wealth satisfy need, or utility? Those questions drew thinkers' attention, igniting heated debates. Opponents of classical economics stepped into the limelight, such as the French economist Jean-Baptiste Say (1767–1832), author of *Traité d'conomie Politique* ([1803] 1997); the British economist Thomas Robert Malthus (1776–1834), author of *Principles of Political Economy* ([1820] 1962); and adherents of David

Ricardo's theories such as James Mill (1773–1836) who formed the Ricardo school.

Since the 1830s, especially after the 1830 French Revolution, the momentum of landowning aristocratic attempts to restore feudal order had been frustrated and the capitalist system in Western Europe was strengthened. As mainstream economics gradually launched its public justification of capitalism, theoretical systems emphasizing compromise and harmony took shape, and the first comprehensive system was formed. Representative figures included the British economist Nassau William Senior (1790–1864), author of *An Outline of the Science of Political Economy* ([1836] 1997), and the French economist Claude Frédéric Bastiat (1801–1850), the author of *Economic Harmonies* ([1850] 1995). The first comprehensive system was introduced in *The Principles of Political Economy: with some of their applications to social philosophy* ([1848] 1991) by Britain economist and philosopher John Stuart Mill.

The introduction of capital into the determination of value

One divergence between classical economists and their opponents was whether capital, being labor that has accumulated while the value of goods is formed, is creating new value or just transferring old value.

Opposing Ricardo's views, Malthus argued that only when goods are produced by labor alone can consumed labor be considered the measure of value. In most circumstances, goods are produced by capital and labor, and profits became necessary for the supply and components of value. Labor purchased or commanded by goods, rather than that consumed in production, becomes the measure of value. This includes accumulated (materialized) labor, direct (living) labor, and profit on advances.

James Mill likewise, in arguments with opponents, also included capital in the determination of value. Not only direct labor, but that which has produced plants, tools, and crude materials provided by capitalists should be considered a source of value. He gave the example of mature wine, which is more expensive than new wine because it has been cellared for longer. Although no more direct labor has been applied, capital (accumulated labor) is still creating value, and the longer the wine is stored, the more value it creates.

42

The introduction of utility into the determination of value

J. B. Say established a utility theory of value, concluding that people judge the values of goods by their value in use. He recognized, however, that utility is a subjective judgment which cannot be measured quantitatively. He used the term "Degree of utility" as a scale of utility and a measure of value. This is however a comparative measure, determined by the capability of different goods to be exchanged. Since exchange usually involves currency, degree of utility is to be measured by the amount of currency for which something is exchanged, in other words its price. Value is then determined by price (supply and demand), but also by cost of production. The chaotic nature of this theory indicates the inevitable theoretical obstacles that arise when utility is brought into the determination of value. Being subjective, it cannot be quantified, and is inherently flawed as an objective standard, such as a measure of value.

Senior expressed similar views. He equated value with wealth and summarized three of its properties: utility, supply limitation, and transferability. Utility was for him an objective expression of value in use, and he analyzed its relation to supply. Because of limitation, the pleasure derived from any good declines as more is consumed. Two items do not necessarily create twice as much pleasure as one item of the same kind. Ten would certainly not provide five times as much pleasure as two. Thus, with a sufficient supply of a good, an increasing number of people feel no need to buy more. However, when goods are rare, demand is greater and more urgent. The degree of utility of goods as well as the pleasure derived from possessing them increases correspondingly.

Senior himself did not establish the utility theory of value, but focused on the limitation of supply; he proposed a production cost theory of value. His opinions on utility and its relation to supply were later absorbed by the Marginal Utility school.

The introduction of service into the determination of value

Bastiat introduced service into the theory of value, making it the cornerstone of a theoretical system of economic harmony. J. B. Say had already attempted a theory of production in which utility is the outcome of three productive factors: labor, capital, and land (natural resources). "Service" is their synergy in production. Inspired by this, Bastiat treated service as effort to meet needs. Value is the proportion or exchange ratio between two services during exchange. It appears in the comparative ratings of the two services involved, reflecting the effort the provider has made and the receiver has saved. The magnitude of value is merely proportional to the labor or effort saved by the receiver. Bastiat thus disagreed with Ricardo's theory, finding it unreasonable to perceive labor as the production of material wealth.

In a laissez-faire market, exchange is based on the equal value of mutually offered services. Through it, people help each other, offer each other services, and work for each other. Thus, a capitalist society built on the exchange of services is a harmonious one.

Comprehensive value theory

In the 1840s, John Stuart Mill's theory emerged as the first comprehensive Western economic system, attempting to reconcile conflicts with Ricardo's opponents like J. B. Say by seeking an explanation acceptable to both sides. He agreed with Ricardo's opponents that value is relative, and denied that the entity 'value' exists.

Like Adam Smith, he distinguished use value from exchange value. Use value refers to the want-satisfying capacity of goods or services – that is, their utility. Value or exchange value (the two were usually identified in political economy) refers to their purchasing power. It should be distinguished from price, a relation between goods and currency. Price is the currency value of goods.

Two essential factors confer value: utility and rarity. The reasons for rarity vary. Sometimes supply is limited absolutely: beyond a certain point it cannot increase. Some goods can only be acquired through the expenditure of labor and capital, while some are infinite, except that beyond a certain production level, each unit of growth in production requires an incremental consumption of labor and capital.

He distinguished market value, referring to the short-term market price determined by demand and supply, from natural value, referring to long-term price which depends on the goods concerned. Like Ricardo, he classified goods according to the effort needed to acquire them. The natural value of absolutely limited goods depends on the ratio between affordable demand and supply. The natural value of the second category of goods, available through production, is determined by production costs. Goods of the third category, mainly agricultural products, demand more costs as their supply increases. Their natural values are in line with the maximum cost of producing them. The common factors of production costs are wages and profit.

Mill introduced the concept of international value to account for the determination of value in international trade. Since labor and capital could not be transferred freely between countries, production costs could no longer determine international value. However, if the international division of labor accords with comparative costs, international value is determined by the exchange ratio between the imports and exports of two trading countries. The law of international value is thus an extension of the general law of value, insofar as this concerns the equality of demand and supply.

J. S. Mill's value theory thus combined production cost theory with demand–supply theory, abandoning the labor theory of value.[2]

The labor theory of value of Karl Marx

In the 1840s, the German philosophers Karl Marx (1818–1883) and Friedrich Engels (1820–1895) co-founded Marxism, the ideological system that represents the interests of the proletariat. After graduating, Marx dedicated the rest of his life to the proletarian revolution, as did Engels from his early youth. Both were eminent leaders of the proletarian revolutionary movement.

Marxist political economy, a great revolution in political economy, is integral to Marxism. Its foundation is its theory of value, progressively enriched through the critical appropriation of classical political economy.

2   Some western scholars hold that Ricardo's value theory can be regarded as a primal production cost theory of value.

The fact that labor creates value has several implications for Marx. First, this labor produces both the commodity and value; this distinguishes it from the labor that exists in all societies as the precondition for human production. Historically, labor that creates value and surplus value appears after labor comes into being in primitive and non-commodity economies; it can thus be regarded as a historical concept.

Second, such labor is productive. Productive labor in general is that which produces materials, but as regards capitalism the term has a special meaning: it is the labor that creates value and surplus value. When Marx talks about productive labor, he combines the general meaning with its special meaning.

Productive labor under capitalism includes both manual labor, such as that of a factory worker, and mental labor, like that of an engineer. This is because, in capitalist society, the socialization of production promotes the division and co-operation of different labors. Labor becomes a co-operative activity; it refers, in other words, to the combination of division and collaboration. Its meaning is thus richer than it would be, if confined to individual commodity producers under simple conditions of commodity production. Marx refers to this as *general labor.* In general labor, the functions of manual and mental labor are separated: they no longer belong to the same producer. Instead they become integrated parts of the general and productive labor that create value and surplus value. Workers do not necessarily do the work themselves, but as long as they fulfil their job as an organ of general labor and perform their own function, we can say that their labor is productive. Productive labor thus includes labor that is indirectly linked to the object of labor, as well as that directly applied to it.

Productive labor includes the guidance and management of large-scale socialized production. Marx points out that any large-scale socialized labor or co-operative labor needs guidance and management to coordinate each member's work. Any integral part of general labor belongs to productive labor. In general labor, some people work as manual workers, such as craftspeople, and some as mental workers, such as managers and engineers, but all create value.

Labor is abstract

The third consequence of Marx's definition is that labor refers to "undifferentiated" or abstract labor: that is, productive, simple, average labor. This concept is abstracted from all concrete useful forms of labor. For example, sewing and spinning are two kinds of labor yielding different products with different uses. If we abstract from this only one thing remains in common: the consumption of human labor, that is, the productive consumption of the brain, muscle, nerves, hands, and so on.

Concrete labor, in contrast to abstract labor, creates use value. To do this, we apply particular tools and methods to specific objects to produce particular products. The labor in each case is a specific type of concrete labor. Concrete and abstract labor are thus two aspects of labor with different functions. The first creates use value, the latter value.

Why is it abstract labor that creates value? Because different commodities like cotton, cloth, and coats have incommensurate quantities. In exchange we must ignore the differences in their use values, and hence the concrete labor that produced them, and find a common standard: the undifferentiated consumption of human labor – that is, abstract labor.

The magnitude of value is determined by the length of abstract labor time. Since the labor that this consumes is general labor, its content must be converted into the consumption of average and simple labor. Simple labor is the average consumption of an ordinary worker without expertise. This is distinguished from complex labor, which contains many skills and much expertise, and is consequently a multiple of simple labor.

The basic categories of Marx's scientific system

Karl Marx's theory of value is a rigorous scientific system founded on a set of basic categories. *Capital* starts with the commodity, the representative of the simplest social form in modern society. Externally, the commodity is an object satisfying a definite need by virtue of its properties. It is not simply a subjective concept; it is an objective entity that people come across in their everyday life. It can also be exchanged for other products; but it differs from products of labor in general, which become commodities only in the commodity economy. The commodity is therefore a historical, rather than an eternal, natural concept.

The two properties of commodity: use value and value

For Marx, the commodity is a dual concept, uniting the property of being a usable article with that of bearing value. As a use value it can be used by people and meet their needs; this concept also ascribes to it inherent objective material utility exhibited in its use and consumption. Its representative characteristic is that a commodity is produced for others and for social use. It has use for its consumer, not its producer. This is also the case for pre-commodity societies. Use value is thus more of an eternal, natural category making it a component of material treasure. Because of its material nature, it functions as the material bearer of exchange value. Articles with no use value cannot be exchanged in the market and therefore have no exchange value.

Value is an inner component of the commodity and can only be expressed in exchange value. This refers to the property of being exchangeable for other commodities to meet the owner's needs. As such it expresses a quantitative relationship, the proportion in which one kind of use value exchanges for another.

The equation that represents this relation – for example

$$1 \text{ quarter of wheat} = X \text{ tons of pig iron}$$

implies that the two commodities are equivalent not only in quantity but also in quality. There must therefore be *some third thing* or common measure equivalent to both the wheat and the pig iron in quantity and quality. Since the two commodities have disparate use values due to their different material properties and units of measure, they cannot be compared and measured directly. Therefore, we must remove the use value that functions as the exchange standard, leaving only the undifferentiated abstract labor of human beings.

Value is hence actually the abstract labor of human materialized in the commodity. It is the content and foundation of exchange value; conversely exchange value is the form and expression of value.

Individual and market value

Marx distinguishes individual value, created when the laborer produces commodities through their individual labor time, and market value, which refers to the value realized in the market. Since it is formed through competition in the market it is also called social value, and this is what is socially necessary labor time creates. This competition, within a single sector, means that enterprises producing the same product compete with each other to obtain excess profits. Because production conditions, and hence individual values, differ between producers, each will try to sell the product at a price beneficial to himself or herself. But competition establishes a single average value and price, reflecting the combined social effect of individual producers in the sector. This can thus be regarded either as the average value of the product in that sector, or as an individual value created under average conditions of production with average individual labor time.

The monetary expression of market value is market price, which is determined by market value but fluctuates with supply and demand. For various reasons, market value and market price are usually not equal to each other. Although market price usually rises above or sinks below market value, it fluctuates around market value as its center, and the fluctuations balance out. When value is converted into social price of production, market price becomes its monetary expression and fluctuates around it in the same way.

Value and price of production

In capitalist society, producers in different sectors compete with each other for favorable investment locations and higher profits. This competition converts these varying profits into average profit, bringing about the conversion of the commodity's value into its price of production, with two components: cost price and average profit.

The law of value does not exert its influence directly through value but through production price. Since price of production can be regarded as the actual form taken by value in the presence of competition, this accords with the law of value.

Although a commodity's value can be converted into its price of production, the two are not always equal. In those sectors with a higher organic composition of capital, the commodity's production price exceeds its value; for those with a lower organic composition, the commodity's value exceeds its production price. The two are equal only when the organic composition is equal to the average in society. However, for the whole of society, the total of the prices of production of all commodities must be equal to their total value, because the total average profit is equal to total surplus value.

The development from commodity exchange by value to commodity exchange by production price requires the capitalist mode of production to advance to a point where the commodity is exchanged not just as a commodity but also as the product of capital. It takes a long time for society to achieve this.

National value and international value

To analyze international exchange, Marx proposes the concept of international value, which refers to a commodity's market value in the international market. This is the opposite of its national value, which is what we usually mean when we refer to its value. Since the measure of value is an average unit of labor, the international value of a commodity is determined by the socially necessary labor time consumed in producing it in all those countries where it is produced. National value is determined by the socially necessary labor time only in an individual country, representing the average level and intensity of labor in that country.

National labor with higher intensity creates more value than national labor with lower intensity, within the same period of time, being more efficient. When capitalist production is more advanced in a country, the intensity and productiveness of its national labor are more advanced, compared with the international average. Different countries may therefore produce the same kinds of commodities in the same time, but national values may still differ from each other and from international values.

The international value of a commodity develops on the basis of its national value. With the development of the international division of labor and international trade, the exchange of commodities gradually expands from the domestic market to the international market, where they can only be exchanged at their international values. Therefore, we say that international value comes into being only when the commodity economy develops to a relatively higher stage.

The analysis of pricing

The determination of the magnitude of value

Since labor creates value, it is the representation and materialization of abstract labor. Its magnitude is the amount of labor that creates this value. How do we measure it? It has a natural measure, labor time. We can thus say that the magnitude of the value of a commodity is determined by the labor time consumed in producing it. However, producers operate under different conditions and with different skills, so the individual labor time consumed in the production of the same commodity varies. Yet its value is determined by socially necessary, not individual, labor time. This refers to the labor time needed to produce a certain use value under existing normal production conditions with average labor proficiency and intensity in the given society.

The magnitude of value and labor productivity

The magnitude of value varies with socially necessary labor time, which in turn changes with the development of labor productivity, the laborer's capacity to produce, whose use is reflected in individual labor. S&T development is the main cause of changes in labor productivity, which translate into changes in the commodity's unit value. If labor productivity is higher, the same laborer will produce more within the same unit of time; in consequence less socially necessary labor time will be spent producing each unit of the commodity. The unit value of the commodity thus varies in proportion to the labor consumed in producing it, but in inverse proportion to labor productivity.

Dual definition of socially necessary labor time

Marx offers a dual explanation for the idea that the value of a commodity is determined by the socially necessary labor time consumed in producing it. On the one hand, this refers to the normal conditions of production with labor of average proficiency and intensity. On the other hand, it refers to average labor time in the sector, as opposed to that of an individual producer.

The two definitions deal with different issues. The individual labor time consumed in producing the same product varies between the enterprises in a single sector, and because of competition between them, socially necessary labor time, that is the labor time required if labor of average proficiency and intensity is employed, comes to form the social value of commodity. Nevertheless, the exchange of commodities of different types brings about competition and labor comparisons in different sectors, placing a question mark over whether the commodity's social value can be realized.

Actually, the realization of social value relates to supply and demand. If the proportion of labor time consumed in producing a certain commodity, as a part of total social labor time, accords with social need and the labor time that society allocates to this activity, then supply and demand in the market are roughly equal and the commodity's social value can be realized. If this labor time exceeds what society requires, supply exceeds demand, and part of the commodity's social value cannot be realized, the value of the commodity then surpasses its social value. Therefore, the first definition of socially necessary labor time yields an internal, intrinsic standard of the commodity's unit value; while the second defines what is required for the commodity to realize this value magnitude.

The form of value

The form of the value of commodity

In daily life, people usually exchange commodities for currency. But why can they do so? Marx's theory of value form is a scientific response to this question and the theoretical paradoxes that underlie it.

The value form of the commodity is its expression in exchange. Use value has a natural and directly perceptible form, but value, as the embodiment of abstract labor, cannot be felt or touched like a material object, nor is it directly expressed. It is expressed only in exchange. The value form of the commodity is the form in which its value, or its exchange value, is expressed.

Marx analyzed this in terms of four phases of development corresponding to different stages of commodity exchange.

The stages of development of value forms

The simple value form is when the value of a given commodity is accidentally and simply expressed as the quantity of another kind of commodity, for example

$$20 \; yards \; linen = 1 \; coat$$

This is the simplest value form of the initial period of commodity exchange. Marx held that all the secrets of the value form are embedded in this, its most simple expression.

This value form involves two parties: relative and equivalent. Linen, whose commodity value is directly expressed in the equation, is on the positive side of the relative value form. The magnitude of its exchange value is influenced by two factors: its own size and variation, and the size and the variation of the commodity on the other side. The coat, in whose material the value of linen is expressed, is the equivalent, placing it on the passive side.

The commodity on the side of the equivalent – the coat – has three characteristics: its use value is the form in which the value of other commodities is expressed; its concrete labor is the form in which abstract labor is expressed; and its private labor is the direct form in which social labor is expressed.

In the expanded value form, the value of a given commodity is expressed in the value form of a series of commodities. For example:

$$20 \; yards \; linen \begin{cases} = 1 \; coat \\ = 10 \; pounds \; tea \\ = 1 \; quarter \; wheat \\ = 2 \; ounces \; gold \\ = Other \; commodities \end{cases}$$

This manifests three traits which distinguish it from the simple form. First, the value of the commodity truly embodies abstract human labor. Second, it implies an expansion of the social relations of commodity exchange. Third, it shows that the value form of the commodity has nothing to do with the natural form of its use value. Since commodity exchange is frequently seen in the market, the magnitude of value of a commodity is basically settled quantitatively. The proportions in which commodities exchange are very close to socially necessary labor time.

The general value form means that the value of any commodity can be expressed by the value form of another particular kind of commodity. For instance,

$$
\left.\begin{array}{r}
\textit{1 coat} = \\
\textit{10 pounds tea} = \\
\textit{1 quarter wheat} = \\
\textit{2 ounces gold} = \\
\textit{Other commodities} =
\end{array}\right\} \quad \textit{20 yards linen}
$$

The general value form is a qualitative leap. In the first two value forms, the value of a commodity is expressed in an arbitrary commodity with a different use value, while in the general value form, the value of various kinds of commodities can be uniformly expressed by the use value of a particular commodity. The primary property of commodity value, which is the embodiment of undifferentiated human labor, is thereby expressed completely and sufficiently. As a general equivalent, one commodity becomes the material expression of the value of all commodities. As a result, exchange between individual articles can develop into commodity circulation with a general equivalent as the medium.

In the monetary form, the value of all commodities is uniformly expressed by currency. For example:

$$
\left.\begin{array}{r}
\textit{1 coat} = \\
\textit{10 pounds tea} = \\
\textit{1 quarter wheat} = \\
\textit{2 ounces gold} = \\
\textit{Other commodities} =
\end{array}\right\} \quad \textit{2 ounces gold}
$$

The nature of the monetary form has not changed compared with the general value form. The difference is that in the general form, the commodity serving as general equivalent is not fixed or unified; in the monetary form, it remains unchanged for a long period of time.

When one particular commodity is separated from the commodity world and acquires the permanent status of general equivalent, this special kind of commodity becomes currency. The appearance of currency divides the commodity world into two parts: the various commodities with distinctive use value in need of conversion into value, and currency, directly representing the value of each kind of commodity. Furthermore, with the appearance of currency, the unity of opposites between use value and value develops into that between commodity and currency.

Commodity fetishism

Currency introduces a sense of mystery into the world; for the first time, the value of all commodities is uniformly expressed in something that can be directly exchanged for any commodity, and which thereby becomes the main representation of value and wealth. The sense of mystery that currency evokes is a kind of commodity fetishism.

Fetishism reveals itself when an object acquires the mysterious ability to control human destiny; people worship it as an idol because of this sense of mystery. Once the product of labor becomes a commodity, it acquires the capacity to be fetishized, because the various concrete labors against which it can exchanged revert to undifferentiated and equivalent abstract labor. This equivalence of labor means that all products of labor have value in common.

Second, the labor consumed in producing the commodity, which ought to be expressed and calculated as time of labor, is now expressed and calculated as a value magnitude. Third, the social relationship formed in production cannot be expressed directly, but only in the exchange relationship between commodities. The sense of mystery comes from the fact that the phenomenon conceals the essence. By nature, the commodity is produced by humans for exchange; yet it appears to be a mysterious creature with a separate existence apart from and above human beings, capable of controlling people's economic activities and destinies, leaving people no option but to worship and obey it. Marx uncovered its mysterious veil by explaining that the commodity and currency actually reflect social relationships between commodity producers.

The relationship between supply, demand, and market price

The deviation of supply and demand from price and value magnitudes

Price is the currency name of the labor materialized within the commodity, or the monetary expression of its value. In its role as the expression of value, it is the index of a value magnitude; in its role as the expression of the exchange ratio between a commodity and currency, it is the index of that ratio. The two do not always accord with each other. In its latter capacity, price only indicates the amount of currency that a commodity can exchange with, which does not necessarily mean that the magnitude of value of the commodity accords with its price. In short, price deviates from value.

The reason lies in the form of value, which reflects a commodity's value in a certain amount of currency. Their exchange ratio is influenced by many factors, including supply and demand. When these balance social productivity, price and value are equal to each other. If socially necessary labor time is expressed in the value of 1 quarter of wheat and 2 pounds of gold, then when they exchange with each other, the wheat price of 2 pounds is the index of both the exchange ratio of wheat for currency, and the value magnitude of wheat. If the market is in short supply, then it may raise the price of 1 quarter of wheat to 3 pounds; in excess supply, the price of the wheat may drop to 1 pound. In this case, 3 pounds or 1 pound is the price of wheat, or the index of the exchange ratio of wheat for currency. But as an index of the value magnitude of wheat, this figure is too large or too small. Such an imbalance of supply and demand is normal.

Supply and demand triggers the deviation of market price from market value and regulates social production

Market price is the monetary expression of market value. When goods are in short supply, their market price rises above their value; in oversupply, it falls below their value. When the market price rises, this brings about a fall in demand and increased production in search of additional profits, leading towards oversupply; when it decreases, the result is rising demand and a contraction in supply to reduce losses. Thus, in the long term, market price fluctuates with its center on market value, and the fluctuations balance out on average.

When value is converted into price of production, market price becomes its monetary expression, and fluctuates with price of production as its center.

Supply and demand influence the variation and realization of market value

Drastic changes in supply or demand lead to drastic changes in both market price and market value. When supply is well below demand, the price does not fall even though the value of the commodity is created under the worst conditions; these worst conditions thus determine the market price. Conversely, when demand is well above supply, price will not increase even though the commodity is created under the best conditions, which then regulate the market price. Though variations in the market value of a commodity are triggered by variations in supply and demand, it remains essentially determined by the labor time socially necessary to produce the commodity under either the best, average, or worst conditions, depending on whether the market is understocked, well stocked, or overstocked

The relation of supply to demand also influences the realization of market value. When there is oversupply, the labor time consumed in producing a given commodity exceeds the time that would be needed if labor time were proportionally distributed to its sector by society, and it can only be exchanged at a relatively lower market value. In other words, part of its value cannot be realized; that is to say, the realized commodity value is higher than its own value. Only when supply equals demand, that is, the commodity of a certain sector is produced with a proportion of society's labor time that accords with society's needs, can all the commodities in this sector be sold, and their market value be completely realized.

The marginal revolution

The tendency towards subjective and quantitative analysis

From the 1870s to the early 20th century, capitalist economies enjoyed a period of relative internal stability. Free competition was giving way to a system in which monopoly played an increasing role. Non-mainstream schools like the Historical school emerged and thrived; and Marxism was born.

The most popular mainstream theory, J. S. Mill's, neither corrected the flaws of classical political economy to withstand the challenges from the Historical school and Marxism, nor offered solutions to the problems of this transitional period. Capitalist economics needed new instruments of analysis and more up-to-date content. In the 1870s, a group of economists proposed a "revolutionary reconstruction," and reformed traditional economics. Their three distinguishing figures were Menger in Austria, Jevons in England, and Walras in France, who published works with similar theoretical propositions at almost the same time, founding the Marginal Utility school. This had a lasting impact on economic thought, and was later called the marginal revolution.

The Marginal Utility school's priority was to analyze how agents obtained maximum utility, or the greatest satisfaction, and to explore the optimal distribution and allocation of resources. It focused on consumption, utility, and demand, enquiring into the laws governing the actions of agents by such means as marginal equilibrium. Its members illustrated their views with mathematical approaches or models, especially marginal analysis. They transformed economics into a systematic theory organized around consumption, exchange, and production, which since then has been dominated by subjective and quantitative analysis.

Derivative schools emerged in many countries, such as the Austrian school, the Swedish school, and the American school. All were based on the theory of marginal utility, though their views and research priorities varied.

Value theory derived from subjective analysis

Karl Menger (1840–1921) founded the Austrian school (also called the Vienna school), and was its representative figure together with Eugen von Böhm-Bawerk (1851–1914) and Friedrich von Wieser (1851–1926). All paid close attention to the subjective and psychological aspects of value.

Menger defined value in terms of agents' subjective judgments, inseparable from their minds and consciousness, on how their possessions affected their lives and well-being. Wieser also argued that value was subjective, and Böhm-Bawerk distinguished between subjective and objective value. Subjective value expressed the relationship between possession and well-being, need, or satisfaction. If people thought certain possessions brought well-being, then they could satisfy needs and obtain pleasure, or exempt themselves from pain, by acquiring them. The marginals, for these reasons, all regarded value as the outcome of subjective judgment.

The Marginal Utility school divides things into economic and non-economic categories, depending on the supply–demand scenario. Only economic goods for which demand surpasses supply have value. Böhm-Bawerk proposed two prerequisites for a thing to have value: utility and scarcity. For a person sitting by a stream, a cup of water is useful but not scarce; it is required for happiness and satisfaction but has no value. For a man struggling in the desert, it is the last hope for survival and indispensable for happiness. Without it, this man faces inevitable pain and so the water has priceless value. This illustrated Wieser's opinion that value exists only subject to the relationship between needs and limited supply.

Since value is subjective, its measure also has to be subjective. Menger and Böhm-Bawerk believed it is determined by the utility of an item in meeting the most minimal needs, while Wieser proposed that marginal utility determines value, the view that economists most widely recognized subsequently.

The Austrian school also analyzed what determines the prices of goods, which Böhm-Bawerk's objective value theory sought to represent. He defined objective value as an item's capacity to be exchanged for other items. This purchasing power actually relies on the owner's subjective judgment: in other words, it is a subjective value. Normal exchange involves not just one buyer and one seller, but many competing parties, which Böhm-Bawerk illustrated with the market in horses. Market prices are determined by the subjective judgments of marginal pairs: the two pairs of buyers and sellers who offer the highest and lowest prices. Market price must lie where supply and demand are in equilibrium. Though termed objective, this theory is clearly based on a subjective foundation; psychological analysis supplies the determination of market price.

The quantification of value analysis

After the marginal revolution the major trend was to apply mathematical formalism, such as equations, formulas, and geometric patterns, to facilitate the descriptions of economic theories. This affected all value theory but especially the Mathematical school, which shared the Austrian school's main opinions on value theory, but expressed them using mathematical language.

The British economist William Stanley Jevons (1835–1882) opposed labor value theory but regarded labor as one of the conditions that determine value on most occasions. Labor or production costs determine the supply of goods. Supply affects the ultimate degree of utility, which determines the exchange rate or value. Thus, he raised the ultimate degree of utility value theory.

For Jevons, utility reflects pleasure and pain and is not inherent to the commodity, but related to people's demands. As the supply of a good increases, its marginal utility diminishes, leading to Jevons's idea of the final degree of utility, the ratio between an additional unit of goods and its utility. This is the unit utility of an infinitesimal increment. In mathematical language, suppose X to be the quantity of goods and U their total utility, and suppose U = f(X). The degree of utility of a small increment Δx is then $\frac{\Delta U}{\Delta X}$ and final degree its limit as ΔX tends to zero, that is $\frac{dU}{dX}$, the derivative of U with respect to X.

Jevons denied that value is a property inherent in a good. He used the exchange rate in place of value to express the quantitative relation between goods. Driven by profits, the parties to exchange always compare the ultimate degree of utility of goods to decide how much they are willing to forgo to secure the most profit. When both sides achieve equal degrees of utility, exchange is in equilibrium and ceases. Therefore, the ultimate degree of utility decides the exchange rate (value) of goods. The exchange rate of two goods is the reciprocal of the ratio of their ultimate degree of utility.

Take an isolated exchange between two people for instance, and assume that this happens in under perfect competition subjected to the principle of indifference. No matter how big or small, a certain good has only one exchange rate at a certain time. When X is exchanged for Y, there is only one exchange rate Y/X ($\frac{dY}{dX}$) if infinitesimal quantities are exchanged).

Assume that exchanger A has a pounds of grain while B has b pounds of beef. Following the existing ratio (e.g. 10 pounds of grain = 1 pound of beef), A offers X pounds of grain to exchange for Y pounds of beef. After exchange, A has $(a-X)$ pounds of grain and Y pounds of beef, while B has $(b-Y)$ pounds of beef and X pounds of grain. So, the ultimate degrees of utility of grain and beef, for A, are $\varphi_1(a-X)$ and $\varphi_1(Y)$, and for B, $\varphi_2 X$ and $\varphi_2(b-Y)$. When $\varphi_1(a-X)/\varphi_1(Y) = dy/dx$ and $\varphi_2(X)/\varphi_2(b-Y) = dy/dx$, both A and B have maximized utility. According to the principle of indifference, the function $\varphi_1(a-X)/\varphi_1(Y) = y/x = \varphi_2(X)/\varphi_2(b-Y)$ is the outcome.

Walras (1834–1910) proposed a similar theory. He believed scarcity was the source of value. This is the ultimate intensity of desire which could be satisfied by consuming goods. Satisfaction diminishes as supply increases. The price of goods is the ratio in which they are exchanged. To maximize the satisfaction from exchange, the exchangers have to ensure, mutually, that the ratio of their ultimate intensities of desire is equal to the price.

Assume that, under perfect competition, quantities m and n of goods A and B are exchanged at prices P_a and P_b, while V_a and V_b are their exchange values per unit. The following conclusions can be drawn.

1. The ratio of price or exchange value is equal to the inverse ratio of the amount exchanges, which is

$$P_a=V_a/V_b=n/m;\; P_b=V_b/V_a=m/n.$$

2. Realized utility is maximized when the ultimate intensity of desire of every good is equal to its price:

$$P_a=R_{a1}/R_{b1}=R_{a2}/R_{b2}=R_{a3}/R_{b3}=\ldots P_b=R_{b1}/R_{a1}=R_{b2}/R_{a2}=R_{b3}/R_{a3}=\ldots\ldots$$

where R stands for the ultimate intensity of desire.

3. Since that price is equal to the ratio of exchange values and also the ultimate intensity of desire, exchange value is in proportion to the ultimate intensity of desire, that is:

$$P_a=n/m=V_a/V_b$$
$$\therefore R_a/R_b=V_a/V_b;$$
$$P_b=m/n=V_b/V_a,$$
$$\therefore R_b/R_a=V_b/V_a.$$

Walras concluded that the ultimate intensity of desire is the source of exchange value. In distinction from Jevons, he employed the concept of equilibrium. The above prices apply when supply is equal to demand. This formed the basis of general equilibrium, which Walras used to analyze exchange and the formation of prices.

Comprehensive value analysis

In the late 19th century, Western economics underwent a synthesis under the *aegis* of Alfred Marshall (1842–1924). This British economist published *Principles of Economics* ([1890] 1964) taking J. S. Mill as his point of departure.

Marshall saw value as relative. Most countries measured value in gold or silver, showing that value is a reference to price. Past economists had emphasized either supply, when discussing manufacture, or demand, when discussing utility. Such theories had merits and flaws: Marshall claimed to draw on all of them to arrive at a comprehensive analysis of the determination of value which, he concluded, depends on both demand and supply. Only when these are equal will both determine value and price, which therefore obtains in equilibrium.

The starting point of his theory of value was, however, demand. This, he held, depends on utility, the pleasure or other benefits that commodities provide, and hence on the psychological state and subjective judgment of the buyer. This could be measured indirectly in currency, the price offered by the demand side. The law of diminishing marginal utility became Marshall's law of diminishing demand price: the more goods are offered for sale, the lower the sale price has to be, in order to reach enough consumers, since the quantity demanded decreases as price goes up, and increases as it goes down.

This law can be illustrated with a chart in which the horizontal axis represents quantity demanded and the vertical axis sale price. Different points can be drawn and connected to yield a curve slanting from the top left to the bottom right, which is the demand curve of a given consumer. Marshall proposed the concepts of elasticity and consumer surplus, and thus elaborated the principles of consumer choice.

Supply in Marshall's theory depends on the cost of production, which is the sum of the costs of the labor and capital expended in manufacture. Labor is disutility since laborers dislike working both spiritually and physically. Capital is anticipation, comprising delayed pleasure for capitalists. Both disutility and anticipation are psychological, and indirectly measured by currency. This yields the cost of production in currency and the supply price of a good, allowing Marshall to deduce the relation between sale price and the quantity of that good which would be supplied. To illustrate this, he developed concepts such as the supply curve, elasticity of supply, the short and long term, external and internal economies, and the principle of substitution.

To explain the formation of an equilibrium price, Marshall drew upon J. S. Mill's approach. He argued that the supply–demand scenario would affect price differently in the short and long term. The shorter the period, the bigger the role of demand, and the longer the period, the bigger the role of supply. Marshall analyzed this through partial equilibrium. He assumed that the value of currency and other factors were stable, confining his enquiry to the effect of changes in the supply and demand functions on the value (price) of a commodity. He elaborated this theory in mathematical appendices, using functions and geometrical patterns.

In summary, Marshall took equilibrium price theory from the Marginal Utility school and incorporated into it views and approaches taken from the Ricardians.

3
After Marx: research into the labor theory of value

Western scholars of labor value theory

The concept of *Western scholars* is not geographical, being borrowed from political theory. It refers to scholars in so-called Western countries, excluding the socialist countries of the former Soviet Union and Eastern Europe. Japan is an exception; although geographically speaking it is an oriental country, we treat it as Western because it has a capitalist system and has acquired a political and intellectual heritage from Western countries such as the United States. Western scholars studied Marxist economic theory extensively, developing a range of views on many theoretical issues. Here we focus on their work on labor theories of value.

Representatives of Western bourgeois theory

Eugen von Böhm-Bawerk

The Austrian economist Böhm-Bawerk was the first bourgeois economist to criticize Marx's theory of value and surplus value in a systematic way. He set out these views mainly in *Capital and Interest: A critical history of economic theory* (1884) and in *Karl Marx and the Close of His System* (1936). He questioned three aspects of Marx's labor value theory. First, he claimed that Marx's procedure for transforming values into production prices used pure logic without any experiential or psychological proof, and that Volume 3 of *Capital*, and the relatively more abstract Volume 1, offered contradictory explanations of the labor theory of value. This contradiction, he argued, contributed to the collapse of Marx's theoretical system. Second, he argued that Marx's value theory should be replaced by marginal utility theory because Marx's system failed to recognize the contribution by other factors of production to the creation of value. In this regard he singled out three deficiencies: its neglect of demand, its failure to recognize any reward for the use of capital, and its denial of the relationship between prices (Marx 1979, p. 74). Third, he questioned Marx's reduction of complex to simple labor. The presence of heterogeneous labor, he argued, contradicts the hypothesis that the level of exploitation is the same under all conditions, unless different labors are reduced to homogeneous abstract labor according to their wage level. The reduction of complex to simple labor is therefore an arbitrary fabrication. However, he did not support this criticism with sufficient reasoning.

Paul Anthony Samuelson

Paul Samuelson questioned Marx's transformation of values into prices. In an article written in 1957, he first changed Marx's model of simple reproduction into a simple input–output table, drawing three sets of conclusions. First, the relative prices of commodities can be calculated directly from the quantitative relations between the material and technical conditions of production, without recourse to the concept of value. Second, if this is done, values do not need to be transformed into prices. Third, existence of exploitation destroys the proportional relationship between price and value (Samuelson 1957, p. 888). He repeated this in Samuelson (1971), where he argued that transformation arises from the need to establish a certain proportional relationship between commodity prices, but since this can be calculated from the material and technical conditions of production, value and transformation are unnecessary intermediate links. Samuelson also questioned the applicability of labor value theory, arguing it applied only in the "Garden of Eden in the initial period of history" (Samuelson 1987, p. 317), and was no longer relevant in capitalist society.

Piero Sraffa

The Production of Commodities by Means of Commodities was an influential masterpiece written by Sraffa in 1960 (Sraffa, 1979). In this book, he further developed the price theory of Ricardo to replace the marginal utility theory of orthodox neoclassical economics. His research findings included two points. First, we should not measure absolute value in terms of labor, but should measure the relative prices of commodities, using the relationship between materials and their quantities employed in commodity production, in order to identify a standard commodity as the measure of value. Second, in establishing the standard commodity and production system, he made a vital contribution to the argument of converting values to production prices, thus opening up a new way to resolve transformation.

Ian Steedman

Steedman presented his main critique in *Marx After Sraffa* (1977). He showed that the profit rate can be calculated from material relations, real wages, and the direct quantities of various kinds of heterogeneous labor in different sectors. There is no need to reduce one kind of labor to another. He then argued that relative commodity prices are determined by the physical conditions of production without introducing labor value, which is itself determined by the physical conditions of production. Moreover, under conditions of joint production, commodity values can be indeterminate or even negative, which is economically meaningless. In consequence he believed that Marx's labor value theory should be abandoned. Finally, he held Marx's transformation procedure to be logically contradictory. Both the social average profit rate, and relative prices, should be calculated directly from the wage level and the material conditions of production as manifested in the proportions between input and output.

Michio Morishima

Michio Morishima studied four aspects of labor value theory. He thought heterogeneous labor posed a dilemma for Marxist value theory, since if its value contribution depended on the wages awarded to it, labor value theory would have to be discarded. Further, in *Marx's Economics: A dual theory of value and growth* (1973), he used to a simple example to prove that the same commodity could have several different values under a variety of technical conditions; he held that this made the magnitude of value ambiguous. He thirdly regarded the negative values and surplus values noted by Steedman under joint production as a kind of *pseudo-value*. Value, he argued, should be defined in terms of the minimum required labor, which should be calculated by linear programming techniques: these yield *true values*. Fourth, he argued that since transformation is not a historical concept, value is only a logical concept.

However, he showed sympathy for Marx's opinions. He first distinguished between value as a creation of abstract human labor, and value as the labor time socially necessary to produce a commodity. He also applied some mathematical logic to transformation, proposing a solution based on the result of an iterative Markov process beginning with value and converging on a correct and consistent production price. He believed this showed Marx's two "equalities" – total value equals total price, and total surplus value equals total profit – were both true. Nevertheless, he did not adhere to labor value theory. Given joint production and other issues, he advocated its abandonment and believed value could not form the foundation of prices of production.

Representatives of Western Marxist economics

Maurice Herbert Dobb

Dobb's main work on value theory was *Political Economy and Capitalism: Some essays in economic tradition*, published in 1973. This book correctly explained the indisputably significant position occupied by Marx's value theory within political economy. As regards transformation, Dobb thought Marx had never satisfactorily explained how production price is related to or derived from value. Marx might have known his own solutions were not perfect, but he died before the third volume was completed. Although Marx insisted that individual production prices did not accord with values, their total was still equal to total value and total profit was equal to total surplus value. Against the critics' claim that the first and the third volumes of *Capital* were mutually contradictory, Dobb advanced the concept of the *method of approximation*.

Paul Sweezy

Paul Sweezy's *The Theory of Capitalist Development* ([1942] 1993) was an introduction to Marxist economics. It laid the foundation of Sweezy's historical reputation as an important Marxist economist. He founded the left-wing magazine *Monthly Review* in 1949 and served as its chief editor for the rest of his life.

Sweezy published many works critical of capitalism. His research into labor value theory can be summarized as follows. First, under what conditions would exchange rates correspond precisely with the time of labor? Using an example based on Adam Smith's deer–beaver economy, he suggested that exchange conditions had to hold, which Marx had failed to notice. Exchange value could only be proportional to labor time when supply was equal to demand. Therefore, the theory that the equality of supply and demand determine market price did not differ from labor value theory, but was integral to it. Second, he held that monopoly did not change the basic social relationship of commodity production, and hence did not change the qualitative nature of value, but that unlike the difference between production price and value, monopoly price diverged from value in such a way that the precise quantitative relationship embedded in the law of value no longer applied. Third, Sweezy held that Marx's transformation procedure was logically deficient and that Bortkiewicz had supplied a logically superior solution.

Marx's analysis started from value instead of price. Sweezy argued this was because the value calculation was vital in recognizing profit as a deduction from the total social product of labor, and that the value calculation would help people see the underlying relations between people and classes below the superficial phenomena of currency and commodity.

Sweezy's transformation procedure aroused decades-long debate between bourgeois economists and Marxist economists.

Ronald Lindley Meek

Meek's masterpiece *Studies in the Labor Theory of Value* (1956b) studied the history of Marx's theory, drawing attention to the unreasonable rejections, and inconsistent alternatives, offered by its opponents. As regards transformation he thought it was reasonable for Marx to explain price through value. The purpose, he argued, was to criticize vulgar economics for determining commodity price from wages, profit, and land rent. As regards value, he further held that Marx needed to analyze capitalist commodity production and exchange from the standpoint of a simple commodity society.

He made three basic points about transformation. First, he thought the equality of total profit and total surplus value was more significant than the equality of total production price and total value. Second, he thought production price should be calculated in a different way, by means of an analysis based on the commodity, not an analysis based on value. Finally, he thought that the transformation from value to production price theoretically reflected a historical transformation from exchange at values to exchange at prices of production.

M. C. Howard and J. E. King

Howard and King are best known for their comprehensive three-volume *History of Marxian Economics* (1985). They contributed to the discussion on complex and simple labor.[1] They argued that in citing training costs as the reason complex labor was a multiple of simple labor, Marx had offered an inadequate explanation. First, skilled workers' wages do not entirely depend on training costs. If these are paid by the workers, wages would be lower than labor costs in the short term, but the opposite would be true in the long term. If training costs are paid by capitalists, wages would be higher than

---

1   Editor's note: much of the Western literature does not distinguish, as Marx does, between *complex* labor and *heterogeneous* labor. Complexity for Marx refers to "more intense" labor, which typically arises when workers engaged in the same occupation, or at least in the same branch of industry, contribute more or less value in the same time, either because some work harder than others or because they are better trained or more apt. Heterogeneous labor is closer to Marx's concept of the differences in *concrete* labor, laborers engaged in different activities. Since some activities are typically more skilled than others, the two concepts are not always separated, and in the literature discussed in this chapter are generally speaking simply merged. We have throughout this chapter used the term "heterogeneous" labor and counterposed it to "uniform" labor, but many of the terms used – such as "reduction" – derive from Marx's discussion of complex versus simple labor.

labor costs in the short term, but lower in the long term, since the profit from skilled labor would be regarded by capitalists as a profit on past investment. Second, workers' capabilities are not necessarily the result of training: gifted workers could also be paid more. Finally, some dirty, unpleasant, and even dangerous work could also be better paid.

King believed that the existence of a variety of technical conditions could contradict Marx's logical analysis. Value is not determined prior to the rate of profit as Marx maintained, since first the production technology and profit rate are selected. He also believed that the co-existence of various technologies means the magnitude of value loses its uniqueness, so that value determination becomes ambiguous.

Referring to the definition of value, King pointed to a weakness in the concept of "true value" advocated by Michio Morishima (1973) and Kate Foss: these could not be aggregated. The idea that value could be aggregated was a pillar of Marx's theoretical system: for instance, his theories of the capital circuit and capital turnover, as well as the reproduction schemata, were based on aggregated value. King proposed to calculate value magnitudes using socially necessary labor time, defined as the labor consumed under the worst production conditions.

S. J. Pack

Pack proposed to base his research on Sraffa's commodity value theory instead of Marx's labor value theory. He believed that this did no harm to Marx's theory and circumvented the transformation of value into production price. He elaborated this theory in *Reconstructing Marxian Economics: Marx based upon a Sraffian commodity theory of value* (1985). In his opinion, the key to commodity value theory lies in comprehending the dual use value of the commodity, for individual and productive consumption.

On the basis of this commodity value theory, he rewrote those parts of the first four chapters of the first volume of *Capital* dealing with labor value, including those covering the commodity, currency, commodity fetishism, the function of currency, and the transformation from currency to capital. He noted two differences between commodity and labor value theories. First, the value of the commodity is no longer determined by the socially necessary labor time materialized in it, since labor is now only one among many factors contributing to production. Second, the quantitative relations in which commodities are exchanged are determined by the production process as a whole. The value magnitude of the commodity is inseparable from both the direct and indirect conditions contributing to its production. For automated production in particular, Pack found commodity value theory more convincing in explaining the existence and origin of profit and value; this made it a superior and more promising theory.

Bob Rowthorn

Rowthorn responded to opponents of labor value theory on the reduction of heterogeneous to uniform labor. Marxists had proposed two approaches based on production cost and indirect labor. Rowthorn saw two disadvantages of the production cost approach. First, it does not respond to Böhm-Bawerk's proposal to use wages for the reduction. Second, it fails to notice the role of education in reproducing labor. According to the indirect labor approach, various unskilled workers all make contributions to training the skilled laborer. These are all transferred by the labor of the skilled worker into the value of the product. If we trace backwards, we can treat the contribution of skilled labor as a total of unskilled labor applied to its creation at each specific time. This method relieves us of reliance on the wage level, the criticism advanced by both Böhm-Bawerk and his critics.

As regards the value of labor power, Rowthorn thought Marx proposed three different scattered and confused definitions, though these are in agreement on one point: that wages are determined by the minimum living standard.

The concept of the monetary equivalent of labor time: new explorations in value theory (He and Liu 2002)

Foley (1982), and Duménil (1980), writing separately but at the same time in the early 1980s, and following in the footsteps of Aglietta (1979), developed a critique of Western orthodox economic objections to the Marx's labor value theory in which they stressed the relation between money and labor time. They laid the foundations of a range of approaches that Kliman and Freeman term *single system* interpretations of Marx's theory, following the terminology introduced by Ramos and Rodriguez (1996), who characterized the orthodox Western calculation as a *dual system* method. By this they meant that values and prices are determined in two separate and unconnected systems of equations, one in which values are determined by labor proportions, and another in which they are determined by the market.

Foley, and Duménil and Lévy, set out to rebuild the interpretation of Marx's labor value theory by stressing the relation between money and labor time. In their opinion, an important standpoint of Marx is that socially labor time is expressed in money. They proposed to explain labor value theory by studying the relation between the two. Foley referred to this as the "value of money." Following Ramos (1995), usage has converged on the term "monetary expression of labor time," which is conventionally abbreviated to MELT. If this is properly defined, a quantity of money in any actual capitalist system can be converted to a quantity of labor time, and *vice versa*, instead of building a separate system to determine labor value independent of price.

Foley argued that Marx's first equality (total value equals total price) should be rewritten to show that the total price of the net product is equal to the total value of the net product. Distribution should be then be defined by specifying that the value of variable capital, and hence the value transmitted to the worker by her purchases using the wage, is equal to the price of the consumer goods then purchased, after this has been converted into a labor value magnitude, by dividing by the MELT.

If the above two principles are accepted, any value magnitude could be converted to a price magnitude; moreover, Marx's conclusion that the two totals were equivalent is upheld. Both sets of writers maintained that the sum of paid and unpaid labor remain equal to labor time. Thus, the unpaid labor yields the magnitude of surplus value in exactly the same way as in Marx's writings and in Western interpretations of these writings, being equal to the value product of labor (given by the time of that labor) less the value of wages.

Subsequent writers built on this foundation, developing a variety of *single system interpretations* in which the new principle of the convertibility of money and labor time is applied to constant as well as variable capital. The results could reproduce Marx's conclusion that total price and total value are quantitatively equal, as well as total profit and total surplus value.

These authors diverge on a number of issues, including the calculation of the MELT. They also fall into two main groups, called *simultaneous* and *temporal*. The first group apply a MELT conversion to arrive at values, but maintain the broad approach of Bortkiewicz, who had reformulated Marx's original ideas as a variant of general equilibrium: that is, a system of simultaneous equations. In contrast temporal authors, including those associated with the temporal single system interpretation (Kliman 2007, Freeman and Carchedi 1996) argue that this subsequent orthodoxy has fundamentally misrepresented Marx by confusing Bortkiewicz's reformulation with Marx's original approach in which general equilibrium does not figure, and neither values nor prices are calculated by using simultaneous equations.

However, all these authors concur that the MELT allows us to organically combine value determined by labor time with production price after the equalization of the profit rate. Thus, we could say that the MELT is a universal concept, for it explains not only the determination of value in production, but price fluctuations in circulation. There is wide agreement that the concept of the MELT has successfully responded to the critics of Marx's transformation, amended some deficiencies within Marxism, and opened up new areas of research into labor value theory.

A summary of Chinese economists' views on Marx's labor value theory

Labor value theory, as the core of Marxian political economy, has been under attack from bourgeois economists since its birth. However, these attacks do not change the fact that labor value theory is science-based, and holds true for modern bourgeois society as well as for a socialist market economy. Nevertheless, as society continues to move forward, existing theories need to evolve to keep up with the times, or they exert negative instead of positive influences. Since China's socialist society is quite different from what Marx envisaged, there has been intense debate on the content of labor value theory among Chinese economists. Since the 1950s, there have been four major rounds of debates, each round focusing on different aspects of the theory. The debates mainly focus on the following four aspects.

Economists have questioned the theory's applicability from two angles. First, when advances in technology change the way people work and reduce the living labor involved in wealth creation, how does labor value theory account for rising commodity prices and other new economic circumstances? Second, is the theory applicable to China, which is in the primary stage of socialism and runs a socialist market economy?

Song Tao (2000) believed that labor value theory holds in a modern market economy. Even unmanned factories are still under the control of human beings, so the theory's premises remain valid. Cheng Enfu and Wang Guijin (2003) argued that labor value theory underlies the theoretical analysis of not only a capitalist market economy, but also a socialist market economy. A multi-ownership structure in which public ownership is the principal element, and a distribution system in which distribution according to work remains dominant, as is in practice the case in China, can be dissected using the labor theory of value, which in turn promotes the sound development of the socialist market economy. He argued that all the misunderstandings surrounding labor value theory, such as the false assumption that the theory was born out of an era of small commodity production, can and should be dispelled.

Wei Xinghua (2002) argued, against those who maintained the theory cannot deal with practical phenomena, that this arose because they did not have a comprehensive or profound understanding of the theory. Basing his work on the opinions of several other economists, Su Xing (1995) dealt with three aspects of the theory: whether tertiary industry creates value, whether S&T create value, and how to understand the role of non-labor factors in the distribution of income. He thought that Marx's value theory was a scientific system which could be a useful tool to illustrate economic phenomena provided that it was grasped and understood thoroughly. Wu Yifeng (2001) emphasized that the theory arose from the processes of commodity production and circulation, two stages of the circuit of capital shared by different modes of production, which made a case that the theory was universally applicable, being relevant to simple commodity production, bourgeois commodity production, and socialist commodity production. Xu Xingya (2002) compared labor value theory with Western price theory, concluding that the latter places more emphasis on the analysis of phenomenon, and technical processing, making it less profound than the former, which could be employed to analyze both the capitalist and the socialist market economy.

Other academic voices dissented. Yan Zhijie (2001) argued the theory could only explain a simple barter economy, offering little guidance about the general laws that determine market price. Bai Baoli (2001) countered that Yan had attributed three premises to Marx's value theory, namely barter, the free use of all other factors of production, and the idea that labor is inherently manual. Yan, he said, had falsely isolated these three premises from a chain of interconnected premises of the theory, and therefore erred in his judgement that labor value theory can only work for a simple commodity economy or fix exchange ratios in barter. Jiang Xuemo (1996) argued that labor value theory would not become obsolete as long as it kept evolving and developing.

According to Li Jiangfan (2001), labor value theory originated in the study of the material production sector, and is applicable when non-material production is negligible. The situation is quite different today, as tertiary industry has assumed much greater importance. Thus, it is wrong to think that only material production creates value. Based on the views of Gu Shutang and Liu Xin (1993), he claimed that traditional theory is *unitary*, assuming that only labor in material production creates value. This approach is out of date and cannot explain modern economic phenomena. Pluralism, which would incorporate both labor and non-labor factors, has given Marxian theories new life, thus providing more convincing accounts of reality.

The distinction between productive labor and unproductive labor

Discussion on the distinction between productive labor and unproductive labor, which began in the 1960s in the academic field, have now been raging for nearly half a century. Consensus is still elusive.

Cheng Enfu (2001) based his work on Marx's scientific notion that living labor creates the value in commodities produced for market exchange, while the circulation of these commodities creates no value, instead making it possible to convert the form of this value. He argued that the labor employed to produce material commodities and intellectual products for market exchange, as well as that which produces and reproduces labor power itself, can be counted as productive. Cheng's new theory of living labor value did not reject Marx's core methodology and ideology, but expanded it to all socio-economic sectors.

Jiang Xuemo (1996) argued that living labor engaged in manufacturing material products, intellectual products, and service products creates value and therefore is the source of value, providing a scientific basis for analyzing the status and contributions of the primary, secondary, and tertiary industries in national income and gross national product (GNP). Wu Yifeng (2001) however held that labor only creates value if it is engaged in commodity manufacture, or is part of the preparatory or follow-on stages. Productive labor of the same form does not necessarily create value. Some productive labor creates both use value and value, whereas some creates only use value. In the tertiary sector no definite answer is possible, because the productive or unproductive character of labor depends on its specific properties. According to Wei Xinghua (2001), productive labor includes both manual and mental labor. He also thought that the managerial expertise of private entrepreneurs is a kind of advanced labor and creates more value. Li Jiangfan (2001) also argued that labor in tertiary industry is productive, and employed the ratio of tertiary industry turnover to gross domestic product (GDP) to illustrate his point. His train of thought is as follows: there are non-material products of labor. These include service products, which have a use value. They also have a value, and so the labor that renders these services is productive. Qian Bohai (2001) also concluded that tertiary industries produce value, proceeding from the new system of national accounts, as did Li Ruicheng (2003).

These conclusions were disputed. Su Xing (1995) argued that the difference between productive and unproductive labor lies in the nature of the labor, not the sector in which the person works. One reason a consensus on this issue continued to evade us is that we have failed to apply this distinction. Therefore, we should use unitary theory to investigate which types of labor create value when employed in tertiary industries.

Similarly, Zhang Weida (2002) argued that within the tertiary sector, only productive service labor creates value. In a market economy, the tertiary industries make profits by setting prices. However, just because labor brings income, this does not establish that it creates value. Wang Tianyi (2001) and Bai Baoli (2001) warned against sweeping generalizations. Bai thought that productive labor manufactures goods that could meet the needs of the bulk of the people. If the goods only serve a minority, then the labor cannot be said to be productive. Wang Shuying (2001) stated that as long as the labor can satisfy social needs, it is productive. Luo Gengmo (1990, pp. 18–19) argued that since China is still in the primary stage of socialism, labor employed to produce goods for individual or family use, and the labor of workers hired by individual families, are both unproductive. Only labor engaged in small commodity production or production for public needs is productive.

Most economists and scholars agreed that labor employed in material commodity production in some parts of the tertiary industry sector, as well as managerial expertise and scientific technology, is productive, only a small proportion arguing that only labor engaged in material commodity production is productive. The latter argued that value does not come from nothing, and must be based on the use value of a commodity which can serve as the bearer of value. Thus, You Lin (2000) stated that only abstract labor responsible for manufacturing material products can create value. While labor that promotes technology, knowledge, or artistic work is important, its function in meeting people's demands is not sufficient to guarantee its status as productive labor. The same applies to labor in the education and public health sectors, which is not productive, even though it is indispensable for society. If we confuse these sectors with material commodity production, we fail to recognize that they serve different purposes and work on different subjects.

Bai Baoli (2002) argued that we should consider this issue from a different perspective, in the light of the wide extent of labor that Marx recognized as productive. First, because of its use value, labor employed in producing material commodities is productive. Second, if commodities are made for exchange, then the labor involved is productive. Third, commercial labor is also productive in the broadest sense that it creates surplus value for capital. Guo Xiaolu (2001) stated that intermediary services affiliated to material commodity production, such as consultation, create value and should be categorized as productive, whereas those services that cannot be separated from material commodity production do not create value and are not productive.

Is the theory of value unitary or pluralistic?

Though classical economics contributed to identifying and defining the source of value, it failed to make a scientific distinction between value and use value, offering only a vague understanding of the nature of the commodity. After more than a century, Marx came up with the labor theory of value, for the first time offering a scientific conception of the source of value. However, on the basis of Adam Smith's second definition of value, capitalist economists began constructing vulgar economics, in which value was said to be created by the combined action of all factors of production. These two opposed viewpoints regarding the source of value still exist side by side.

Cheng Enfu (2001) argued that labor value theory could not be separated from the core notion that labor is the source of value. He proposed a new unitary theory of living labor value. He argued that in addition to the production of both material commodities and cultural goods, the production and reproduction of the commodity labor power, which includes managerial expertise and scientific technology owned by individuals or legal persons as well as domestic labor, requires productive labor which creates value. He further argued that labor that has already been materialized creates no value. First, it differs from labor power and has different characteristics; second, the laborer cannot create value many times by laboring only once; third, if materialized labor is held to create value then no clear quantitative relation can be established between materialized labor and the amount of value it creates.

Su Xing (1995) likewise believed it is wrong to argue that capital, land, and labor all combine to create value. Living labor creates value whereas materialized labor only transfers value. Natural resources like land have no role to play in value creation and value transfer.

Wu Yifeng (2001) stated that labor is the only source of value, whether in a capitalist market economy or a socialist market economy. Other factors of production create no value. Attempts to expand the boundaries of labor to incorporate capital and land deny the definition of labor and undermine labor value theory.

According to Xiang Qiyuan (2001), it cannot be concluded, from the fact that developed countries have seen a surge in their total output, that non-labor factors of production create value. As living labor intensifies, total output will increase. The phenomenon that value quantity increases while the employment of living labor decreases relatively can be explained using labor value theory. Even though the amount of living labor is reducing, its increased complexity contributes to more value creation in a given period of time.

Lu Congming (2001) argued that a fundamental truth in Marxian economics is that labor (abstract labor) is the only source and entity of value. Although living labor and other non-labor factors are essential conditions for the creation of value, its social nature indicates that human abstract labor is its only direct source.

Opposed viewpoints also exist. Yan Zhijie (2001, pp. 8–10) argued that the key to understanding the role of capital, technology, and managerial expertise is to shift from traditional labor value theory to a theory based on factors of production or the theory of wealth.

Qian Bohai (1999) denied that only living labor creates value. His reasoning is as follows: if we deny that materialized labor can create value, then the statement that S&T constitute a primary productive force cannot hold water. Further, relative surplus value, including excess surplus value, would disappear. Third, the dual character of the commodity and of labor would no longer exist. Fourth, creating value does not necessarily mean adding value.

Wu Xuangong (1998) countered Qian's opinion with reference to a case study, demonstrating that materialized labor cannot create or add value, all the surplus value being created by living labor. Tang Guozeng (2001), Gu Yumin (1996), Xi Zhaoyong (2002), Chen Zhenyu (2002), Li Shanming, Xiao Ying (2002), and other scholars reached the same conclusion by various other routes.

Some scholars have unique opinions. For example, Wu Zhaozhen (2001) agreed that materialized labor does not contribute to value creation. However, he also found it incomplete to regard living labor as the sole source of value. Instead, he suggested that "combined labor" creates value, by which he meant that only when a dialectical unity is achieved between use value and value, concrete and abstract labor, material and service goods production, and living and materialized labor, can we harness use value and value, and handle the inherent contradictions within commodities or the conflicting interests between different owners, and facilitate the development of a socialist market economy and social productivity.

Some writers have argued that capital, productivity, scientific technology, knowledge, and information all create value, in some cases seeking to create a new general value theory on this foundation.

There has been an intense academic debate around S&T, and their relation to value, reflecting their growing role and influence in modern society.

Some hold that S&T itself creates no value, but the living labor of scientists and technicians does. Cheng Enfu (2001) thus stated that S&T is not attached to living labor and therefore cannot create value. Its effect is to multiply the efficiency of living labor. To say it creates no value is not to deny its critical role in value creation. Finally, it does not follow that because something is a factor of production, it creates value by itself. It only transforms the value already there, which is not the same as being a source of new value. As Yang Guochang (2001) put it, S&T equipped human beings with stronger labor capacities, but labor capacity is different from labor and therefore creates no value.

A second group think that S&T does create value. Qian Bohai (1995) argued that to identify materialized labor with capital and confine the creation of surplus value to living labor is a theoretical distortion in labor value theory. Relative surplus value and excess surplus value arise mainly from materialized labor. S&T creates surplus value through materialized labor, proving that it constitutes a primary productive force. Gu Shutang (2001) noted that since the Second World War, S&T has evolved exceptionally fast, playing an ever-increasing role in the creation of social wealth. Thus, it is wrong to say that technology, as one of the factors of production, only creates use value, and creates no value. Wu Xuangong (2002) in contrast argued that means of production, including high technology, are not capable of creating value.

Yet a third group argued that S&T can create value under some conditions. Li Dingzhong (1994) explained that when new technology and equipment are introduced into the production line, the resulting products will be produced with less than the socially necessary labor time. In this case, new technology and equipment not only transfer value but also create new value, bringing excess surplus value to the owner. Feng Wenguang (1997) stated that though other factors do not directly create value as labor does, they participate in the process as important determinants, just as fixed assets can work to increase relative surplus value. Zheng Zhiguo (2002) argued that we should not isolate knowledge and technology from labor. Instead, we should think of them as incorporated into labor. As for whether knowledge can create value, it depends on specific conditions. It is unwise to make sweeping generalizations. Likewise, we should not jump to the conclusion that technology and equipment create value.

A final group argued that the role of knowledge and technology in value creation should be approached by studying the production process. Yang Jirui (2001) stated that judgment should be based on specific situations. For example, when the knowledge economy made its debut in the production process, knowledge and technology that were internalized in the means of production did not create value. They mainly transferred value and enhanced living labor's capacity to create value.

The relation between value creation and value distribution

Cheng Enfu (2002) drew attention to a number of misunderstandings concerning value creation and its relation to distribution. It had been claimed that living labor value theory laid the theoretical basis for distribution according to work, that factors of production and their owners create value and therefore participate in its distribution, and that only those who create value should share in its distribution. The common origin of these misperceptions is a confusion between the creation of value and its distribution.

Li Qiqing (2001) argued that Marx's labor value theory explains mainly what to distribute, and how much of it. However, it does not deal with how to distribute, as this is the task of distribution theory rather than value theory. Marx once said the socialist practice of distribution according to work had nothing to do with labor value theory. Therefore, China's current distribution system is not based on Marx's labor value theory, but on Marx's theory of ownership.

Gu Shutang (2001) held that the principle of distribution according to work runs counter to reality, because current economic conditions cannot justify this practice. Instead, we should distribute according to contribution. Workers should receive income based on their work, and other factors of production such as capital or land should likewise be rewarded according to their contribution.

Zhou Xincheng (2002) argued that the creation and distribution of value are two separate processes. The fact that all factors participate in the distribution of newly created value does not necessarily mean that they all play a part in value creation. Value is created by labor both under capitalism and under socialism, but its distribution depends on the relations of production, which are quite different in the two systems, and also in different economic sectors. Thus, it is wrong to say that the factors of production create the income they receive through distribution, nor can we attribute changes in the modes of value distribution under different social systems to changes in the factors that create value.

Zhang Leisheng (2001) disputed the idea that China's distribution system, where distribution according to work remains dominant and a variety of modes of distribution coexist, is based on the principles of Marx's labor value theory. Marx's labor value theory, he argued, deals with the origin of value, whereas distribution is determined by ownership of the means of production. To regard labor value theory as the basis of the distribution system has to cause confusion.

Lu Congming (2001) argued that although there is no direct causal relation between labor value theory and the principle of distribution according to labor, some relations do exist. Labor value theory reveals that abstract labor is the only source of value, and that the value created by complex labor is a multiple of that created by simple labor. Therefore, distribution should favor workers who undertake complex labor, such as mental work.

Economists and scholars agree that the distribution of the factors of production is unavoidable in the current stage of China's evolution, even though they remain divided on the relation between value creation and distribution. What are their opinions on how value should be distributed?

Cheng Enfu (2003) thought that distribution according to the contributions of factors of production is merely the form whose essence is distribution according to ownership. The amount distributed to owners of different factors of production is decided by different criteria. For example, under the law of competition and the formation of an average rate of profit, owners of non-labor factors of production will receive gains commensurate with their capital, with specific manifestations in the forms of rent, interest, and profit. Hu Jun (2001) noted that in capitalist society, workers are only paid the value of their labor power, while capitalists appropriate the surplus value that workers create. Even among capitalists, value is not distributed by how much each enterprise creates, but by the amount of capital invested in the production process. Gu Shutang (2001) believed that value should be distributed by the marginal productivity of each factor of production.

A final area of contention is exploitation

Cheng Enfu (2002) argued it is well known to all that private enterprises pursue surplus value. Therefore, there should be no doubt that exploitation exists in capitalist society. The private entrepreneurs' managerial expertise and scientific knowledge are complex labor. The result is therefore a product of labor, and does not arise from exploitation. Exploitation is a historic phenomenon which will persist until productivity reaches an advanced level.

Wei Xinghua (2002) also noted the convincing evidence that exploitation exists in private enterprises. In China's current circumstances, however, playing down the theory of exploitation is conducive to the development of the non-public sector. If as a consequence China gave too much publicity to the "factors of production" value theory and its denial of exploitation, denying the labor theory of value and surplus value would have negative consequences.

Shi Zhengfu (2002, pp. 120–1) argued that private enterprises in China have assumed new characteristics, specifically the separation of ownership from management. Private capital and public joint capital have become interchangeable under certain simple conditions. Thus, we can no longer regard returns to private capital as the result of exploitation. Exploitation in a socialist market economy means making an undue profit in conflict with other people's rightful interests, by breaking the principle of equality and free will in the marketplace. Three specific manifestations are compelling others to accept unfair trade terms by force, cheating others so that they fall victim to unfair trade deals, and acquiring excess economic profit by means of privilege and monopoly, to the disadvantage of other economic entities in the marketplace.

Wang Dachao (2001) argued that exploitation should be analyzed from a historical materialist point of view. In the primary stage of socialism, various economic elements coexist. Therefore, exploitation is to be expected. It has played some positive role in capital accumulation, resource allocation, and the development of productivity. Thus, in some sectors, it cannot be replaced by the system of distribution, and should be encouraged to some extent as long as it meets the standards of the "Three Favourables."[2]

In summary, though economists and scholars in China have debated labor value theory for almost half a century, they continue to disagree and hold completely opposite opinions on some issues. We celebrate the theoretical achievements of this discussion but do not want to lose sight of a number of deficiencies, as follows.

(1) Most research dwells on abstract theoretical study, citing classic works without going deeper to make independent discoveries and new findings. This leads to a lack of theoretical depth. This is compounded by the tendency to shy away from empirical or practical investigation. Even a very logical theory becomes quite dull in such research.

(2) No in-depth study has been made of how labor itself has evolved. Some researchers just follow their instincts and jump to the conclusion that the nature and meaning of labor have changed, so that both scientific technology and managerial expertise can create value. More discussion is

---

2   Deng Xiaoping raised three fundamental criteria for judging a proposal or a policy: whether it is favorable for promoting growth of the productive forces in a socialist society, whether it is favorable for increasing the overall strength of the socialist state, and whether it is favorable for raising the people's living standards. The criteria were called the "Three Favorables."

needed on why these two forms of labor create value and what determines the quantity of that value.

(3) Most scholars approach labor value theory in political economy through normative analysis, which means they devote too much time to expounding the nature of a theory with insufficient positive and quantitative analysis. Viewpoints arrived at in this way do not stand up to closer examination and may lead to misunderstandings.

(4) The labor theory of value is a well-knit theoretical system. Instead of trying to break it up, the right approach is to take it as a whole and make a thorough analysis of its role in today's new circumstances, especially as regards the nature and scope of labor in the market economy. So far, most research has focused on one issue, which risks missing the whole picture.

4

Main theoretical positions on productive labor[1]

As the situation changed, adherents of Marx's value theory began to voice doubts and objections. The truth is, we should note, always relative, and there is no absolute truth. Basing himself on the characteristics of the mode of production and the basic contradictions of the capitalism of his time, Marx, through painstaking research, developed a theory of the economics of the capitalist mode of production, the relations of production corresponding

1   Editor's and translators' note: This book employs the term "productiveness." This requires two clarifications, the first semantic and the second conceptual. First, semantically, the more modern term "productivity" is used in the Penguin edition of *Capital* that has become the Western standard, but the older term "productiveness" used in the Progress Publishers/Chicago edition is the best known to Chinese scholars. We opted for "productiveness" where this is used to render Marx's own usage.

Second, the authors treat "productiveness" and "labor productiveness" as two different conceptions. "Productiveness" refers to the concrete productiveness of labor, namely its ability to act on objects using means of labor to produce use-value. This from the outset includes labor power, natural power, and the power of science and technology. It contains three elements, namely the laborer, implements of labor, and the subjects of labor. The result of efficiency in productiveness is the rate of production. Labor productiveness measures the efficiency of productiveness by calculating the use value produced in given period of time. However, labor productiveness results from not only productiveness but also labor intensity. The two terms "labor productiveness" and "productiveness" can only be regarded as the same if labor intensity is constant. In practice, labor productiveness is usually influenced by both productiveness and labor intensity (Zhang Xunhua 1999, 8–9).

to it, and the relation between the two. Labor value theory is the foundation of Marxian economics, on which are based many other theories such as the theory of surplus value. Now 150 years have passed since the birth of this theory, during which the world has undergone profound changes. Modern science and technology, in particular, has modified the mode of production.

For this reason, it is far-fetched and not objective to criticize the theory for not keeping up with the current situation. We face many new problems absent in Marx's time. Nevertheless, the facts show that labor value theory can still serve as a guide to our practice. Therefore, the authors argue, we should stick to the basic theoretical positions while improving Marx's labor value theory as it applies to modern economic development.

Changes in the means of labor: an analysis of the connotation and the denotation of labor

As forces of production develop and social and economic formations change, so do the means of labor – the means by which humans exist. This chapter studies these changes, and their general law, in history. It does so from the standpoint of the expenditure, and objects, of labor.

Different uses of "productiveness" and "labor productiveness" are to be found in different versions of *Capital*. On page 53 of *Capital Volume 23* published by People's Publishing House, the word "productiveness" is used, instead of "labor productiveness." On page 560, however, the word "labor productiveness" is used. On page 47 of the English version of Capital, "productiveness" is used, rather than "productive power," "productive force," or "productiveness" (Marx 1972, p. 47). On page 562, "productiveness" is mentioned again. On page 54 of the German version of *Capital*, the phrase used is "Die Produktivkraft der Arbeit," instead of "Die Produktivität der Arbeit" (Marx 1972, p. 54). On page 535, however, the phrase "Die Produktivität der Arbeit" is used. There is an obvious difference between the two German words.

From the uses of these two words in various versions, we can see that "productiveness" and "labor productiveness" are two different conceptions. The English word "productiveness" is more accurate, while the Chinese translation fails to express the exact meaning of the original German word "Produktivkraft."

Labor, an exchange process between human beings and nature, is the fundamental economic activity of humans, and the foundation of their existence and development. To this extent labor, a relationship between humans and nature which is permanently present, does not change with the social formation. If we set aside their specific nature and hence their use values, all forms of production boil down to the expenditure of labor power.

This takes various concrete forms, such as the production of grain and steel, which are productive activities of different kinds. Setting aside their specific means of labor, however, both are productive expenditures of human brain, muscles, nerves, and hands, and therefore both expend labor power. The labor that produces a given use value is hence a combination of the laborer's manual and mental labor, which are inseparable and vary only in their share in total labor.

The proportion of manual to mental labor depends on economic development and the level of the productive forces, the latter being the most direct influence and the most dynamic factor of production, which is itself "determined by various circumstances, amongst others, by the average amount of skill of the workmen, the state of science, and the degree of its practical application, the social organization of production, the extent and capabilities of the means of production, and by physical conditions" (Marx 1965, p. 29). From Marx's analysis, we can discern two influences on the productive forces: labor power, and science and nature.

Labor power, an attribute of living persons, is a combination of the manual and mental labor performed when producing a given use value. It changes with the intensity and complexity of work as well as the skill of the workers. Therefore, stronger labor power suggests a higher level of productive forces. Science is not only a system of knowledge, but also a general social productive force: a potential or indirect productive force, which can be transformed into a direct one through the means of labor. It mainly manifests itself materially in the form of instruments of labor.

The impact of science on productive forces was already quite salient in Marx's time, as he notes in the *Poverty of Philosophy* (1962). Human productive activities are carried out under certain natural conditions. Free natural forces such as wind, abundant forest, and fertile land participate in and contribute to production, exerting great influence on the productive force of labor. Moreover, joint labor in production leads to the division of labor and the coordination of work, giving rise to the cost-free productive forces of social labor which, as with natural forces, participate in production and promote the development of productive forces.

As this happens, Marx argued, human economic activities broaden and deepen. More frequent and broader exchanges lead to the further division of labor, which in turn promotes exchange, with a consequent huge impact on the way labor is expended.

In the early stage of primitive society when productive forces are less developed, people unite into communities to defend themselves against threats of nature, and to conduct such simple productive activities as hunting a limited number of animals and picking fruits for mere subsistence. Although this labor is almost entirely manual, mental labor also contributes to production because human labor is a conscious activity guided by the brain. As the productive forces develop and productive experiences accumulate, people invent various instruments that can perform or supplement the functions of human hands and feet, leading to a gradually decreasing proportion of manual labor. Under capitalist development, with scientific technology advancing by leaps and bounds, machinery dominates the mode of production, production is conducted on an ever larger scale, further extending the division of labor, social combination in production reaches a new historical level, and laborers contribute in a great variety of ways to the direct process that forms the commodity, or more appropriately here, the product:

> *one working more with his hands, another more with his brain, one as a manager, engineer, or technician, etc., another as an overlooker, the third directly as a manual worker, or even a mere assistant, more and more of the functions of labour capacity are included under the direct concept of productive labour, and their repositories under the concept of productive workers...*

> *If we consider the total worker constituting the workshop, his combined activity is directly realised materialiter in a total product which*

*is at the same time a total quantity of commodities, and in this con-
nection it is a matter of complete indifference whether the function of
the individual worker, who is only a constituent element of this total
worker, stands close to direct manual labour or is far away from it.
(Marx and Engels 1994, pp. 443–4)*

Thus, when productive forces develop to a certain level, they bring great changes in the proportion of manual to mental labor. Some are engaged in technical work as engineers, some in managerial work as managers, and it is the workforce as a whole that produces products collectively.

As technology advances, the role of mental workers becomes more ever important and their proportion in the total workforce ever greater. It is estimated that in capitalist countries, people educated to a medium standard account for more than half the workforce of those enterprises with a high degree of automation, while more than a third have higher education. Generally, the ratio of manual work to mental work stands at 90:10 in enterprises with a low level of mechanization, at 60:40 in enterprises with a medium level of mechanization, and at 10:90 in fully automated enterprises.

Thus, technicians account for almost a quarter of the workforce of the US company General Motors, with more than 6,000 people in its technical center. All these facts show that as the productive forces have developed, and exchange has expanded, labor has shifted from a manual-labor-centered to a mental-labor-centered mode, in which manual work plays a supplementary role. The connotation of human labor is changing, as mental-work-centered technicians and managerial personnel create as much or more value than manual laborers.

Denotation: how the object of labor is changing

Humans are social beings with various desires and needs, both material and spiritual. Whether on our own or in a developed economic system of exchange, we allocate our time and resources rationally according to the urgency of our needs in order to meet them. Even Robinson Crusoe on his lonely island has to meet various needs by allocating his time between different labors, such as making tools or catching fish.

The time allocated to each type of activity depends on the difficulties Robinson surmounts to achieve the expected results. The same applies to an economic system based on exchange: the time allocated to each activity varies with the urgency of the needs it meets, and with general labor productivity. Higher labor productiveness allows less time to be spent on some needs, and that time to be reallocated to other needs. The division and coordination of labor generates social productive forces, which promote productive efficiency, and hence save more time.

These needs may be tangible like grains, or intangible like consultation, but given limited time and resources, production cannot meet them all, so resources are allocated according to the importance of their needs. When productivity is low, time is mostly spent producing the basic means to survive. As the productive forces develop and with them the number of surplus products, people can spend time on literature, art, fortune-telling, and other activities to meet the needs of the minority. In modern capitalist society less and less time is required to produce basic materials, leaving more time for other things.

When more time is spent to produce the means of subsistence, less is allocated to other social needs. By the middle of the 19th century, machinery began to displace hand work in production, and productivity was greatly advanced, but workers still had a low cultural level. The labor process was relatively easy, and workers tended to shift from one sector to another. Most social labor time was allocated to the material sector, with not much time left for others. For example, according to Lange (Marx and Engels 1996, p. 208), of the population of 18 million in England and Wales at that time, 11 million were engaged in producing materials. The share of population producing materials in the total population reached 61.11%, and the share of the 4.64 million middle class such as officials, writers, artists, and teachers stood at only 25.83%. Most social labor time was allocated to material production, and only a small proportion to the spiritual (cultural) or service sectors.

As the forces of production developed and technology advanced, human labor has developed through hand labor, workshop handcraft, modern mechanical industry, and mechanized industry to automated systems. Mechanization is today applied basically throughout all the sectors of production.

With such levels of productive forces, only a small proportion of aggregate social labor time is needed to meet the whole of society's material needs, and much more time can be allocated to services and society's cultural needs, and to promoting human development. Industrial structure nowadays thus differs considerably from Marx's time. The proportions of primary, secondary, and tertiary industry were 2.2: 42.6: 55.2 in 1980, reaching 1.8: 31.5: 66.7 in 1996. The figure for China in 2001 was 15.2: 51.1: 33.6.

Aggregate social labor time is fixed, and its allocation depends entirely on the level of development of the productive forces and the intensity of effective needs. Human needs are both material and spiritual, so society naturally spends more time producing cultural goods and services that meet the latter needs and raise quality. This in turn raises the capabilities of labor. We cannot now therefore limit productive labor to material production, and should extend the denotation of labor. We should acknowledge as productive both the labor of creating commercial goods and that of producing both tangible and intangible cultural goods, and the labor of services.

The theory of productive labor

In this section we discuss three issues. First, what is the source of value and the scope of productive labor – that is, labor that creates value – in current society? Second, what is the source of wealth, and what relationship does it have with the source of value? Third, can materialized labor create value?

Productive labor creates value

According to Marx, labor creates the value of a commodity, while circulation that only changes the form of this value does not. We can infer that all those kinds of labor that produce marketable material and intellectual goods, or that serve to produce and reproduce commodity labor power, including management labor and the S&T labor of natural persons and legal entities, are value-creating, or productive, labor. Therefore, productive labor value theory, rather than negating Marx's central point, is the natural conclusion of his approach to the study of value creation in the material production sector, and even in all social economic departments. To be specific (Cheng 2001):

First, labor that produces material goods is productive. This includes agriculture, industry, construction, and material technology. Marx has already illustrated this point.

Second, labor engaged in transporting tangible or intangible commodities is productive. This covers the conveyance of commodities or personnel in the market, as well as post and telecommunication labor which passes information through letters, messages, telegraphs, telephones, and so on. Changing places or transferring information constitutes the generalized labor of communication, a special productive department in the circulation sector. Marx also illustrates this point.

Third, labor engaged in producing tangible and intangible intellectual commodities is productive, including education, social science, natural science, culture, literature and arts, broadcasting, film and television, news media, libraries, museums; also teaching, performing, and creating other intangible commodities and services. Value creation is not limited to the labor that produces material goods.

Fourth, labor that serves to produce commodity labor power is productive. Besides those productive sectors close to people's daily lives that have already been mentioned, sectors such as medical treatment, health care, sports and games, hairdressing, the beauty industry, and the bathing industry are also involved in the production and reproduction of special commodity labor power (Cheng 2001).[2]

Fifth, the private owner of a productive enterprise creates value through operational and management activities. China's traditional political economy accepts that in publicly owned enterprises, the management activities of the director and manager are productive. But for capitalist enterprises, its attitude is negative or evasive. It is self-contradictory to maintain that management activities that originally created value cease to do so when combined with the private property of the enterprise. If the major investor or owner of a productive private enterprise is, at the same time, the actual manager

2   This is Cheng Enfu's "fourth breakthrough." He surmounts Marx's hypothesis that productivity increases while the magnitude of value stays constant, and establishes the theory that the productivity resulting from the increase in labor complexity (such as through S&T) and proficiency will increase the value of the commodity this labor produces.

of the enterprise, then management activities take on a dual character. That aspect that provides necessary management of collaborative social labor objectively creates new value. However, the aspect that exploits this necessity to secure benefits arising from property rights objectively extracts surplus labor for free. In real economic life, the two functions can be qualitatively distinguished by scientific analysis even if they are intertwined with each other and shouldered by one person (Cheng 1995).[3]

Sixth, improvements in the productiveness of labor may arise from changes in labor complexity which modify the amount of socially necessary labor, leading to changes in the magnitude of value. When Marx explains the relation between the magnitude of value and labor productiveness, he ignores subjective effects on labor productiveness, and believes that increased productivity resulting from a change in objective or natural conditions will change only the magnitude of use value, with no influence on total value. He concludes that the magnitude of value changes in the opposite direction to labor productiveness.

However, the major factor that promotes labor productiveness is technological advance, which raises labor's complexity, proficiency, and intensity, and hence the amount of value it produces, as follows:

1. If the change in labor productiveness results only from an alteration of labor's objective conditions, its subjective conditions remaining unchanged, then productiveness and the amount of value vary in the opposite direction. This situation exists under certain condition in certain periods.

2. If the change in labor productiveness results only from the alteration of labor's subjective conditions, with its objective conditions remaining unchanged, then labor productiveness and the amount of value vary in the same direction.

3. If the change of labor productiveness is caused by joint variation of both subjective and objective conditions, then labor productiveness and magnitude of value may vary in opposite directions or the same direction, or both may remain unchanged.

4. Since, overall, the amount of value produced shows an upward tendency along with the increase in labor productiveness, total value tends to increase rather than remain unchanged.

---

3   Marx accepts this conclusion but does not stress it. This is "the third breakthrough" of Cheng Enfu in 1995.

The definition and reinterpretation of the relation between magnitude of value and labor productiveness clearly illustrates the role of management labor and S&T labor during the process of value creation.

The academic community remains divided on the source of value. Some scholars hold that the issue is actually the source of use value. They think that human labor creates value in combination with nature, various means of production, S&T, and managerial experience. That is, they think commodity value is created by various factors of production. Some scholars propose, on the basis of multivariate labor productivities or production functions, that non-labor elements also influence value. Other scholars try to distinguish between creating and increasing value. They think that from the perspective of a single enterprise, materialized labor creates value and serves as the major source of surplus value. Some scholars even distinguish between productivity determined by the use of capital and that determined by the use of land, calling these the capital productivity and the land productivity of labor respectively. They think these kinds of productivity also create value. In addition, there is also general value theory, resource contribution value theory, and so on.

In essence, this dazzling variety of value theories falls into two categories, with different scopes. On the one hand we find living labor value theories, and on the other, generalizations of productive factor value theory. For example, the idea that materialized labor creates value actually belongs to factor value theory, since it holds that means of production create value. The assertion that the capital and land productivity of labor create value also assumes that means of production – land and capital – can create value.

Such theories fail to stand up to theoretical examination. First, factor value theory does not distinguish abstract labor from concrete labor, thus confusing value with use value, and the labor process with value expansion. Logically, it confuses two different levels: factors are concepts arising from the value process, while capital (including constant and variable capital) arises from value expansion. This expresses a confusion between value formation (how value comes into being in production) and value expansion (how capitalists acquire value in excess of the value consumed in production). In production, concrete labor transfers the value of means of production C to the product. The same labor is also the abstract labor that creates the new value V+S. So the value of the product is C+V+S. Now, no enterprise or capitalist will be satisfied to receive only C+V, the original value and the cost of labor power. Value expansion refers to the production of surplus value S over and above this magnitude. The owner of the surplus value can be an individual, a collectivity, or the state, depending on the property system.

The total factor theory of wealth

Living labor is the only source of value, but it is obviously far from sufficient on its own. Land, capital, technology, information, natural resources, and the eco-environment are required to conduct real productive and service activities, and provide use value capable of meeting a variety of demands. Therefore wealth – that is, utility or use value – comes from several sources, all directly created by all relevant means of production.

Marx's theory clearly distinguishes wealth from value. The commodity has a dual nature –value and use value. Use value (wealth) is the material bearer of value, and the material content of wealth. In *Capital,* Marx (1965, p. 31) criticizes the idea that labor is the only source of material wealth. Humans can only change the material form of a product with the help of natural forces. "Labor is not the only source of material wealth, i.e. of the use-values it produces. As William Petty says, labor is the father of material wealth; the earth is its mother."

Engels echoes Marx's criticism in *Dialectics of Nature*, stressing that labor, together with nature, comprises the source of wealth. Nature provides labor with materials, which labor then turns into wealth (Marx and Engels 1972a, p. 508).

In the *Critique of the Gotha Programme* (Marx and Engels 1972a, p. 508), Marx further presents the class origin of the viewpoint that labor is the source of all wealth and culture, pointing out that it actually comes from the capitalist class, since it avoids mentioning the objective conditions of production. Labor is the sole source of wealth only to those who own the labor and treat the natural world as their private property. When the capitalist class controls the means of production and becomes the ruling class, they are willing to consider that labor has a supernatural creativity. But the proletariat and their political party cannot accept this opinion. Therefore, contrary to the arbitrary criticisms that Marxist economics ignores wealth and factors of production, Marx paid great importance to both.

The total factor theory of wealth does not contradict the living labor theory of value. The two complement each other, and together constitute the complete theory of commodity and wealth creation. The former illustrates the relation between production factors (representing concrete labor) and social wealth (representing the use value or utility of commodities). Its aim is to lay bare the relations between people and objects, and between objects and each other, as concrete labor creates use values. The latter explains the relation between living labor (representing abstract labor) and commodity value. Its aim is to lay bare the relations between people as abstract labor creates new value under a definite mode of social production.

At the same time, the inner relations between the two theories show that living labor, the subject of labor, is the source of both value and wealth; while the tangible or intangible means of production, which are the objects of labor, are the source of wealth and a necessary economic condition or basis for value to be created. However, factor value theorists claim that the source of wealth is the source of commodity value. Since labor is not the only source of wealth, they reason, then neither can it be the only source of value, which must therefore be created jointly by labor and other means of production. This confuses a series of concepts, including wealth and value, concrete labor and abstract labor, constant capital and variable capital, and labor process and value creation.

The report of the sixteenth National Congress of the Communist Party of China points out that we should "unleash all the vitality contained in work, knowledge, technology, management and capital and give full play to all sources of social wealth for the benefit of the people." The total factor theory of wealth indicates that in modern society, the three substantial means of production, including abundant objects of labor, advanced means of labor, and high-caliber laborers, together with the organization factor of management, the subtle factor of science and education, the connecting factor of information, and the restrictive factor of environment, are the direct source and constituents of society's material, spiritual, and management wealth. To meet people's increasing material, cultural and service demands, we must give full play to the function and potential for wealth creation of all means of production.

Materialized labor cannot create value (Cheng and Gu 2001)

The central point of labor value theory is that living labor is the only source of value, and no other means of production can create value. To justify the unitary nature of value, there has to be a reasonable answer to the question: can materialized labor and S&T create value by themselves? Once this problem is solved, there is no need to respond to other value theories, which are all variants of factor value theory. We discuss whether S&T create value in the section dealing with S&T labor. Here, we offer a theoretical explanation of why materialized labor cannot create value.

Materialized labor cannot create value because the material means of production cannot do so, for the following reasons

1. Materialized labor is an object, which does not have the same properties as labor power. It takes the form of means of production, a static factor. Labor however constitutes the action of the laborer who, in the process of production, uses the means of production to act on the object of labor to produce use values. At the same time, value comes into being and expands. This is a dynamic process, enabling labor power to create value. The means of production can only be used by laborers; they cannot initiate this process; for this reason, they cannot create. To say materialized labor creates value is to say that the means of production can initiate the living labor process. This conflicts with common sense.

2. Labor can only create value once. Every time the laborer works, value is created. The process of value creation stops when the labor process ends. The idea that materialized labor can create value leads to the wrong conclusion that labor creates value several times over. As the fruit of previous acts of creation, it already contains value in itself. In production, this is gradually transferred to the new product through the application of living labor. If materialized labor creates value, this means previous living labor can create value many times over.

3. The idea that materialized labor creates value cannot quantitatively specify the relation between this materialized labor and the value to which

it allegedly gives rise. Various means of production play totally different roles in production. Each is combined with specific technologies and skills, and has a distinct quality. How they create value and how much each creates cannot be calculated. The Cambridge school already furnished this criticism in the 1950s. Scientific empirical analysis thus shows that despite claims to be quantitative, the theory that materialized labor creates value cannot produce quantitatively accurate results.

Research on the reduction of complex to simple labor

The relation between complex and simple labor, and the reduction of the former to the latter, are central to Marx's theory of value. Opponents of his theory frequently cite this issue as a basis for rejecting it, making further research on it of great theoretical and practical significance.

The main views of Chinese and foreign scholars on the conversion of complex to simple labor

We begin with a brief introduction to the views of foreign scholars.

Böhm-Bawerk (1936) launched the first attack, arguing that with the introduction of heterogeneous labor, Marx's theory would contradict his assumption that the rate of exploitation was the same everywhere, unless different labors were reduced to the same abstract labor in accordance with wage rates. He deemed this reduction a causal fiction and a forgery.

Ian Steedman offered mathematical proofs which suggested that the profit rate could be calculated from the input and output of material factors, the real wage, and the direct consumption of heterogeneous labor in different sectors. The profit rate could therefore be determined without reducing different kinds of labor to any common type.

Michio Morishima held that Marxists confronted a dilemma: whether to use the wage rate to calculate multiplying factors. He also used mathematical approaches to justify his views, and concluded that labor value theory should be abandoned.

M. C. Howard and J. E. King opposed Marx's statement that complex labor is the simple multiplication and accumulation of simple labor. Marx, they argued, thought that complex labor required training costs, which they regarded as a partial analysis.

Rowthorn proposed two reduction methods: the cost method, which he found to be flawed, and the reduction of indirect labor. The latter was first discovered by Rudolf Hilferding, who stated that all unskilled and skilled workers contribute to the training of skilled workers. The whole value they contribute is gradually transferred to products through the labor of the skilled workers. All skilled labor can thus be decomposed into unskilled labor. This removes any dependence on wages, and the circularity that Böhm-Bawerk alleged.

In China, Zhu Zhongdi (1989) argued that Marx had not treated the reduction of complex labor comprehensively. He agreed with Rowthorn and Hilferding's approach of reduction of indirect labor, but did not agree that skilled workers' labor constitutes a transfer of old values. The value created by complex labor could surpass this, leading to a bigger multiplying factor.

Qian Jin (2001) agreed. He pointed out that in modern society, the conversion of complex to simple labor is not that clear. Within a certain range, the two kinds of labor differ in magnitude, but out of that range they differ in nature. The reduction of complex to simple labor at the level of abstract value is realized through the market.

Peng Biyuan (2001) said that the foreign scholars confused complex with skilled labor, leading to a wrong conclusion. The reduction was realized through exchanges between products created by the two kinds of labor. The so-called "circular argument" does not exist, because the reduction is not a process of calculation.

Tang Meilian (2003) proposed two further ways to reduce complex to simple labor: the factor analysis approach and the complexity coefficient approach. The former yields a reduction multiplier by analyzing the elements of complex labor and their influences on value. The latter considers training expenses, time needed, and the value it creates, to define an indicator that can be used to calculate the complexity coefficient.

On the reduction of labor to simple labor, Marx stated that

more complex labour counts only as intensified, or rather simply multiplied simple labour, so that a smaller quantity of complex labour is considered equal to a larger quantity of simple labour. Experience shows that this reduction is constantly being made. A commodity may be the outcome of the most complicated labour, but through its value it is posited as equal to the products of simple labour, hence it represents only a specific quantity of simple labour. The various proportions in which different kinds of labour are reduced to simple labour as their unit of measurement are established by a social process that goes behind the backs of the producers; these proportions therefore appear to the producers to have been handed down by tradition (Marx 1965, p. 32) ...

All labour of a higher or more complicated character than average labour is expenditure of labour-power of a more costly kind, labour-power whose production has cost more time and labour, and which therefore has a higher value, than unskilled or simple labour-power. This power being higher-value, its consumption is labour of a higher class, labour that creates in equal times proportionally higher values than unskilled labour does. (Marx 1965, p. 138)

Engels agreed with Marx in his *Anti-Dühring* (Marx and Engels 1972a, pp. 236–40). He criticized Dühring's statement that working hours were the same for everyone at the very beginning, and all labors were of the same value with no exceptions. Engels argued that most labors in society are complex labor, and even in the same period, value created by complex labor differs from that created by simple labor.

Basic positions on the reduction of complex to simple labor

The conversion between complex and simple labor actually has a twofold meaning: whether the conversion is possible, and how to realize it.

(1) Both complex and simple labor are abstract labor. Simple labor is the labor power that all ordinary humans possess in their bodily organism, without being developed in any special way. It has different natures in different countries and at different times, but remains stable in a given society, and serves as the measure of value. Complex labor is a higher labor power surpassing the average. These two kinds of labor exist in every country and every historic period. Two products must be measured by the amount of labor in them, in order to be exchanged. If complex labor could not be converted into simple labor, exchanges in the market could not exist, because these two kinds of labors could not be compared quantitatively.

(2) The value created by complex labor surpasses that created by simple labor. The intensity of different labors that take up the same amount of natural time must be taken into consideration here. Marx mentioned this concept but did not develop it, which did not arouse attention in Chinese academic circles. Professor Cheng Enfu advanced the concept of labor natural time (external scale) and labor intensity time (inner scale) for the first time in academic circles, and this offers a better instrument for understanding the reduction of complex labor (Ma and Cheng 2002).

Labor intensity time refers to the time a laborer needs to produce a certain use value employing a given labor intensity. As we know, labor is the substance of value, and the magnitude of value is determined by the consumption of labor, which is expressed in terms of labor time, usually measured in natural time. The labor consumed determines the magnitude of value created. The labor consumed by the application of complex labor is greater than that of simple labor and creates more value, because a complex laborer must be trained. During the training, the individual laborer spends time, which we assume to be A hours, and incurs training expenses embedded in goods, for whose production we assume the labor time needed is B hours. So the labor time consumed for this training is A + B, which is hence the labor time necessary for training complex labor. This is reflected in the subsequent process of production. For instance, a worker could work for a total of 100,000 hours in their lifetime and invest 50,000 hours of simple labor equivalent in their training. Then every hour they work should be calculated as one and a half hours of simple labor. Sweezy (1997, p. 61) uses this example to show that the value created by complex labor surpasses that created by simple labor.

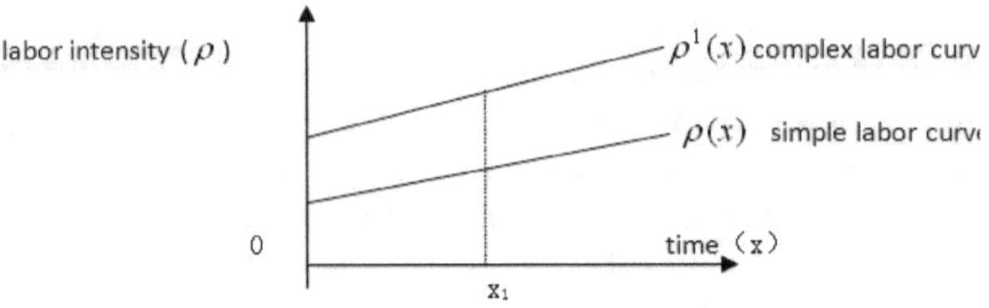

Figure 4.1 The value created by complex labor and simple labor

As is shown in Figure 4.1, in a unit of time X_1 the value created by complex labor is $\int_0^{x_1} \rho'(x)dx$, and that by simple labor is $\int_0^{x_1} \rho(x)dx$. The first appears to be greater. With a longer production period and fewer gaps, however, complex labor is more intense, and more labor is consumed when it is used. It thus creates greater value, as can be seen from Figure 4.2.

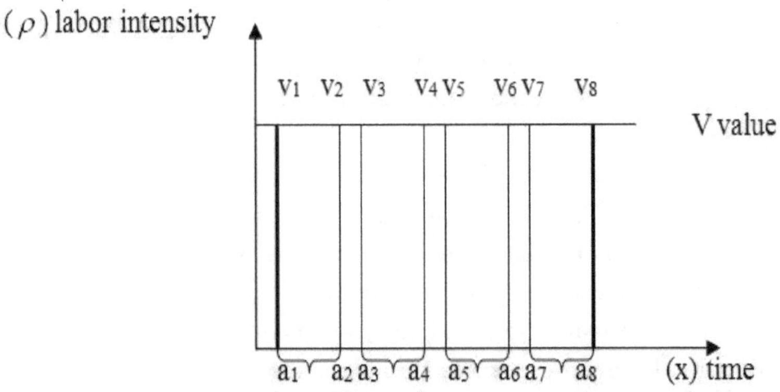

**Figure 4.2 The value created by complex labor and
simple labor with advanced labor intensity**

104

As is shown in Figure 4.2, if continuity is weaker (more gaps in the application of labor during production) with lower labor intensity and shorter labor intensity time, the value created by simple labor is $\int_{a_1}^{a_2} x dx + \int_{a_3}^{a_4} x dx + \int_{a_5}^{a_6} x dx + \int_{a_7}^{a_8} x dx$. With greater continuity, more labor intensity, and hence longer labor intensity time, the value created by complex labor is $\int_{a_1}^{a_8} x dx$ which is obviously bigger than that created by simple labor.

(3) The concept of labor in human history begins with its simplest form. As the productive forces grow and experience accumulates, labor becomes more complex. The gradual progression from the simplest to complex labor happens to any laborer. A specific such individual laborer would clearly know how much more time complex labor consumes. When it happens to other laborers, owing to the connections between labors and the relative simple form of complex labor, then the laborers can also discover this quantitative relation. In a specific exchange, one side might feel unfairly treated, but in the market, the exchange rate is adjusted and tends to a certain level. For instance, in the 1960s and 1970s, an ironworker made a hoe and gave it to a farmer. The farmer did three days' farm work for him rather than pay him with currency. The people in the village all recognized that a hoe equals three days' farm work. Why did not they think that it equals one or four days' work? Because they all knew that the exchange was fair and acceptable.

Complex labor was thus reduced to simple labor through a progression from the simplest to the most complex form, with its own law. In mathematical language, the sequence was A–B–C–D…, rather than A–D. But no quantified approach exists for comparing the labor consumed in car design and that of a receptionist, which can refer to such a historical progression. The social process determines the real exchange rate behind the back of the laborers.

(4) Complex labor creates more value than simple labor, which is expressed in the amount of products exchanged, but cannot be understood as wages. A wage is the value of labor power expressed in money. Setting aside the effects of fluctuations in the currency value, the wage does not necessarily equal the value created by the worker. In times of small hand-mills or small-scale production, the wage might be equal to a certain amount of the resulting exchanged products. But under capitalist production, to use the

wage rate to reduce complex labor it is putting the cart before the horse; it is a faulty theoretical method.

(5) The reduction of complex to simple labor is realized in the market. Before exchange, no one can calculate their labor complexity, since this is expressed in the exchange products the other side offers. Therefore, all attempts to figure out a stable reduction rate or coefficient are methodologically in vain.

(6) The theoretical explanation of reduction can however offer practical guidelines. It confirms the merits of training in enhancing the results of labor. It proves that mental labor creates value, and even more value than ordinary manual laborers. Third, it shows that the principle of labor-based distribution should be followed, with priority given to laborers in the field of S&T and managers.

5
Value creation in material production

No matter what the form of social production, material production is always the basis of human existence and social development. With S&T progress and the accumulated experience of production, capitalist societies have created more wealth in less than a hundred years than all preceding generations. As the world enters the 21st century, capitalism has developed to a new high, and social productiveness has great potential for development.

Although the industrial structures of developed countries today are quite different from those in Marx's time, material production still accounts for a certain proportion of social labor. Moreover, material production (namely the primary and secondary sectors) provides a strong material foundation for the growth of the service sector. Experience demonstrates that without highly developed material production, a large-scale and high-level service sector is impossible. Thus, material production is even more important for developing countries than for developed ones.

When analyzing economic development in capitalist societies, Marx focused on production, exchange, circulation, and distribution in the material production sectors.[1]

His analysis starts with the cell of capitalist economy – the commodity – extending it to cover the dual character of commodities, the dual character

---

1   This is required by theoretical analysis. To treat material production sectors as the object of study is not only consistent with the social conditions at that time, but also sets aside the influence of other factors required for abstract research, in order to explore the essence of the capitalist economy.

of labor, necessary and surplus labor, absolute surplus value and relative surplus value production, and finally establishing the labor theory of value. However, in modern society, with the unprecedented development of social productiveness and of S&T, the economic situation is very different. Can Marx's labor value theory still be applied to today's capitalist societies and to socialist societies with socialist market economies? To cope with these new situations, do any of the conclusions of Marx's labor theory of value need to be improved? These problems await answers in this era. This chapter does not address all the issues related to the labor theory of value in material production, but focuses on some of the difficulties.

The creation of value under automation

Introduction

Labor is a process of metabolism between humans and nature, a historical process in which people learn about, conquer, and change nature. In expectation of more material gains, people keep inventing all kinds of tools, to increase labor intensity and improve productiveness. To do so they gradually apply S&T in production. With the capitalist mode of production, this occurs on a large scale, in return accelerating S&T process. As the world enters the 21st century, S&T have attained a new historical high. In Marx's time, steam was the only motive power for industrial production. Now we have nuclear power. In Marx's time, factories contained only low-level machines; today automation is widespread. Workers used to act directly on the means of production, but today production is more often controlled through computers in the control room. Since the 1950s, the number of "white collar" workers in manufacturing in the United States has exceeded "blue collar" workers, the ratio standing at 75 to 25 in the year 1960 and 84 to 16 in 1990 (Li 1998, p. 23). Automated production has become more and more widespread, with the problem that the number of production line workers are declining and with it the living labor engaged in industrial production, yet aggregate social value is increasing.[2]

2   Yang (2002) estimates that world total GNP in the 20th century grew over 20-fold, from over US$1 trillion to US$30 trillion.

According to Marx's theory, value is created by living labor, yet simple labor, mostly physical, is becoming less and less prevalent. Does Marx's theory still apply to highly automated capitalist production? Is value created by living labor, by automated systems, or both?

Some writers (Li 1998) argue that with the rapid development of S&T, certain hi-tech means of production also create or form value. This refers mainly to intelligent automated systems in production, service, operations, and management. They illustrate this argument with a thermal power station which once required 1,000 workers. After automated intelligence systems were installed, the plant required only 30 graduates from vocational secondary schools. Under such circumstances, it is considered unreasonable to say that 30 simple laborers whose job is to press some buttons generate the same amount of power, or create even more value. The intellectualized hi-tech capital element, they conclude, also creates and forms value. We consider this idea in the next section.

Why automated machines do not create value

The discussion has long antecedents. The view that the means of production create value can be traced to the French economist Jean-Baptiste Say, the father of bourgeois vulgar economics, who believed that the three factors of production – labor, capital, and land – were sources of value, being rewarded with wages, profits, and rent. Alfred Marshall later listed entrepreneurs as a factor of production, and argued that they created profit. When machines replaced hand labor and became widely used in production, some people claimed that since they had greatly improved productivity and capitalists had gained huge profits, the machines had created value and surplus value. Lauderdale proposed that machines could replace labor to create value, and that capital could create value without labor. The application of machines in industrial production was still at a low level, but Marx had foreseen that machine production under capitalism would move in the direction of automation: "But, once adopted into the production process of capital, the means of labor passes through different metamorphoses, whose culmination is the *machine,* or rather, an *automatic system of machinery*" (Marx and Engels 1979a, p. 207).

However, he developed the classical economists' idea that labor creates value to form the scientific labor theory of value, criticizing the idea that machines create value and surplus value:

From a viewpoint [that of machines creating value – author's notes) ... fixed capital – namely that whose physical presence or use value is machinery – is the form which gives their superficial fallacies still the greatest semblance of validity. (Marx and Engels 1979a, p. 216)

From what has been said, it is clear how absurd Lauderdale is when he wants to make fixed capital into an independent source of value, independent of labor time. This statement is an absurd bourgeois cliché. (Marx and Engels 1979a, p. 214)

The belief in question confuses the labor process with the value-creation process. If the labor process is studied independently of social form, the product of human activity is use value, an object that has been adapted to people's needs by changing it. However, capitalists hire workers to produce surplus value, rather than use value; this is the purpose of capitalist production. Thus, the production process combines the labor process and the value-creation process.

Moreover, since the value-reproduction and labor processes are integrated, the production process is both a capitalist process and a capitalist form of commodity production. Marx pointed out that:

[T]he surplus value (= surplus labour, absolute as well as relative) which capital brings into existence through the employment of machinery does not arise from the labour capacities replaced by the machinery but from the labour capacities employed by it. (Marx and Engels 1988, p. 328)

The automatic system of machinery replaces most living labor; this is the use value of machines. Before this use value was employed in production, it had value as a commodity. The value of the machine was determined by the quantity of necessary social labor bestowed upon its production. It is used in the production process, and workers' living labor gradually transfers its value into the new product until the original value is restored. In the process, no value is created. Marx made it clear that ***"Machinery, like every other component of constant capital, creates no new value"*** (1965, p. 268). The machine is only a means used in producing value and surplus value, not an instrument that creates value and surplus value itself. The automated system of machinery is still the machine, with the added element only of certain artificial intelligence. In essence, it is still fixed capital and does not create value.

How can the value and surplus value of the products increase when there are fewer workers in the automated factories?

There are five answers to this question.

First, a high-level automaton means a massive investment in fixed capital in the sector and a high organic composition of capital (OCC). In a market economy, competition between enterprises leads to equalization of profits. All participating enterprises receive profits proportional to their investment in capital. If total surplus value is fixed, part of the surplus value in sectors with a low OCC will transfer to sectors with a high OCC. Thus, the relatively high value in automated factories is not created by machines, but comes from the surplus value produced by workers.

Second, as S&T develop, and more machines are used in production, fewer operating workers work directly on the means of production. However, there will be more mental laborers in other parts of the enterprise. What changes is not the capitalist mode of production, but the specific means of labor. The labor process as a whole is not confined to workers operating the machines, but to the combination of scientific laborers, managerial staff, and production workers in the enterprise. The scope of production workers becomes larger as the number of mental laborers grows. By the 1960s, 76 per cent of all workers had been converted from manual workers into supervisory workers. Manual and mental workers together create the value of commodities.

Third, automated factories have high requirements for qualified scientific workers, and even higher requirements for supervisory workers. All kinds of workers in the enterprise have quite high education levels. According to the calculations of foreign experts, electric steel workers in modern society spend 70 per cent of their total labor time on mental labor. Controllers of automated production lines spend 90 to 95 per cent of their time on mental labor. This kind of high-quality labor is more complex, and creates much more value, than average social labor in the same amount of time. Thus, even though the number of production line workers declines, more value and surplus value are created.

Fourth, automation arises from the labor of scientific workers. The value of the automatic machine involves not only those scientists and technicians who directly participate in the research it embodies, but also the research findings of their predecessors. The realization of the value of S&T products has unusual features; the value of scientific labor can only be realized indirectly. The value they created is owned by those who own the automated system of machinery. However, "the productiveness of labour that serves as its foundation and starting-point is a gift, not of nature, but of a history embracing thousands of centuries" (Marx and Engels 1965, p. 361). Therefore, the study of value creation in highly automated sectors should not be confined to the means of labor in a particular enterprise, but should consider the comprehensive and historical picture of relevant human labor value.

Fifth, in automated factories, since the enterprise adopts means of production with high productiveness, the individual value of a commodity is lower than its social value. But the value of commodities is determined by social value. The margin between individual and social value, namely excess surplus value, will be appropriated by the owner of the automated factory. Their high productiveness results in declining individual labor time, but the excess surplus value they attract comes not from the system of automated machinery, but from the value and surplus value created by workers in other sectors.

Sixth, because advanced machinery greatly improves productiveness and increases output, workers can transfer more value in the same amount of time. But this additional value is not created by the machinery. It is workers' living labor, which absorbs and transfers more value from the means of production. Thus, high levels of automation make workers' labor more intense and more complex, so that living labor creates more value by absorbing more capital.

A correct understanding of automated factories' role in the production of wealth

Automated factories are a result of modern S&T, whose deployment greatly raises productivity and transforms the means, process, and results of labor, which gives it a special role in production in human society. Marx stated in the *Communist Manifesto* that "The bourgeoisie, during its rule of scarce one hundred years, has created more massive and more colossal productive forces than have all preceding generations together" (Marx and Engels 1972b, p. 471).

By transforming the workers' means of labor, automation reduces the number of workers acting directly on the subjects of labor, and raises the number of knowledge workers in control, maintenance, and design. Wealth production no longer depends on line workers, but on advanced machines. Marx once said that:

> *[under the system of automated machinery], labour appears, rather, merely as a conscious organ, scattered among the individual living workers at numerous points of the mechanical system; subsumed under the total process of the machinery itself, as itself only a link of the system, whose unity exists not in the living workers, but rather in the living (active) machinery, which confronts his individual, insignificant doings as a mighty organism. (Marx and Engels 1979b, p. 208)*

> *Labour no longer appears so much to be included within the production process; rather, the human being comes to relate more as watchman and regulator to the production process itself. He steps to the side of the production process instead of being its chief actor. (Marx and Engels 1979b, p. 209)*

Marx further pointed out that:

> *As the basis on which large industry rests, the appropriation of al-*
> *ien labour time ceases, with its development, to make up or to create*
> *wealth, so does **direct labour** as such cease to be the basis of produc-*
> *tion, since, in one respect, it is transformed more into a supervisory*
> *and regulatory activity; ... but then also because the product ceases to*
> *be the product of isolated direct labour, and the combination of social*
> *activity appears, rather, as the producer. (Marx and Engels 1979b, p.*
> *218)*

This enhanced productivity obscures the true picture, making it seems that machines create large amounts of wealth and hence create value too.

The relationship between productiveness and value

What is the relation between productiveness and value? Some scholars argue it is incorrect to say that value varies directly with the productiveness of labor. They offer two accounts of the labor theory of value. In the first, which we shall call theory A, the value of a commodity is determined by the amount of labor crystallized in it; in the second, theory B, this value is determined by the labor time necessary to produce it. These theories are the same when qualitatively identical labor is involved. But they diverge when social labor is complex and heterogeneous, and logical contradictions arise. First, in both versions there is a conflict between subjective and objective views. Second, in theory A the value of a commodity does not necessarily vary inversely with the productive forces. Third, theory B cannot explain how the complexity of labor in different eras affects the value of a commodity. Other scholars argue that Marx once asserted that the value of a commodity varies in direct proportion to the productiveness of labor (Zhu 2001).

Scholars who agree with Marx (for example Gu and Liu, 1993) believe that the productiveness of labor changes inversely with the value of a commodity, which they illustrate with Marx's words:

The value of a commodity is, in itself, of no interest to the capitalist. What alone interests him, is the surplus-value that dwells in it, and is realisable by sale. Realisation of the surplus-value necessarily carries with it the refunding of the value that was advanced. Now, since relative surplus-value increases in direct proportion to the development of the productiveness of labour, while, on the other hand, the value of commodities diminishes in the same proportion; since one and the same process cheapens commodities, and augments the surplus-value contained in them; we have here the solution of the riddle: why does the capitalist, whose sole concern is the production of exchange-value, continually strive to depress the exchange-value of commodities? (Marx 1965, p. 224)

Clearly there are two quite different explanations for the relationship between the productiveness of labor and the value of a commodity, which remains in dispute. It is worth studying why there are such disputes. Let's first look at Marx's views.

After showing that the value of a commodity is determined by socially necessary labor time, Marx further points out that the labor time necessary to produce a commodity changes with the productiveness of labor, which is determined by many factors. Thus,

> *the greater the productiveness of labour, the less is the labour time required for the production of an article, the less is the amount of labour crystallised in that article, and the less is its value; and vice versa, the less the productiveness of labour, the greater is the labour time required for the production of an article, and the greater is its value. The value of a commodity, therefore, varies directly as the quantity, and inversely as the productiveness, of the labour incorporated in it. (Marx 1965, pp. 29–30)*

Here, Marx made it clear that the value of a commodity varies directly as the quantity, and inversely as the productiveness, of the labor incorporated in it.

This statement is taken from the first section in Chapter 1 of *Capital* ("The two factors of a commodity: use-value and value"). As we know, in the early parts of his work, Marx abstracted from many concrete facts in order to establish the substantive basis for his theories. The establishment of any theory has certain prerequisites or hypotheses, and Marx's are no exception. What does the proposition that the productiveness of labor is inversely proportional to the value of a commodity presuppose?

First, what kind of labor creates the value of commodities? Marx employed three hypotheses to analyze the labor time necessary for the creation of value: first, the amount of labor is measured in natural time; second, the productiveness of human labor is treated as the same across society, with no essential differences; third, this same productiveness can be regarded as the social average. Under these hypotheses, labor time is equal to natural time, and this gives the magnitude of value created in a given time.

However, we should also take into consideration those factors that impact the productiveness of labor. Marx deemed these to include the average proficiency of the workers, the level of development of science and its application to production, the integration of society and production, the scale and efficiency of the means of production, and natural conditions. Any change in any of these five factors will also change the productiveness of labor. Since value is calculated as the natural time of labor of average productiveness, any change in the productiveness of labor must change the natural time required for the laborers' productive activities. The value of commodities will alter accordingly. Moreover, a rise in the productiveness of labor means that less natural time is necessary to create use value, and *vice versa*. Therefore, the productiveness of labor is inversely proportional to the value of commodities. Marx's conclusions are reasonable given these hypotheses. However, if these hypotheses are modified, different conclusions could follow.

When studying the labor theory of value, the most important thing is to clarify the hypotheses or prerequisites that lead to Marx's conclusions. Otherwise we might mistakenly think his conclusions are wrong. The hypotheses themselves arise from the requirements of developing the theories, and cannot be judged as right or wrong. Obviously, different hypotheses lead to differential conclusions.

Thus, to understand the relation between the productiveness of labor and the value of commodities, we need to study the labor that creates value. Today the means of labor in socialized production has changed fundamentally compared with over 100 years ago. Under such circumstances, is it reasonable to assume that the labor power across whole society equals the average labor power? If we moreover consider the differences in the labor power between individual laborers, and between labor of various complexity and quality, what conclusion can we draw about the relations between the productiveness of labor and the value of commodities? And how significant are the conclusions for our research and study?

It is only a supposition that changes in objective factors improve the productiveness of labor. In fact, any such change also leads to changes in subjective factors. For example, when new equipment is adopted, the intensity and complexity of the labor of the workers who operate it may improve or decline. However, as the qualifications of laborers improve, they can operate more advanced machines and therefore improve productivity. Improvements in labor intensity, complexity, and proficiency, combining changes in both objective and subjective labor factors, promote the development of labor productiveness. This is a major reason for the paradox of the Marxist "law of movement of the value of commodities and the productiveness of labor."

Generally speaking, as a result of scientific progress, the productiveness of labor also improves. This is shown in Figure 5.1 (Ma and Cheng 2002).

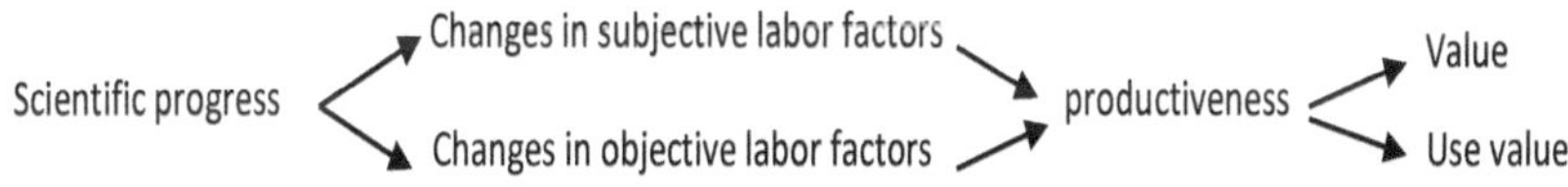

Figure 5.1 The impact of scientific progress

As the diagram shows, Marx's conclusion that the change of productivity itself will not affect the labor that creates value – that is, no matter how productivity changes, the total value of commodities created by the same labor in a given time will remain the same – is no longer consistent with reality. Changes in social production are partly due to changes in the labor that creates value. Labor intensity has changed. Therefore, when subjective labor factors are added to the prerequisites of Marx's theory, the relation between the productiveness of labor and the value of commodities could reverse.

Having discussed the consequences of changes in subjective labor factors and the productiveness of labor, we now turn to natural time as the unit for calculating value, and study further the relations between the productiveness of labor and the value of commodities.

As noted, Marx supposed that the amount of labor is calculated by the natural time required to create value. Although he noted the issue of the density of time, he did not differentiate natural time from density time, and drew the conclusion under discussion. But if the labor intensity and complexity are considered, and socially necessary labor time is differentiated from natural labor time and density time, labor complexity and intensity will vary even if natural time remains unchanged. The productiveness of labor may then vary directly with the value of commodities.

Thus, as labor density time – that is, labor intensity and complexity – increases as a result of changes in objective factors, more value is created in the same time. The consequences can be summarized thus.

First, if labor productiveness changes because of objective factors, it will vary in inverse proportion to the value of commodities. The formula is:

$$V = \frac{T}{Q} = \frac{1}{P}$$

where Q is the quantity of use value of a commodity, V is its unit value, T is the labor time required to produce it, and P is the productiveness of that labor.

Second, if labor productiveness changes because of subjective labor factors, it will vary in direct proportion to the value of commodities. There are two possibilities. One is that the socially necessary labor time changes (increases or declines); the other is that the socially necessary labor time remains unchanged, but the density of socially necessary labor time increases – that is, when labor intensity and complexity improve, more value is created in the same amount of socially necessary labor time.

Third, if labor productiveness changes because of both subjective and objective labor factors, the direction of movement of the productiveness of labor and the value of commodities can be direct or inverse.

In general, when the productiveness of labor improves in a particular enterprise, sector, or the whole of society, the total value of commodities will also increase. This is because the improvement is generally related to an increase of labor complexity or proficiency, so more value is created in the same amount of natural time.

This new analysis is significant for inheriting and developing Marx's theory.

(1) It further confirms that living, materialized labor creates value, which is the fundamental principle in the labor theory of value. According to this principle, changes in value caused by changes in the productiveness of labor can only arise from changes in the nature of living labor itself, not other factors. This helps avoid the mistakes of David Ricardo and his followers, and removes any need to diverge from Marx's theory.

(2) It helps solve a problem in traditional labor value theory, namely the contradiction between increasing social value and declining labor time.

(3) It confirms the role of scientific labor and labor management in creating value. We have to accept that more value can be created if socially necessary labor time is constantly decreasing.

Productive and unproductive labor in material production

The definition of material products and their existing forms

The notion of material products involves two layers of meaning. The first refers to material products produced by labor, such as clothes or freightage, but excludes "immaterial" products like statues or concerts. The second refers to products in "materialized forms" which exist outside the material production process and can be consumed either at the instant of production or afterwards. "Materialized products" in this sense can be found in both "material" and "immaterial" production fields, including grain production which is classified in the field of material production, or statues and books which are classified in the field of immaterial production. But it excludes products in the forms of "labor activities," like transportation, which Western accounting systems treat as services, but which Marx (see below) treated as material production, and concerts, which are classified as immaterial production. These two layers of meaning cannot be mixed, and must be clarified to avoid ambiguity.

As results of human labor, there are two existing forms of product. Materialized products exist outside the production process, and can be consumed or used in different places and at different times. Other types of product exist only in the production process, and can only be consumed at the instant of production; they are classified as "labor activities."

Within material production as such, we find both types of product: machines, equipment, and clothes have a materialized form, while transportation and telecommunication systems can only be consumed in the instant of their production, and are classified as "labor activities." Both types of product also exist within "immaterial" production: artists' works like statues or published books are materialized, while musical and drama performances are not, being products consumed in the production process. Production and consumption are combined.

These distinctions help us to identify the scope of material production, and differentiate productive from unproductive labor.

Productive and unproductive labor

As mentioned above, a heated issue in the labor theory of value is how to define productive and unproductive labor, and differentiate them from each other. Not only theories but approaches to classification are disputed. The disputes have lasted for half a century in the academic world in China, and so far no common view exists. We believe there are two reasons for this situation. First, there are different understandings of the conception of labor. As noted, with improvements in the social productive forces, the definition and extent of labor have changed profoundly. Obstinate adherence to unchanging definitions of labor impedes both theoretical research and real work. Second, as we have noted, human labor, being social, relates at one and the same time to natural objects and to the relations of production. A reasonable analysis of productive labor should be based on specific conditions which we now analyze, drawing on the analysis already presented in the last part of Chapter 4.

(1) Regardless of social relations, certain use values must always be produced to satisfy material and cultural needs, and are considered to be products in which labor is materialized. These are distributed between material, spiritual, and service activities, but insofar as the productive forces develop, more of the latter two are produced, and labor expands its scope and extent.

Moreover, with progress in S&T, different types of labor emerge and are distributed among laborers. Unskilled workers remain near the machines and act directly on them. As the labor of control, motive power, and operation become separated, the connotation of labor engaged in production extends from manual to mental labor. Scientific workers, managerial staff, and production workers coordinate, and it becomes difficult to clarify who created this or that product. The products become results of collective labor.

(2) Human production takes place within different societies with varying relations of production, giving rise to varying concepts of the labor of production. In capitalist society:

> *the notion of a productive labourer implies not merely a relation between work and useful effect, between labourer and product of labour, but also a specific, social relation of production, a relation that has sprung up historically and stamps the labourer as the direct means of creating surplus-value. (Marx 1965, p. 359)*

> *Capitalist production is not merely the production of commodities, it is essentially the production of surplus-value. The labourer produces, not for himself, but for capital. It no longer suffices, therefore, that he should simply produce. He must produce surplus-value. That labourer alone is productive, who produces surplus-value for the capitalist, and thus works for the self-expansion of capital. (Marx 1965, p. 359)*

The notion of productive labor narrows, and here refers only to labor that produces surplus value and "exchanges with capital directly." To make this understandable, Marx gives an example. Milton, he says, received £5 for writing *Paradise Lost* but was an unproductive laborer since he wrote the book of his own volition. However, the proletarian writer from Leipzig, who compiled the book under the instruction of the publishers, was a productive laborer. This is because his labor was exchanged with money acting as capital, and produced surplus value for capitalists.

(3) Capital itself is based on relative rather than absolute productiveness. The term "absolute" here means that value created by the laborer is compared with the value he consumes. If the two are equal, the labor is defined

as productive. If the value he consumes outweighs the value he produces, he is called unproductive. "Relative" means that the value created is compared with his salary. Surplus value is produced when the former is greater than the latter, and only then is the labor considered to be capitalist productive labor. This also applies in a socialist market economy. When the value produced by the laborer exceeds the value he consumes, surplus value is created, and his labor is productive.

Productive and unproductive labor can thus be analyzed from three perspectives. These give rise to different standards of classification, so when studying or discussing the definitions, we must specify the perspective or there will be unnecessary disputes. China is still at the primary stage of socialism, and implements the socialist economic system. The purpose of socialist production is to satisfy people's increasing material and cultural needs. From this perspective, the productiveness standard is not only theoretically correct for defining productive labor, but also significant for practice and future research.

To sum up, we believe that productive labor includes the direct production of material or spiritual commodities for exchange in the market, activities that serve the production and reproduction of labor power as a commodity, management activities, and scientific labor. To be specific:

First, labor that produces material commodities for the market, as in agriculture, industry, construction, and technology, is productive.

Second, labor that displaces tangible and intangible commodities, such as the transportation of goods and personnel, along with post and communications which transmit information by letters, messages, telegraphs, and telephones, is productive. Such activities can sometimes take place in certain production sectors in the circulation field.

Third, labor that produces tangible or intangible commodities, such as spiritual commodities in education, social sciences, natural sciences, culture, technology, literature and art, broadcasting, publishing and news, libraries and museums, is productive. These include services that deliver intangibles, like lecturing and performing.

Fourth, service labor that helps produce or reproduce the commodity labor power is productive. Besides the role played in daily life by the productive sectors already mentioned, such sectors include medical care, health, sports, beauty care, and baths (Cheng 2001, pp. 179–80).

The transport industry: a special sphere of material production

Marx expressed his understanding of capitalist transportation in the following words:

> [i]n addition to extractive industry, agriculture and manufacture, there exists yet a fourth sphere of material production, which also passes through the various stages of handicraft industry, manufacture and mechanical industry; this is the transport industry, transporting either people or commodities. The relation of productive labor – that is, of the wage-laborer – to capital is here exactly the same as in the other spheres of material production. Moreover, here a material change is effected in the subject of labor – a spatial change, a change of place. (Marx and Engels 1972c, pp. 444–5)

Marx thus clearly considered transportation to be part of the material production sector. The criterion for his classification differentiates transport from other spheres of material production, for which there are two criteria, that of productivity and the historical stage of social development, and that of social relations. When productiveness was very low, people could only get the basic means of subsistence from the earth or forests. As productiveness improved they learned to plant crops or raise poultry, and human society entered the age of agriculture. The invention of tools and machinery then facilitated the production of many material products. All these were still material products because society had not yet generalized the mass consumption of spiritual or intangible products. The second criterion is that labor products have certain materialized forms, such as coal, grain, and clothes. These exist independently of producers and consumers, and can be consumed at an appropriate time and place.

Marx classifies transport as a fourth sphere of material production from the perspective of the means of labor in the transport industry. This industry has two basic characteristics. First, no new material products are created, but the subjects of labor are moved to a new place. This change, brought about through tools specific to the activity of transportation, is a production process in its own right. Second, the result of labor – transportation – has no materialized forms. It is a kind of activity that is "consumed at the instant of production." The means of transportation move goods or passengers from one place to another, which is a production process but also a consumption process from the point of view of the goods or the passengers. Generally, passenger transport is individual consumption, while goods transport is productive consumption. Due to the particular form of existence of the labor product, Marx appears to have regarded the transport industry as a fourth material production sphere. Thus, by the criterion of either productivity or relations of production, the transport industry is a productive sector in which labor creates value.

Goods transport is generally acknowledged to be productive, but arguments persist about passenger transport. A change in place of a good constitutes a new use value, so transport costs are included into production costs and transferred to new commodities; producers can thus get these costs repaid. As for passengers, some scholars believe that although a change of place provides use value, tourists or people visiting their relatives have nothing to do production, so their transport adds no value. Passengers pay transport fees from their income, so they cannot gain an equivalent for the change of place. Thus, scholars argue, passenger transport is unproductive, and the labor of transport workers is unproductive.

This argument is not entirely correct. The transport industry is productive in essence. Both passenger and goods transport provide use value and add value. Passenger transport is productive because the labor of transport workers is productive. However, we should clarify that this does not mean passengers themselves deliver productive labor.

Some scholars (see Luo 1990, pp. 259–60) offer a more detailed analysis, distinguishing productive from unproductive passenger transport. Unproductive passenger transport means personal income or public revenues are used to buy transport services from an enterprise, for a change of place by land, sea, or air, for purposes such as visiting friends, tourism, or public service. Since personal income or public revenue are consumed without return, this is classified as individual or unproductive consumption.

124

Productive passenger transport then means the consumption of transport by business people. Their transport costs are a component of the value of products, for which an equivalent return can be obtained by selling these products, hence such transport is passenger transport.

The production of surplus value and exploitation

For Marx, the purpose of capitalist production is to obtain surplus value, which Engels considered one of his two discoveries. In current discussions, Chinese scholars do not disagree about the theory of surplus value, but they do disagree on the source of value, on which they hold two basic views, as we have noted: that living labor produces value, or that it is produced by the factors of production. There are still further theories of value, such as the knowledge or science theory.

If factors of production are the source of value, then the theory of surplus value collapses by itself and exploitation cannot exist. Therefore, to understand Marx's basic views about the production of surplus value, we need to recognize living labor as the source of value. Only thus can we understand exploitation in a socialist market economy.

Marx's basic views on the production of surplus value

The capitalist production of commodities combines the labor process and the value process. To carry out production, capitalists use money capital to buy means of production and labor power, use technological breakthroughs to coordinate the production process, and then sell products to the public. But the money they get from selling these products must be greater than the money they advance. Otherwise, there would be no motive to continue producing.

The capital they advance is composed of two parts: means of production (C) and labor power (V). Their value is determined by socially necessary labor time, so that advanced capital (C+V) can be expressed as a definite quantity of labor time. The value of the commodities that the capitalists sell on the market is C+V+S: beyond the advanced capital C+V, there is a surplus S, which they appropriate.

Where does this surplus value come from? For Marx, the capital advanced on means of production is gradually transferred to products during production and is repaid by the exchange value obtained from selling these products. This part of capital merely completes a circuit of production, and no value is added thereby. Thus, surplus value can only come from labor. The value of labor power is determined by the value of the means of subsistence necessary for the production and reproduction of laborers. However, capitalists hire workers not only because they want to compensate for the advanced capital but also to get more value than they advanced. If the value of the productive power they purchase is 4 hours of socially necessary labor time, they will make the laborers work not just 4 hours, but for 6, 7, or 8 hours. This labor time is thus divided into two parts; socially necessary labor time, which compensates for the advanced capital, and surplus labor time, during which laborers produce surplus value. Workers however only retrieve the value of their labor power, and have no access to surplus value, which is appropriated by the capitalists.

Capitalists appropriate surplus value in two forms: absolute surplus value and relative surplus value. Absolute surplus value is the expansion of surplus labor time to produce more surplus value by lengthening labor time. Because of physiological limits and working-class resistance, the length of working days is limited nowadays. Thus, it is very difficult for capitalists to produce more surplus value by prolonging labor time. But as always, this is relative. Walmart, the leading American retailer corporation, once cancelled the 15-minute tea break in its working days so that workers could work without stopping. Even these 15 minutes could bring them huge profits. Workers opposed the policy, and eventually the corporation reinstated the tea break.

Relative surplus value is produced by lowering the value of labor power by improving productiveness, reducing the labor time socially necessary to produce the means of subsistence. With the number of hours in the working week constant, surplus value is extended by prolonging surplus labor time relative to this fixed magnitude.

Capitalists are not concerned what kinds of use value are produced. What interests them is the surplus value they can appropriate when these use values are sold. Thanks to relative surplus value, they make every effort to improve productiveness so as to appropriate as much surplus value as possible. This is why they are dedicated to employing S&T to improve productivity.

Doubts concerning the source of surplus value

From our earlier review, we know that value is created by living labor, not means of production. Surplus value is in turn produced during the workers' surplus labor time, which is also created by workers' labor. Thus, the theory of surplus value is based on the labor theory of value, and is not tenable without it. However, in economics for most people the concept of profit is more familiar, and surplus value is a more abstract concept. Opponents of labor value theory see factors such as machinery, technology, management, and the operational activities of capitalists as increasingly important, and conclude that profits arise from a combination of these factors, not labor alone. This leads to doubts about Marx's theory. We now assess some of these views on the sources of profits, which are described by Erik Olin Wright (1979).

(1) The causal-agnostic account

This view has been propounded by four scholars, Anthony Cutler, Barry Hindess, Paul Hirst, and Athar Hussain. They wrote in *Marx's "Capital" and Capitalism Today*, published in 1977, that if the processing of raw materials is viewed as a complex process (under the influence of required factors including machinery, labor, technology, and knowledge), then all products arise from the combination of all factors in the production process, and cannot be viewed as the results of labor or labor time. They believe profits are produced by those factors, without explaining the specific effect of each factor. This is illustrated in Figure 5.2, drawn from Wright (1979).

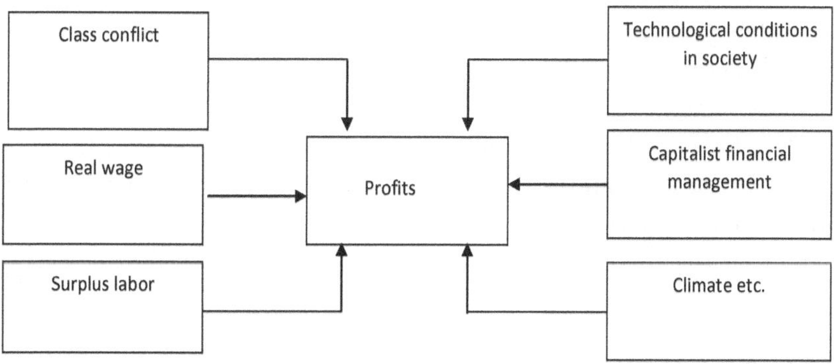

Figure 5.2 The causal-agnostic account

(2) The Sraffian account

These scholars think that there exists a concept of surplus product instead of surplus value. A given level of wages with a given production technology, they argue, can produce more commodities than are consumed as input. They see no need to be concerned about the source of surplus products, which are the material foundation of profits. This is illustrated in Figure 5.3, also drawn from Wright.

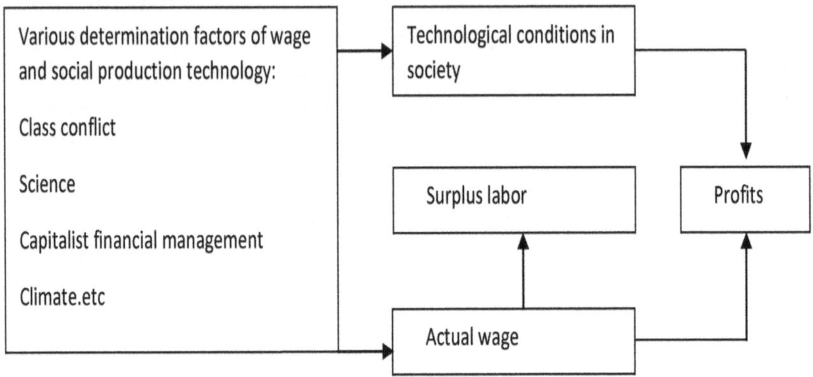

Figure 5.3 The Sraffian account

(3) The Marxist account

For the Marxists, according to Wright, the mass of profit may change even though surplus value remains the same, as a result of changing technology. There are two forms of determination: structural limits, and choices made within these limits. Given the important influence of class conflict on profits, these may be determined in another way – through an adjustment of all the factors that influence profits across society. Figure 5.4 shows Wright's illustration of this view.

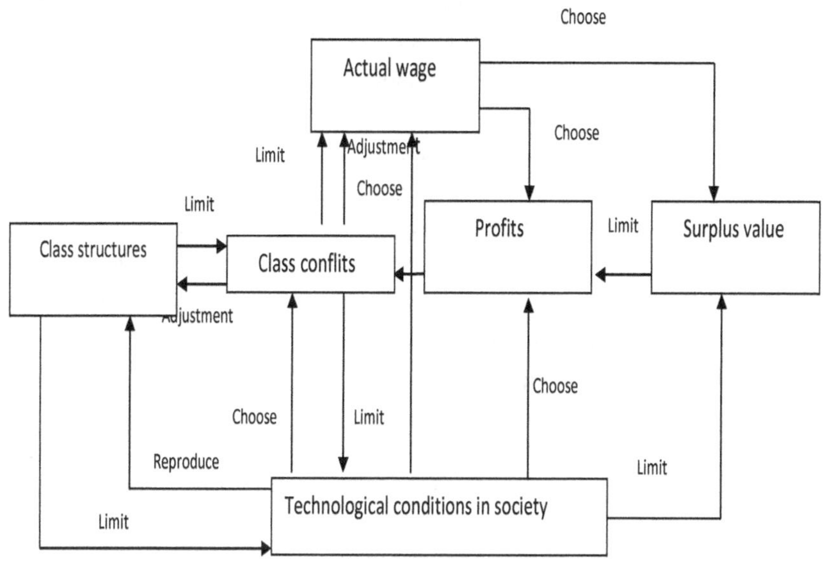

Figure 5.4 Marxist account (complex formula)

A correct understanding of exploitation

Some western Marxists mistakenly think Marx's labor value theory has many defects, and cannot serve as the foundation of exploitation theory. They believe that an exploitation theory can be established without the labor theory of value, many basing themselves on a theorem developed by Western scholars in the 1960s called the fundamental Marxian theorem (FMT), which states that positive surplus value is a necessary and sufficient condition for a positive profit rate, but which abandons the requirement of any precise numerical relation between the two.

American economist John Roemer (1981) abandoned the labor theory of value, and with it the idea that wages and surplus value are related to the distribution of value. He sought to explain the determination of wages through class conflict, to demonstrate the intensity of capitalist exploitation imposed on workers.

Similar views exist among Chinese scholars, such as Shi Zhengfu (2002), who argues that a return on capital is a long-standing phenomenon in the socialist economy. Whether surplus value can be appropriated on the basis of equal exchange depends on the institutional structure in which capital and labor interact with each other. Under new institutional structures, capital return cannot be explained using the traditional theory of exploitation. Some other ideas on exploitation exist, but are not listed here (Shi 1999).

We believe that the error in all such views lies in a failure to understand the essential features of economic exploitation. There is a widespread belief that discussion on exploitation should be confined to the academic world and not mixed with ideology.

Consider, however, the academic definition of exploitation offered by the *New Palgrave Dictionary of Economics*. Capitalism has its historical characteristics – its exploitation relationships are almost entirely covered by the surface phenomena of exchange relations:

> *Orthodox economics, encapsulated within its magic kingdom of production functions, perfect competition, and general equilibrium, manages to avoid such issues. Indeed, it concerns itself primarily with the construction and refinement of an idealized image of capitalism … the firm hires "factors of production" called capital and labour in order to produce an output, paying for each factor according to its estimated incremental contribution to the total output (i.e. according the value of its marginal product) … this conception puts a thing (capital) and a human capacity (labour power) on equal footing, both as so-called factors of production. This enables the theory to deny any class difference between capitalist and workers by treating all individuals as essentially equal because they are all owners of at least one factor of production …. Finally, since capital and labour are mere things, they cannot be said to be exploited. In this sense, exploitation is defined as a discrepancy between an actual and an ideal "factor payment" … more importantly, exploitation as defined above can in principle apply just as well to profits as to wages. Capitalism thus emerges as a system in which capitalists are just as liable to be exploited by workers as vice versa. With this last step, the very notion of exploitation is reduced to utter triviality. (NPDE 2, 1996, p. 250)*

This authoritative comment is clear and profound. We believe that the definition of exploitation under private ownership refers to the legal appropriation, for free, of surplus labor (including feudal rent and surplus value) by means of the ownership of the agents of production. Capitalist exploitation, specifically, refers to the legal appropriation, for free, of surplus value by means of the ownership of agents of production. All illegitimate income can only be seen as exploitation in a broader sense.

To arrive at favorable national policies for developing the private economy, treating the phenomenon of exploitation under private ownership scientifically (Cheng and Wang 2002), we should study it from the perspective of historical materialism. The following six points summarize our suggested approach.

1. We need to understand the private economy under a socialist market economy correctly. The private economy refers to economic activities carried out by private capital on a certain scale. According to Marx's analysis of the capitalist mode of production and his labor value theory, private economy, like foreign capital, aims to pursue private surplus value. We should not doubt that exploitation exists. Otherwise, problems such as the denial of capitalist exploitation will ensue, confusing people's understanding of contemporary capitalism in the primary stage of socialism, which would be unfavorable for developing productiveness.

2. Private owners participate in the management of production to different extents. Management activities appropriate for the needs of socialized production also create surplus value. Therefore, all or part of the wages of private owners belongs to labor income. The management and scientific labor of private owners is probably more complex, and their resultant high income is still labor income, not exploitation income. That is, if a capitalist is also the chief executive and takes part in management activities, some of these activities create new value (obviously, not including activities such as prolonging the working day or defaulting on wages). The part of their income that derives from the ownership of capital is, however, exploitative.

3. Currently, China's private economy is developing rapidly, but there is not a complete mechanism for regulating employee–employer relations. These are very tense, which is unfavorable for both sides. The relevant authorities are improving legislation to handle these better, protect workers' legal interests, and supervise the activities of private companies. They

131

should also control exploitative behavior, including violations of labor laws and the infringement of workers' legal rights. At the same time, they should strengthen the macro-management of the market, dealing with such violations of the law such as tax evasion, counterfeiting, bribery, and pollution. The aim is to ensure private companies gain their income through lawful activities under state laws and regulations.

4. Economic exploitation is a historical phenomenon which existed long before the advanced development of productiveness. In the primary stage of socialism in China, the private economy will exist for a long time, and plays a positive role in promoting the development of productiveness, reducing unemployment, and increasing state tax revenue, so it should be developed appropriately. Lenin (1986, p. 239) remarked, during the New Economic Policy, "Isn't it dangerous to bring capitalists to Russia? Doesn't that mean we will develop capitalism? Yes, it means capitalism, but it is not dangerous. Because political power is in the hands of the workers and peasants." As long as we study the "Three Represents" Theory from the perspective of Marxism and implement it seriously, the advantages of the private economy, and the exploitation which accompanies it, can outweigh the disadvantages.

5. While developing the private economy, we should be aware that our target is to develop the socialist market economy. The essence of socialism is to emancipate and develop productiveness, eradicate exploitation and class polarization, and finally realize common prosperity (Deng 1993, p. 373). Socialist public ownership remains the mainstay of our system and cannot be sacrificed for the sake of the non-public economy. Socialist public ownership, especially the state-owned economy, represents the interests of the general public and is the fundamental material basis of common prosperity. It should be developed in the market economy or the primary purpose of the reform will be violated. Sun Yat-sen advocated that the country should "control private capital and develop national capital." This slogan is still of significance today. As Deng Xiaoping said, "the fundamental purpose of socialism is to realize common prosperity, rather than class polarization. We will fail if our policies cause class polarization. And we must be on an evil route if new capitalists appear" (Deng 1993, pp. 110–11).

6. Distribution according to the contribution of each factor of production is based on the specific contribution of the owners of factors of production to value and wealth creation. The economic essence is the size of these factors, and the property relations provided by the owners in the process through which living labor produces value and the factors of production create wealth. These are the forms, and the essence, of distribution according to the contribution of each factor of production, which is known in economic philosophy as the "theory of distribution by contribution."

7. Because of class limitations, western capitalists mistake form for essence, while the economic theory of the Shanghai School, as regards the "Three Represents Theory," believes that the form of the "theory of distribution by contribution" reveals its economic essence. This school makes fresh use of the term "distribution by contribution" by combining form and essence. This is not the same as the accounts offered by Western capitalists.

Some scholars think that if the term "distribution by contribution" is accepted, then the owners of factors of production create wealth and value, or contribute to creating them, in person, treating this as the basis of distribution. We disagree. When using the term "distribution by contribution," we only admit that under certain economic systems, the owners of factors of production provide some non-labor factors such as land and capital, which are combined with labor power. Laborers then use the non-labor factors to create wealth and value. Owners "contribute" non-labor factors in the sense of "advancing," "providing," or "taking out" in the purchase phase of the circuit of capital, before the production of wealth and value. However, wealth and value are created by laborers, who employ those non-labor factors to carry out production. In the sale phase, after production is complete, the owners of the factors divide or allocate the results of production based on the size of the factors they have "advanced," according to property ownership.

Hence the factors themselves, rather than its owners, become the source of wealth. It is the factors, not the owners, that contribute to the creation of wealth. Laborers employ these various factors to create or contribute wealth and value, which relates only to the quantity and quality of these factors and is not directly related to the ownership (be it private, collective, state, or mixed) of the factors. This is also the economic basis for the working class and government to expropriate for free or redeem the factors of production of slave-owners, landlords, and capitalists.

Thus, there are three ways of conceptualizing "distribution by contribution": distribution by labor income, distribution by labor and capital income, or distribution by capital. When factors such as management, technology, and information are treated as labor and participate in distribution, this is distribution by labor. When the same factors are treated as capital to participate in distribution on this basis, that is distribution by capital.

Scientists and technicians, for example, get an income for their inventions, which belongs to labor income and hence constitutes distribution by labor. If they convert the invention into a certain number of tech stocks, then the income belongs to technological capital income and hence constitutes distribution by capital. To cite another example, a celebrity acts as a nominal shareholder of a company and is given a certain number of performance shares in return. But he does not have to actually work for the company. Thus, the invisible asset of the celebrity is converted into capital, and this income belongs to capital income and hence distribution by capital. Again, the wage and performance shares offered to staff, or the manager of the company, are on the whole labor income or distribution by labor. A similar analysis can be applied to other factors.

What mechanism or law regulates the volume of each factor's income? The supporters of the factor theory of value believe that marginal analysis can accurately measure the contribution that each factor deserves. In fact, the basis of measurement, and hence the basis for distribution, depends on the form of ownership, which depends on the factor concerned. Wage income is the monetary expression of the price or value of labor power. Its size, which has no impact on the value of commodities, depends on negotiation with owners and competition among workers, rather than the workers' marginal contribution. Owners of non-labor factors, on the other hand, appropriate profits more or less equivalent to their capital under the law of formation of an average rate of profit, taking the form of rent, profits, or interest. This mechanism does not exclude the influence of subjective and objective factors such as monopoly, industry status, transaction costs, and competition strategies.

At present, we should make full use of the various factors of production, including labor, S&T, information, management, environment, and capital so as to protect the lawful interests of all owners of factors, and promote the rapid and healthy development of people's living standards and our public-led economy.

6
Labor and value in cultural production

Chapter 5 discussed labor and value creation in the production of material goods. We now turn our attention to cultural products or non-material goods. We focus primarily on the labor contributed by artists, writers, and teachers in private schools, because this particular group have provided various spiritual products or services for some time. These cultural products are believed to be the most treasured possessions of human society. Not only do they meet humanity's aesthetic needs, they promote progress in human civilization. All these facts suggest that cultural labor is one of the most important aspects of human labor.

In a socialist market economy, can cultural labor create value? If so, can all types of cultural labor can create value? How? What are the differences and similarities between material and cultural goods production? This chapter addresses these questions.

Culture and cultural products

Culture, a social phenomenon, is as old as human history. It came into being in very ancient times. Promoted by commodity production and exchange, cultural activities were increasingly intertwined with human economic activities, and the cultural economy surfaced. But although human society has developed, and its cultural activities have become increasingly plentiful, scholars differ in their definition of culture. Some argue it is the aggregate of human activities on which people and their society depend (Needleman 1941, Cheng Enfu 1999). Some have also argued that culture, or civilization, refers to a complex whole including knowledge, belief, art, morals, law, custom, and any other capabilities and habits possessed by humans as members of society (Taylor 1971). Yet further scholars say culture includes material, spiritual and social-political life; it is in sum all-encompassing (Liang 1920). Some argue that culture does not refer to politics, industries, transport, and military activities, but to literature, painting, music, and philosophy, and so on (Chen 1923). Some believe it is the aggregate of skills, knowledge, mental thinking, and emotions conditioned by history. Elsewhere it refers to the materialization of productive and service technologies, people's educational level, social life and institutions, S&T inventions, as well as literary works (Chesnokov 1965).

The *Grand Dictionary of the Chinese Language* provides an authoritative definition for the term "culture": broadly speaking, it refers to the aggregate of wealth in both material and spiritual form created by human social practice in human history. Narrowly speaking, culture refers to the ideology corresponding to social institutions and organizations. These two definitions of culture were given from different angles, and allow for further theoretical discussion. However, when cultural labor is to be explored, it is important to define socialist cultural labor in a more precise way. In this book, we define socialist cultural activities in the socialist market economy as follows: literary activities and art, the press and publishing, broadcasting, libraries, museums, exhibitions, religion, education, S&T, architecture, parks and gardens, sports, and tourism, and so on (Cheng 1999, p. 12).

It is widely believed that the history of human cultural activities is as long as human history. Engels once argued that:

> *mankind must first of all eat, drink, have shelter and clothing, before it can pursue politics, science, art, religion, etc.; that therefore the production of the immediate material means, and consequently the degree of economic development attained by a given people or during a given epoch, form the foundation upon which the state institutions, the legal conceptions, art, and even the ideas on religion, of the people concerned have been evolved, and in the light of which they must, therefore, be explained, instead of vice versa, as had hitherto been the case. (Marx and Engels 2012, p. 1002)*

As labor productivity grew, surplus products started to emerge, and the division of social labor laid a material foundation for cultural activities by some people. Cultural products began to enter the market, becoming social products that met some customers' spiritual and aesthetic needs. The producers of these cultural products became professional artists, such as the Jie Si during the Han Dynasty, professional troupes in the late Tang Dynasty, and the theatres and Wa She in the Song Dynasty. However, a simple study of cultural activities in history is far from sufficient.

> *In order to examine the connection between spiritual production and material production it is above all necessary to grasp the latter itself not as a general category but in a definite historical form. Thus for example different kinds of spiritual production correspond to the capitalist mode of production and to the mode of production of the Middle Ages. If material production itself is not conceived in its specific historical form, it is impossible to understand what is specific in spiritual production corresponding to it, or the reciprocal influence of one on the other. (Marx and Engels 1972c, p. 296)*

Under the capitalist mode of production, the ultimate goal of all production and marketing of cultural products is the pursuit of surplus value or profit. The goal of providing education and knowledge as well as aesthetic appreciation is secondary to the goal of capital appreciation. The entire function of the education and cultural industries is to secure the economic foundations and development of capitalist societies. For example, in Britain's private educational system, the teachers were purely employed laborers from the standpoint of the school principal. Principals could earn handsome profits by capitalizing on the exchange between their capital and the teachers' labor.

In a socialist market society, the goal of production is fundamentally different from that in a capitalist society. Most cultural products enter the market through exchange, and are transformed into social products. Cultural laborers, who create new value, can receive varying rates of remuneration as a result of this exchange. But the spiritual life of the consumers is expected to be enriched at the same time.

A cultural commodity, simply speaking, is a spiritual or cultural product, service or entertainment sold to consumers by cultural producers.

Seen as fruits of human labor, all cultural products fall into two categories: material cultural products and cultural products provided by living labor. The first can exist independent of their producers and consumers. They include manuscripts, paintings, sculptures, and so on. The second, which cannot exist in a material form, include the performance of the actors in a drama and instructors' lecturing activities. These products are consumed at the time they are produced. Once provided, they perish.

Any cultural commodity, regardless of its form, is content-based. Even if the vast majority of commodities are material in form, their contents are still conceptual. In other words, a cultural product has a strong spiritual coloration. For example, many media products like books, audiovisual products, or films can be viewed as material goods, but their content is purely spiritual.

Most people understand that any cultural commodity has use value as well as value. If a reader needs a book, what they really require is a tangible, well-bound object which can be called "a book." If I want to read *Fortress Besieged* by Qian Zhongshu, I must have a well-bound copy of *Fortress Besieged*. However, it makes no qualitative difference for whom this book was published; when I have finished reading, I experience feelings, whether good or bad. This suggests this book provided me with a use value.

Some people fail to develop a deeper understanding of the use value inherent in cultural products. Since a cultural product is intangible, they feel it cannot have use value. In response, we argue that since a cultural product can enter into the market for exchange and then be transformed into a social product, it must have a use value even though it exists in the form of service. As Marx argued: "a *service*; this is nothing more than an expression for the particular use value provided by labor, just like every other commodity; but it is a specific expression for the particular use value of labor, in so far as labor does not provide services as an *object* but as an *activity*, which however by no means distinguishes it e.g. from a machine, e.g. a clock" (Marx and Engels 1972c, p. 435). "To the producers who provided these services, a service was just a product" (Marx and Engels 1972c, p. 149). For example, suppose we go to see the musical *The Miserable World* at the Shanghai Opera House. The props, lights, set, and actors cannot be moved away. We can choose an appropriate time to attend. The process of performance is actually a production process, which clearly provides a service for its customers. At the same time, the audience's enjoyment is also a process of consuming this service. Once the performance is over, the consumption is also over. Thus, the service synchronizes the performance with the audience's consumption of the service. The use value is simply the emotional content of the drama, which provides the audiences with varying degrees of pleasure. Thus, we argue, it is theoretically correct to say a cultural product in the form of a service can possess use value.

It is known that a commodity is an entity combining use value and value, and hence has dual characteristics. If a given cultural product is a commodity, this suggests that it should contain use value, with particular characteristics, tailored to specific human needs. This use value also serves as a carrier of value, an indication of undifferentiated human labor condensed into the cultural commodity, because its production inevitably consumes a certain amount of socially necessary labor time. In socialist societies, the goal of cultural production is to meet people's increasing needs for cultural products as well as material ones. It therefore forms an important part of the socialist commodity system.

In socialist societies, the real needs of the masses for cultural products are reflected by the pursuit of knowledge, aesthetic appreciation, and pleasure. In short, the masses in socialist societies seek to improve their cultural and intellectual level. In the meantime, they also expect to improve their ethical level. So the use value of a cultural commodity is a combination of its enjoyment, aesthetic, cognitive, and research utility, based in the fact that it can provide the masses with elements of consumption that they need for their spiritual life. It can be either a material or a non-material product.

The cultural product in its material form is characterized by tangibility. Relying on material carriers, cultural labor exists in the form of books, newspapers, magazines, and audiovisual products, which serve as elements of cultural consumption and form an important part of the total social product. In its living labor form, the cultural product is characterized by its intangibility. As discussed, its use is enjoyed by consuming it as living labor at the same time that it is produced.

As well as use value, which is inherent to them, all cultural products also possess the attribute of value. The concrete labor may vary depending on the use value: writers may create different types of artistic works, or scholars from different areas may give lectures. The style of each labor varies, and each creates a different use value. However, they invariably involve living labor. The value of a cultural product can thus be understood as general human abstract labor condensed into whatever is produced, determined not by the individual labor time of the producers but by the socially necessary labor time, with average proficiency and intensity, needed to produce it. As with material goods this can be expressed as C+V+S. C, the aggregate of value consumed by fixed assets and raw materials in producing cultural products, can also be understood as the fixed capital of a producer or, from an operational perspective, as elements of production. V stands for the value of the labor power of the managers, creators, and different types of producer engaged in cultural production. S stands for the surplus, over and above necessary labor. In a market economy, the production of cultural products combines the labor process and the value process, and at the same time involves the process of value expansion.

A cultural commodity thus combines use value and value. However, it differs from other commodities in unique ways. It is a spiritual commodity that serves as a reflection of the ideology of a society during a particular historical period. It also reflects the economic conditions of a particular society; finally, it can also impact these economic conditions. Its spiritual attributes can make a lasting impact on human thinking, intellect, aesthetic appreciation, and pleasure. Cultural commodities, that is, can produce immeasurable social effects. We can summarize their characteristics as follows.

The permanent nature of cultural use value

Conventional wisdom suggests after a material good has been used for some time, its use value gradually wears off or disappears. For example, if a pair of leather shoes has been worn for some years, their user has to discontinue wearing them and buy a new pair to replace them. If a piece of bread is eaten, it no longer exists. So, the use-value of the vast majority of material goods is time-sensitive and they cannot be used indefinitely. But even

142

though the material carrier of cultural products can be used up, their spiritual content continues to be consumed at different times. A superb literary work, movie, or drama can have a lasting influence on human society and became a treasured possession through reprints, repeated performance, or duplication. For example, the Book of Odes collected numerous poems, has survived more than 2,600 years, and its influence continues until this day. It has appeared in the market in the form of bamboo slips, silk, and paper, but its contents remained the same. It is no exaggeration to say that it ranks among the most treasured possession of generations throughout the world.

The high knowledge content of cultural commodities

It is universally acknowledged that the production of any cultural product is actually an intense intellectual activity. Their producers were not born with the corresponding intellectual capacity. On the contrary, acquiring it requires arduous study, long-term real-life practice, and the summation of past experience. It calls for the intense processing of incoming information and an inclination to grasp the laws underlying the creative process. Cultural labor is, moreover, not an intellectual activity in a general sense but a creative intellectual activity. It is widely believed to be the source of cultural products, and the most excellent cultural products are invariably creative ones. The well-known work *Capital* was the end product of 40 years of study by Marx, dealing with tens and thousands of past research works, and with the corpus of classical economics. Such high-level intellectual activities propelled this great work to a peak of achievement. In contrast, nearly all material goods are governed by standards which allow them to be mass produced on a repetitive basis.

The shareability of cultural commodities

Even though cultural products are the result of intellectual activity, the vast majority of them can be materialized in some form of physical carrier, with the sophisticated technologies of modern societies. As a result, more and more people can use them. Not surprisingly, they do not wear away because of this use, but display the prominent attribute of shareability. This benefits the public but gives rise to social problems such as piracy.

The laws of the market economy dictate that producers must consider the expansion of their advanced capital. A cultural producer needs to recoup their costs and earn a profit by exchanging their products with potential customers in the market. But a pirate may also sell cultural products with minimal costs thanks to their shareability, thereby securing handsome illegal gains. Piracy certainly harms the interests of the producers of cultural products, and disrupts the normal operation of the market economy. Governments are impelled to protect copyright and combat piracy mercilessly.

Value creation by cultural labor

Production aimed at generating use value has been present throughout human history, and figured prominently in each historical period. In the socialist market economy, social production, characterized by combining laborers with elements of production, is still the major form of wealth production. Without it, we cannot enjoy the fruits of modern civilization. Cultural labor is more or less the same, although it is not free from the influence of history, and so has some particularities arising from it.

Setting aside these historical particularities, cultural labor in general is not aimed at extracting material resources from nature and using them to produce material goods. Its function is to express human rational thoughts about natural and social events (such as scientific and theoretical knowledge, poetry, drama, or art creation). It may also provide knowledge services, as when teachers impart knowledge to students. From this perspective, we argue that in socialist societies, cultural labor is to be found with five types of economic relationship.

The first, also the most important, aims at providing commercial cultural services and products. China's socialist market economy is characterized by the public ownership of elements of production combined with the co-development of multiple types of ownership. The vast majority of cultural goods are therefore produced not for consumption by the immediate producers but for social consumption by others, so that cultural goods have become social products. In consequence, on the one hand, cultural laborers in various for-profit publications, publishing houses, art performance institutions, or theatres are obliged to engage in cultural production to meet the needs of society. On the other hand, their cultural labor has to be profit-oriented. The reason, as discussed, is that only when survival is guaranteed can cultural workers be motivated to provide society with a stream of cultural goods consistent with socialist mores and practices. Not surprisingly, in the socialist market economy, more and more works of art, science, and culture were destined to become commodities, and formed an integral part of China's commodity-based economy.

The second type is that found in cultural and public service institutions (including not-for-profit institutions). The budgets of these institutions, which mainly provide intellectual services, are set by the state and governments at different levels; they include public schools, public libraries, museums, and others. This type of cultural labor exists because society develops in ways that make it impossible and unnecessary to turn all cultural goods into commodities for exchange in the market. For example, general science cannot be a commodity. Moreover, general science is diametrically opposed to a short-term outlook; this is why the boundaries of this type of activity need to be clearly delineated. To a very large extent, the production and exchange of cultural goods cannot be subject to the law of value; even so, the living labor consumed in the production of cultural goods, and the part of it that is materialized into physical goods, can be measured in value terms. Indeed, the precise measurement of this value will contribute significantly to the reproduction of cultural labor.

The third type is individual cultural labor, which is a certain proportion of all cultural labor. For example, a writer can choose not work under contract with a bookseller, and instead write in their study, and sell the copyright in their productions to the bookseller. Another example is a painter who engages in artistic creation independently and then sells their work to the public. Individuals may also employ a few hands to join them. This type of labor belongs to simple commodity production.

The fourth type is family cultural labor. A family may employ one or more cultural workers, such as tutors. This is independent of social division of labor, since the labor is employed for needs of the family rather than for personal consumption, and hence does not aim at providing services for the whole of society. This form accounts for the smallest proportion of cultural labor.

The fifth type is what we may term "self-use" labor, where a group of people may, for example, write plays which they perform by themselves for amusement. A calligrapher might produce beautiful writing for their own pleasure or present the results to close friends or relatives. This serves the purpose of pure self-entertainment, and the labor involves no social division of labor or relationships of exchange.

As we know, when labor participates in the social division of labor, it produces use value not for self-use but to obtain use values which the producers actually need through exchange in the market. In particular, under the capitalist mode of production, its purpose is to enable capital to create and appropriate surplus value. Therefore, only those products that actually enter circulation can be regarded as commodities, and other products lack the essential attribute of functioning as commodities. Of these five types of cultural labor, which can be considered productive?

We find that the first and third types of cultural labor result in cultural products or services whose use value is other than personal. Producers advance the values of the labor-power engaged in cultural production and expect to recoup these costs in the market. Moreover, those engaged in these two types of endeavor expect to receive more value than they advance, so that their capital expands. The results are therefore commodities and the labor engaged in them is productive.

The second type is normally sponsored by governments which set its budget. The expenses incurred are actually a redistribution of national income in line with the goal of placing cultural products or services at the disposal of the whole of society, for which a monetary reward equivalent to their value is not demanded. They are frequently provided either free of charge or with limited recompense from sources such as donations, souvenirs, tickets sales, and the like, whose composition does not significantly affect their non-commodity nature. This type of cultural labor is not governed by the law of value, and does not expect a profit.

The fourth type provides use value peculiar to family needs rather than for society in general. It is hence not part of social labor and does not create new value. The wage comes from a pool of financial resources and not as variable capital advanced; it cannot be recouped by selling commodities in the market; and finally, any difference between wages and the value of the results can only impact expenditure levels, and cannot create surplus value. The results are hence not commodities and do not create value.

Self-use, the fifth type of cultural labor, is conducted for the individual needs of the immediate producers, bearing little relationship to other people. In consequence, the individual labor time consumed bears little relation to socially necessary labor time, and individual value does not get transformed into social value. However, if the producer determines to sell the product in the market, their work turns into the labor of simple production of a commodity whose value is based on its social value, causing value to be created. Since self-use is not directed to this end, it is not productive.

We now consider a series of features that are specific to cultural production.

The particularity of the subject of labor

Material goods production, as is widely recognized, is a process of material transformation in which humans act on nature. The subjects of their labor are either unprocessed natural materials extracted from nature, such as wood cut from primitive forests, or semi-processed materials such as cotton for spinning yarn. But the subject of cultural labor is neither of these; it is human life. Cultural production distils and processes social life to create commodities and other products. Without rich social life as raw material, cultural production could not even start. Human social life is an endless source of material for artistic creation.

The nature of the mental power consumed by cultural labor

The use made of labor-power consists of labor, of which all types combine, in some way, material force and mental power, characterized by the use of muscular strength, the nervous system, the brain, and so on. However, different types of labor require different specific combinations of these inputs. Cultural labor relies on human mental power; one of the most significant differences between it and material labor is its greater creativeness. As a result, it is much less repetitive. In comparison, although material labor may display some creativity, it is by its nature more repetitive. Not surprisingly, creativity figures more prominently in cultural labor. The production process of a writer, for example, is actually a creative process requiring novelty of subject and distinctiveness of technique.

The uncertainty of the time of labor

In material goods production, laborers cannot work if they leave their post. Workers on an assembly line must operate the machines in accordance with strict rules. If they leave them, their labor terminates. From a spatial perspective, laborers and their positions are an inseparable entity. But because cultural production is dominated by human mental or intellectual activities, it is not conditioned to a particular post. Mental activity accompanies the person, who is its material form.

It could be argued that although there is a shift of space, production in the form of human mental activities does continue. However, the key point is that the calculation of the amount of time devoted to cultural production should not be based on the time spent in one particular spot; time spent in other spatial locations should also be considered. For example, the time a teacher devotes to production includes not only the time spent in class but also that spent on preparing lessons, researching pedagogy, providing after-class guidance for students, grading assignments, and so on.

In this sense, the total time a teacher spends on work is composed of two parts. The second part is almost impossible to measure. Theoretically, a person's active mental activities do not stop until they go to sleep. In other words, under normal material conditions, the upper limit of the labor time a cultural laborer can devote each day is 24 hours, less sleep time. This suggests that there is greater uncertainty about the time of cultural labor. To estimate it, we need a holistic view of the laborer's activities. We could then make an accurate estimate of the magnitude of value of their products.

The periodic nature of the labor process

In distinction from material goods production in a general sense, most cultural production consists of two phases. The first is mental creativity; the second is the production of a material carrier of that creativity.[1] Thus

---

1   This is so in most cases. Each specific cultural production process has its own peculiarities. In this instance we have developed the analysis by citing artistic creation as an example.

the first phase of literary creation is mental: the author produces an original manuscript and sends it for typography and printing. The material carrier of the author's creativity is then produced and sold in the market. The first phase is one of intense intellectual activity. As when bees are busy making honey, the writer is busy creating a literary work, but the consumers do not have the opportunity to enjoy it. When the work is complete, the manuscript has to go to the publisher for editing under an agreed contract. The materialized form of the writer's ideas – the book – is then sold in the market after mass printing.

In summary, the second phase is an extension of the first; but it is not cultural labor. Otherwise, both the printers and the writers would be cultural laborers. We can draw a theoretical distinction between the two phases: the second phase is an extension of the cultural production which typically occurs at best in the first phase. Therefore, the GNP produced in the second phase should be counted as part of the service sector rather than the cultural sector.

A second scenario is when, for example, after a lecturer has completed a series of lectures, it is made into videos and delivered to the market. But while the lectures were being given, they were consumed and were not counted as material goods. Here, the two phases are very discernible. However, the first phase also has some particularities, one of these being that the lectures and the video shooting take place at the same time, laying a foundation for mass production in the second phase. We could argue that the lecturing and video shooting were two inseparable parts of the same process, and the laborers engaged in both parts can be regarded as "workers." Here, the mass production of the second phase is more or less the same as printing in the previous example (Luo 1990, pp. 143–8).

Cultural production thus differs from material goods production in two general senses. The first difference is that the labor productivity of cultural production depends upon the conditions of living labor. According to our analysis above, cultural labor is characterized by exerting a tremendous amount of mental power, in which living labor is central. Capital in materialized form is only secondary, and its impact on labor productivity, accordingly, is also secondary. This contrasts with material goods production, where the key factor that determines the level of labor productivity is the sophistication of the elements of production, especially the machines. For example, one of China's major writers and essayists, Lu Xun, created many literary works amounting to more than 10 million words. This very high literary output is completely attributable to his mental creativity. There were no computers in his time and the basic tools at his disposal were pen and paper, which made little impact on the efficiency of literary creation. Thus, although the instruments of labor in cultural production differ widely, it is undeniable that their impact on labor productivity is much smaller than in material goods production.

The second difference is that the labor productivity of cultural production can only be evaluated on an approximate basis. Cultural living labor, characterized by intense mental activities, is a continuous process free from special restrictions, making it hard to estimate the time of labor precisely. There are also different degrees of complexity of the mental labor involved: the labor of scientists is more complex than that of high school teachers. However, the precise difference could hardly be detected even with the most sophisticated instruments. As a result, what we can do is make a rough estimate of labor productivity in cultural production; a precise estimate proves to be virtually impossible.

Baumol's law

When considering the productivity of cultural labor, a brief introduction to Baumol's law is in order (Baumol 1967, pp. 47–50). Expressing conclusions reached by the American scholar William Baumol when studying the structural problems facing performing art organizations, this law states that the cost of artistic performance should be expected in general to increase faster than that of other industries.

In material goods production, the capitalists are exercised both to recoup their investment and to earn surplus value. One result is that cost-plus pricing became the most common. Mass production being the common occurrence, cost per unit is expected to decrease as the quantity of products rises. However, the sum of values then also rises, as does the wage bill. This can however be offset by increasing output. Consequently, the higher the labor productivity, the less the negative impact on profits of the cost increases imposed by those wage increases arising from increases in the scale of production. Cost price is therefore negatively related to labor productivity.

But in cultural productions, cost price is rarely related negatively to labor productivity because labor costs are hard to reduce. The number of actors needed to perform a Shakespeare play is a requirement of the script, just as the number of musicians needed to play one of Beethoven's symphonies is more or less determined by the score. The increase in actors' wages cannot therefore be compensated by simply lowering the cost per unit. The output of an art performance cannot be greatly increased by increasing capacity. Therefore, if wages have to be increased, the proceeds must be increased. This goal can be achieved either by raising the ticket price or increasing the number of performances. It is thus difficult to maintain the price of cultural commodities by raising labor productivity, if wages increase.

This relationship between labor productivity in cultural production and the cost of the product confirms Marx's argument that labor productivity is negatively related to the value of commodities, if other conditions are constant.

Labor supply and demand in the cultural industries

In the previous section, we discussed the characteristics of labor and value creation in cultural industries, arguing that labor productivity there differs significantly from general material goods production. A key reason is the role of living human labor in cultural production.[2] We argued that it is the well-educated, highly intellectual and creative laborers who deserve serious study.

---

2   As noted, this does not mean that material goods play an unimportant role in cultural production. Without material goods as an economic base, it is impossible for cultural laborers to produce abundant cultural wealth. Thus, we found that when the *Beijing Morning Daily* was published in 1998, it took third place in Beijing's newspaper market with a capital of ¥15 million. After just two years, the capital threshold for such a market share had risen to ¥50 million. It was estimated that in the next 1 or 2 years, the capital threshold for entering Beijing's newspaper market would reach ¥100 million (Zhao et al. 2002, p. 176).

We now move to an in-depth analysis of demand for, and supply of, labor in the cultural industries, taking a traditional medium – the newspaper industry – as an example.

One of the many ways in which mental labor differs fundamentally from manual labor is the absence of hard and fast rules to regulating it. This makes it hard to supervise, or to set down standards that all mental laborers must reach. In a sense, the initiative and creativity displayed by cultural workers largely dictates general attitudes toward work; the initiative and creativity of these well-educated cultural workers, rather than anything else, has the most fundamental impact on the quality of a newspaper. Furthermore, cultural mental labor is endowed with other qualities such as individuality. Much work like interviewing, writing, and broadcasting, can be conducted independently.

These particular qualities inherent in mental labor dictate that talent flow between newspapers is a common occurrence. Competition for valuable talent in media has always been severe. It is quite normal for media institutions to give well-known reporters and editors high salaries. Poaching talents with special qualities is very common in today's Chinese media. Thus, to cover the Top Ten games of 2001, *Sports Weekly* poached the well-known reporter Li Xiang, who was believed to have a close relationship with China's football coach Bora Milutinovic, offering him more than ¥1.6 million over three months. *Football*, however, poached Qin Yun and other highly competent media workers from *Southern Sports* (Zhao et al. 2002, p. 199).

In a competitive labor market, the minimum labor payment is determined by the value of the goods needed to secure the production and reproduction of labor power. However, this assumes adequate competition in the labor market, that all laborers with the same level of skills can receive the same level of wages, and that the market clears.

Since the labor in cultural industries is highly independent, and the process of labor is hard to supervise, the actual outcome is hard to evaluate. Some laborers may not exert themselves and became lazy. In consequence, if a newspaper is determined to make its laborers exert themselves tirelessly and develop their potential, it must offer them a wage level much higher than the equilibrium.

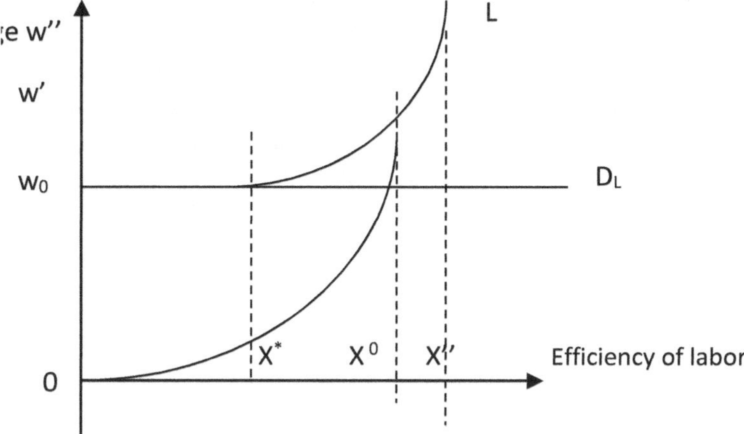

Figure 6.1 Laziness and efficiency-based wages

Figure 6.1 (taken from Jin 2002, pp. 192–3) shows the relationship between laziness and efficiency-based wages. D_L represents the demand curve faced by the laborers, the corresponding wage being w_0. The labor supply curve is L_L, and is divided into two sections by D_L, one above D_L and the other below it. If a newspaper employs laborers for wage w_0, the laborer's work efficiency would be X^0, and the newspaper must be aware that without extra incentives, work efficiency would drop to X^*. To raise work efficiency to X^0, the newspaper needs to raise wages to w'. If wages are raised to w", work efficiency can be raised to X".

Some media institutions choose to provide further incentives like stock options, to secure talents which make special contributions. These laborers could not only enjoy higher welfare benefits, but also display the value of their human capital, using their special talents to get a share of economic benefits. For example, on June 30, 2000, Phoenix TV was publicly listed on Hong Kong's stock market. The stock share received by some well-known anchormen and anchorwomen like Dou Wentao, Chen Luyu, and Xu Gehui was next only to that given to the vice-President of Phoenix TV. These well-known TV stars had the opportunity to buy back the stock issued by Phoenix TV at the original price and resell it in the secondary market. If the stocks performed well, the stars could have expected to earn returns 10 times the original price.

Another example is *Sports Weekly*. This newspaper introduced a new employment contract as early as 1993. All employees, regardless of status or gender, would be treated the same. Employees were remunerated in proportion to the work they had done, and good work got good payment. The monthly income of some extraordinary editors and reporters could be over ¥10,000, higher than the president or editor-in-chief. One anecdote recounts that *Sports Weekly* once paid ¥50,000 for a special article (Zhao et al. 2002, pp. 190–1).

7 Empirical studies in value creation by labor in cultural production

In previous chapters, we approached value creation in cultural production from the theoretical standpoint. We now attempt to examine this empirically, taking the media industry as an example.

Since its reform and opening-up, China's economy has maintained rapid growth for more than 30 years, with an average annual growth of 7.8%. China's GDP has increased 26-fold, from ¥362 billion in 1978 to 9,593 billion yuan in 2001. The output of China's service industry has increased 37-fold, from ¥86 billion in 1978 to ¥3,225 billion in 2001. Statistical data on the output of the cultural industries, defined narrowly as education, culture, art, and broadcasting, shows that their economic size approximated that of the literature industry, likewise defined narrowly. Their economic output in 2001 totaled ¥562 billion, yielding a profit of ¥38 billion. Value added reached ¥239 billion in 2000, when the 156 million people employed in this sector received gross pay of ¥171 billion (China Labor Statistical Yearbook 2002).

The average value created by a worker in this sector thus reached ¥153,800, and the percentage contribution to society, represented by the ratio of profits to wages, was about 22%. By the end of 2001, the number of trained technical personnel in China reached 30.5 million, of whom 11.7 million were concentrated in the cultural industries, making up 38.2% of China's technical personnel and 67% of all employees in this sector. Without doubt, China boasts a high-quality, well-trained and creative technical workforce. In developing its socialist market economy, technical personnel in the cultural industries have proven able to earn high rates of remuneration, at ¥582 per month – higher than the average income level of all employees in the cultural industries.

Let us now reflect on the implications of these data.

A certain amount of material capital is a prerequisite of value creation by cultural laborers, as is true for any type of production. A Chinese maxim tells us that you cannot make something out of nothing. However, the need for capital varies from industry to industry. As discussed, the key factor bearing on labor productivity in cultural production or value creation is the living labor of cultural workers rather than material capital. But as noted, this does not make material capital a dispensable factor. A certain amount of material capital is still required to ensure the survival and promote the development of the cultural industries.

Let's take a look at the following example. The minimum initial funding requirement for entering Beijing's newspaper market and making a profit has risen to ¥100 million. Without funding above this threshold level, the high profit rates expected in this sector cannot be realized and it is impossible even to get a rate of 8 per cent. Clearly, you must have the necessary funds before entering the market.

After several years' fierce market competition, Beijing's newspaper market has been effectively monopolized by several newspaper conglomerates. Behind their successful operation, strong funding support is undoubtedly the key driving force. Let's take a look at the data on four listed media corporations.

Table 7.1. Data on four corporations in the beijing newspaper market

Items / Companies	Assets (Unit: ¥ million)			Liabilities (Unit: ¥ million)			Profit (Unit: ¥ million)			Profit rates on assets (%)
Fiscal year	1999	2001	Growth rate %	1999	2001	Growth rate %	1999	2001	Growth rate %	2001
Oriental Pearl	3,079	3,921	27	1,423	1,139	-20	200	229	14.7	5.85
Gehua Cable	492	1,925	291	198	296	49	109	142	30.3	7.39
CTV	815	969	19	107	231	115	24	267	12.4	2.76
Hunan TV & Broadcast Intermediary Co. Ltd	1,270	4,525	256	418	1,955	826	145	76	-47.5	1.78

Source: Journal of China Securities and Journal of Shanghai Securities

156

As Table 7.1 shows, all four listed media conglomerates reaped large profits, and their success was largely dependent on their financial assets. The assets of all conglomerates increased significantly, as did their profits, with the exception of Hunan TV & Broadcast Intermediary Co. Ltd.

There is a clear positive relationship between total assets and profit rates. Of the four conglomerates, the one commanding the smallest assets had about ¥969 million, while Hunan TV & Broadcast had about ¥4,525 million in assets. Thus it can be seen that cultural industries need at least some material capital, and without it, cultural workers cannot create value.[1]

Among the newspaper conglomerates, the history of the *Guangzhou Daily* Group merits special study. This is actually run by the Municipal Party Committee of Guangzhou. Amid the tide of the market economy, much to the surprise of the public considering it is an official newspaper, *Guangzhou Daily* has not been marginalized but maintains a leading position in Guangzhou's newspaper market. It enjoys a circulation of 1.63 million, next to *People's Daily*. Individual subscribers make up 80% of all subscribers, and advertising revenue totaled ¥1.4 billion in 2001.

Starting from eight editions in its early days, *Guangzhou Daily* now has blossomed into a newspaper with between 40 and 60 daily editions. Its circulation has also witnessed rapid growth. These posed a major challenge to its printing capacity. As early as in 1996, it invested about ¥1 billion to build a sophisticated modern printing center, enabling it to produce 3 million copies per hour in color.

This is an amazing printing speed, regarded as "crazy printing" in the eyes of the world. In the fourth quarter of 2001, the group added two new production lines, increasing its capacity from 3 million copies per hour to 4.8 million copies, using color printing. Guangzhou is now one of the three major printing centers of Asia, alongside Yomiuri Shimbun of Japan and United Daily News of Taiwan (Cao 1999, p. 116). The high capacity of this printing equipment is of great value to the development of the Guangzhou Daily Group. *Guangzhou Daily* simply could not get anywhere without the benefit of these sophisticated machines.

---

1   The total profits of China's top 10 cultural corporations totaled ¥460 million in 2000 (Jiang and Xie 2003, p. 318).

The cultural industries started rather late in China. The media industry, a key component of these industries, has always been regarded as a sunrise industry, and has been believed to have the most exciting prospects. A report on the time taken for 11 industries to blossom into world-class enterprises with international competitiveness, by the well-known investment bank Morgan Stanley, suggests that the time span for an enterprise in the mass media sector to achieve this goal is 8 years, much shorter than for other sectors. In China, where the mass media industry is underdeveloped, it takes only two years for this industry to gain the edge over other industries in a given geographical area. It is precisely in this industry that maximum profits can be reaped.

Not surprisingly, the profit-seeking nature of capital finds its fullest expression here. As is to be expected, large amounts of private capital are already pouring into the media industry. On the other hand, the demand for capital input is enormous in the formative stages, as statistical data from the 2001 *China Media Investment Report* confirm. According to this report, as many as 82% of China's media institutions were strapped for capital.

The reason for such large capital inflows is the high returns that the media industry offers, newspapers being a case in point. Average returns on investment have ranged from 17% to 50% during the past 10 years, much higher than in other industries. Although advertising revenue in the media industry has grown faster than GNP since the 1990s, it is still below 1% of GNP, compared with 2% in developed countries. Thus it is very easy to understand why Tom.com Ltd has taken a keen interest in merging several media institutions in the Mainland, Taiwan, and Hong Kong, including 12 agencies engaged in outdoor advertising and several dotcoms, in the past decade. Tom.com also formed a partnership with the Yangcheng Evening News Group. These mergers produced an approximate capitalization of over HK$3 billion, receiving a blaze of media publicity in all three places.

Living labor in the cultural industries

The history of world economic development suggests that the improvement of S&T usually coincides with the transformation of economic structure, as evidenced by the decline of agriculture and industry and a marked increase in the service sector. By the year 2001, the ratio of agriculture and industry to services in China was 15.2: 51.1: 33.6. In the service sector, cultural organizations capture the lion's share of output. According to the State Bureau of Statistics, they accounted for 8% of the total output of the service sector in 2001. If the output of public health, sports, social welfare, and research and development (R&D) and technical services are taken into account, this reaches 12.9%.

Clearly, China's cultural industries figure prominently in its national economic development. By 2015, the total output of the cultural industries is expected to reach 15% of China's GNP and occupy a market of up to ¥1,000 billion (Jiang and Xie. 2003, p. 19).

Although the commercialization of China's media industry is no more than 5 to 6 years old, it is one of those seeing the fastest development. This is apparent from the huge profit it reaped in the year 2000, during which the total revenue generated by the ten listed media conglomerates totaled ¥4.6 billion. This testifies to the media industry's contribution to the national economy.

However, this value is all created by cultural workers. Laborers working in the cultural industries are the best educated. Generally speaking, there are two important sources of knowledge: education and social practice, of which education has become steadily more important as society evolves. But education calls for not only time but financial input and sacrifice, not to mention opportunity cost. As we have noted, these aspects form an important part of the value inherent in modern labor, unlike in Marx's day.2

Complexity and intensity: cultural labor in the chinese media

Guangzhou Daily illustrates this point. To keep a mental edge over its competitors, *Guangzhou Daily* recruited highly qualified staff majoring in journalism, Chinese language and culture, computer science, law, architecture, and accounting from Peking University, Tsinghua University, Renmin University of China, Fudan University, Shanghai Jiaotong University, and others. Of these recruits, 10 had a doctorate, 28 had a master's degree and the rest had a bachelor's degrees. *Guangzhou Daily* is believed to have developed

---

2   The educational costs of labor power were at that time extremely small and could be neglected (Marx and Engels 1972c, p. 351).

large talent reserves for the upcoming century, and it recently resumed its efforts to lure talent. About 15 more graduates with doctorates, 89 with a master's degree or double BA degrees, and more than 200 elite college graduates have joined the *Guangzhou Daily* Group in recent years.

Guangzhou Daily proved able to optimize the use of its human resources to set its operation on the right track. Starting in 1998, it initiated a program which aimed to send from 6 to 8 outstanding staff to take higher degrees or to study as visiting scholars abroad. For example, it reached an agreement with the School of Journalism of the University of Missouri at Columbus under which it sent outstanding staff there to study for MA degrees each year. It also founded its own post-doctoral research institute (He 2000). Such measures allowed the *Guangzhou Daily* Group to score spectacular successes compared with its counterparts.

Labor intensity in the cultural industries is also high. It would be a mistake to think that laborers in the cultural industry are characterized by education alone and that labor in this particular industry is less intense. These workers are not only well-educated intellectuals, but face pressure just as intense as in other industries, and in some cases their workloads are even heavier. This is illustrated by China's resumption of sovereignty over Hong Kong on July 1, 1997. Phoenix TV dispatched several teams of reporters to cover the handover, with the aim of providing the audience with a panoramic view of this historical event. Well-known anchorpersons on Phoenix TV such as Wu Xiaoli and Dou Wentao wore make-up for 40 hours and reported the event nonstop for 60 hours (Zhao, Yu and Zhang. 2002, pp. 7–8). Moreover the time they spent on the scene does not complete the picture. If preliminary planning and editing work is included, their actual workload is even heavier. The staff of Southern Cosmopolis described the situation in their workplace as follows:

> *We are just like a cog in the wheel fitting together with the bits of another wheel. The movement of the cog appears rather irregular at the outset. As the cog accelerates, we are brought into a right position and then never stop. Another outcome is that if the cog fails to fit with another flying wheel, the cog will fall into disuse and be thrown away. (Dongfang 2002, p. 303)*

160

Staff at Southern Cosmopolis have virtually abandoned the concept of an 8-hour working system, and a 9-to-5 workday has become impossible. Many have their cellphones on around the clock. It is almost impossible for anyone to sleep for five hours without being interrupted by telephone calls. Such an unimaginable condition has become the order of the day. At Southern Cosmopolis, almost everyone is a workaholic, full of vim and vigor. They can get wild with excitement about an important media planning meeting. Having worked nonstop for more than 10 days with 2 or 3 hours of sleep each night, staff may fall ill and have to stay in bed for weeks. A former employee of Southern Cosmopolis said that for two years after he left the newspaper, he did not even know what he should do between 1 and 5 a.m. More often than not, he would sit beside the telephone in a trance, waiting for phone calls. Only after a fairly long period of time did he start to return to normalcy (Dongfang 2002, p. 305).

It could be argued that such an "unhealthy" obsession with work is what has propelled Southern Cosmopolis to such a high status in China's media landscape; it is precisely this huge input of knowledge-based labor, characterized by high intensity, that forms the source of value creation by cultural labor in the media industry.

Labor in the cultural industries is high-level complex labor. These industries are knowledge-based, employing very creative labor. In the media industry, only candidates with a multidisciplinary background or the powerful skills to conduct multidisciplinary assessments are considered qualified. Heavy emphasis is placed on recruiting valuable talents with a wealth of knowledge, scientific methodology, and high ability.

Moreover this knowledge and expertise is not confined to journalism, but refers to a set of comprehensive abilities cutting across many areas of study. The media place increasing emphasis on reporting and editing personnel with a background in humanities, economics, history, or law, or with special analytical skills, combined with training in journalism. The International Division of People's Daily, for example, imposes the following requirements on prospective employees: they must have superb capacity to write news reports and commentaries, and write reference materials for internal circulation (Song 1998). Thus, candidates with strong multidisciplinary backgrounds are regarded by the media industry as both valuable talents and the most important guarantee of success.

Caijing, a commercial magazine known for investigative journalism which cuts a fine figure among myriad other media, is widely recognized as a medium "with a strong mission." One of the most important reasons for its success, rather than its capital, is that its editors and reporters have produced a series of in-depth reports in recent years. Three of its most prominent figures are the editor-in-chief Hu Shuli, editor Yang Daming, and Wang Shuo. They are believed to be its ruling troika, and are the most outstanding figures in the media industry as well. Among them, Hu Shuli is widely believed to be the number one financial reporter in China, and was once rated one of the 50 Stars of Asia by the US magazine Business Weekly. Yang Daming was convinced that a majority of Caijing's cover stories were written by Hu Shuli and Wang Shuo. Yang said that not everyone was capable of writing important news stories, but that having such a capability was a must (Zhao, Yu and Zhang. 2002, 324).

This illustrates the point that complex labor is the aggregate of simple labor: the even more complex labor represented by creative labor counts for several times the aggregate of simple labor, and may create much greater value than simple labor. This allows us to explain why laborers in the cultural industries play a significant role in creating the value of cultural products. This empirical analysis shows that the value created by labor in the cultural industries is significantly greater than that created elsewhere, due to the high level of knowledge of cultural laborers, and the higher level and costs of education.

Because the intensity of labor in the cultural industries is greater not only than normal labor intensity but also than that of complex labor elsewhere, the value it creates in materialized form surpasses that created by other types of industry. This living labor is thus the key factor on which the success of any media organization depends. It is beyond doubt that the cultural industries are making an increasing contribution to the national economy, and play a crucial role in enriching people's lives.

A typical example of value creation by labor in the cultural sector: painter Liu Linghua's story

Painter Liu Linghua is a professor of the Academy of Fine Arts at Xi'an, Jiang and Xie 2002, pp. 297–304). For the Shanghai Art Fair in 1999, he submitted one of his paintings, The Years, for exhibition. The painting attracted the attention of the managers of Shanghai Broadband Television Corporation (SBTC). They believed that Professor Liu's rugged style of painting conveyed a strong impulse to express himself. After a close examination of this oil painting, SBTC signed a contract with Professor Liu, making him the first painter to be contracted to work for it.

In the light of Professor Liu's artistic style and his understanding of life, along with SBTC's marketing research, senior leaders of SBTC had an intense debate over the market potential of his work. It is SBTC's hope that Liu's work will fully convey the essence of Chinese culture by drawing on his understanding of Western art. SBTC finally decided to focus on the Peking Opera, and made it the basis of "Eighteen Paintings of National Quintessence" to be undertaken by Liu. Thanks to his background in the dramatic arts, he gave undivided attention to artistic creation, and finally produced 18 oil paintings related to the Peking Opera, such as A Concubine in Tipsiness and An Appeal to the Emperor by Hairui. At the 2000 Shanghai Art Fair, these works made their debut and caused quite a stir. Later, SBTC mounted an impressive exhibition of Liu's works, which won great acclaim.

The artistic success of Liu's paintings also led to market success. The market value of his award-winning work was less than ¥100,000 at the first Shanghai Art Fair. At the 2000 Shanghai Art Fair, a Hong Kong businessman was willing to pay as much as HK$50,000 for one of his exhibited works. Other works were valued at around ¥300,000, ten times their price before he was contracted to work for SBTC. In 2001, A Concubine in Tipsiness sold for ¥1 million. During the APEC conference, a businessman telephoned Liu to say he wanted to buy it for $600,000, about ¥5 million. By this time, the average price of Liu's works had risen to ¥1 million, and the price of one particular work had risen from ¥38,000 to ¥5 million in only two years, due to the creative labor that combined the technology of Western painting with Chinese themes. During this period, SBTC had invested nearly ¥10 million, but the investment had been recouped and SBTC finally reaped handsome profits. Fine art is notoriously the target of excess financial funds seeking either a haven or a speculative profit. There is quite a lot of work on the formation of fine art prices, which stresses this speculative element together with the role played by branding and recognition.

The role of creativity

The huge value created by the cultural industries comes from creative labor. It includes not only the labor of the creator but their cultural creativity. This has two aspects. The first, narrow aspect emphasizes the individuality of the artist's creation. The second is creativity in a broader sense, referring to the space of re-creation. We argue that only by integrating these two can artists produce the artistic works the masses love. In a market economy, artistic creativity is highly dependent on pooling valuable talents with a multidisciplinary background, which is different from a businessperson's acute sense of the market and the artist's self-initiated exploration.

Artistic creativity is based on a combination of judgments on the market, aesthetics, artistic assessment, social trends and social psychology, and many other factors. The involvement of a businessperson in artistic creation is fundamentally different from an artist's independent creation. Real life suggests that the involvement of businesspeople in artistic creation can not only tap the potential of an artist's creativity, but best meet the cultural needs of the public using market mechanisms. Previously, we have placed heavy emphasis on the individuality of the laborer's creative effort while downplaying the commercialization of cultural products. We argue that it is time to make a fundamental change.

Comparative studies at international level on value creation by labor in cultural production

The official government documents of the People's Republic of China make a clear distinction between "cultural program" and "cultural industries," and argue that "developing the cultural industries is an important avenue to enrich socialist culture under the market economy and to meet the spiritual and cultural needs of the people." This principle provided a solid theoretical as well as policy basis for the development of China's cultural sector in the future. Although the development of China's cultural sector has a history of only 5 or 6 years, their growth rate exceeds that of the service sector in general, reaching 26% per annum.

However, compared with the developed countries, the share of China's cultural sector in her economic landscape is rather small, and there is much space for further development. It is strongly expected that in the next 10 years China's cultural sector will make a greater contribution to economic development in general. A brief multi-country study on value creation by labor in the cultural sector follows.

Amounts of living labor input

Table 7.2 Living labor engaged in cultural production in selected countries

Time Country	1996	1997	1998	1999	2000	2001	2002
China	14,300	15,100	15,500	15,700	15,730	15,750	15,780
USA	7,270	7,550	7,800	7,950	7,890	7,080	7,520
UK	1,360	1,400	1,450	1,460	1,510	1,550	1,630
France	1,450	1,520	1,570	1,650	1,660	1,690	1,720
Japan	3,380	3,530	3,560	3,650	3,760	3,850	3,910

Unit: thousands of workers.

Sources: China Statistical Yearbook, World Economic and Cultural Yearbook, The International Statistical Yearbook, China Statistics Press.

As the definition of the cultural sector varies from country to country, many different factors need to be taken into consideration in a cross-sectional study. However, living labor inputs can be subjected to longitudinal study.

Table 7.2 suggests that all major countries input large amounts of labor into their cultural sector after 1996, and that this amount has increased steadily. The gradual increase in living labor input in the cultural sector has led to its increasing contribution to the national economy and increasing added value.

For example, between 1998 and 2000, the added value of China's cultural sector increased from ¥182 billion to ¥239 billion. The average growth rate was 12.3%, substantially higher than the rate of general economic growth. The number of laborers in the cultural sector also rose 10.4% between 1996 and 2002. During the same period, the number of laborer in the US cultural sector grew by 3.4%. The labor input of other countries was more or less the same. As the classification used by the State Bureau of Statistics differs somewhat from ours, we chose to use the narrow definition of cultural industries, namely, "education, culture and arts and broadcasting."

Table 7.3 Percentage contribution of the cultural sector to China's overall economy and index of added value

Time Content	1995	1996	1997	1998	1999	2000
Added value in the cultural sector (¥100m)	1,124	1,355	1,573	1,824	2,098	2,391
Percentage of cultural sector in services in general	6.3	6.6	6.8	7.2	7.8	8
Index of added value of the cultural sector	108	113	114	110	107	105

Source: China Statistical Yearbook, China Statistics Press, 2003.

Table 7.3 shows that laborers in China's cultural sector created significant amounts of value for China every year. Between 1995 and 2000, the absolute value they created increased steadily, and it had reached ¥239 billion by 2000. The cultural sector's share in output was also increasing steadily, and by the year 2000 had reached 8%. With the development of China's economy and improvement of living standards, the demand for cultural products will be greater than for other types of service. The space for the development of the cultural sector is surprisingly large.

166

Constant capital: the material basis for value creation in the cultural sector

Value formation and creation are actually one process. Although living labor is the only source of value, a certain amount of materialized labor still plays a very important role in value formation, because laborers cannot create value without a certain amount of means of production. On the international market, the value created by laborers with high labor productivity is undoubtedly much greater. Labor productivity is becoming the lynchpin on which value creation depends, and the application of S&T is the most important means to increase it.

Producers are sparing no effort to increase their technological level and upgrade their means of production to increase labor productivity and drive down costs, creating and appropriating surplus value in so doing. This is no different from other types of industry; however, the composition of capital inputs into the cultural sector varies from country to country, as we shall now see.

**Table 7.4 Constant capital inputs to the
cultural sector in major countries (¥ million)**

Time / Country	1998	1999	2000	2001
China	32,500	43,200	50,300	56,200
USA	39,300	42,600	45,300	49,000
UK	3,800	4,300	5,500	6,100
France	7,800	8,500	9,200	9,500
Japan	2,279,700	2,365,300	2,545,600	2,573,600

Sources of data: refer to Table 7.2.

Table 7.4 suggests that constant capital in the cultural sector in these major countries has been growing. China's fixed capital input in its cultural industries in 2001 totaled ¥56.2 billion, and the annual growth rate was as high as 11%. The growth rate of US fixed capital in the cultural sector reached 8%. Similar growth rates are to be found in other countries. These large amounts of constant capital inputs provide an important material basis for laborers to create value, as well as spiritual wealth for the whole of society.

In the market economy, cultural products are sold to consumers in the form of a materialized carrier. Cultural production is thus also a process of economic production in which economic efficiency, the relation between inputs and outputs, also matters. To compute labor productivity in cultural production is not that easy. First, it is dominated by living labor, but the content of a cultural product is more often than not expressed in material form; second, a value index may not precisely express a worker's labor input or the real value of a product. Nevertheless, by examining the ratio of input to output in cultural production, we can study the efficiency of labor in cultural production from a variety of viewpoints. A cross-sectional study of the major indexes shared by China and other countries will give us a basic grasp of the labor productivity level that each of China's cultural industries maintains. We may also find problems to be addressed, and identify gaps between China and other countries.

Table 7.5 is an index expressing the value created per worker (labor productivity) in the cultural sector of a number of countries.

Table 7.5 Index of labor productivity of the cultural sector in selected major countries (current US$/person/year at market exchange rates)

Time / Country	1998	1999	2000	2001
China	875	967	1,352	1,657
USA	48,797	53,645	61,576	69,713
UK	36,745	38,790	42,543	48,759
France	48,563	49,723	47,690	49,806
Japan	48,769	51,326	56,467	61,575

Sources: refer to Table 7.2.

Although labor productivity is computed based on US units in each country, we still find a discrepancy in labor productivity between China and other developed countries. In 2001, labor productivity in China's cultural sector was only $1,657 per person each year, while in the US cultural sector it totaled $69,713 per person each year. Among the developed countries, the UK had the lowest level of labor productivity, at $48,759 per person each year. Comparing Tables 7.1 and 7.4, we find that even though China's laborers in the cultural sector created large amounts of value, this was achieved not by improving labor productivity, but by increasing the number of laborers and reproduction. In contrast, value creation in the cultural sector of the developed countries was achieved by improving labor productivity.

The publishing industry is an example. In the USA, 20 out of 1,000 publishing companies dominate the US book market. In magazine publishing, the circulation of China's most popular magazine is less than 5 million and there are fewer than 25 magazines with a circulation of more than 1 million. For comparison in the USA in 1999, the magazine with the largest circulation (more than 20.64 million) was *Modern Maturity*, now *AARP – the Magazine*. Even *People*, whose circulation was ranked tenth, had a circulation of 3.5 million. In China, the circulation of the top ten magazines was about 400 million, with each person purchasing an average of only two titles, while in the USA, the circulation of the top ten magazines totaled 1.53 billion, with each person purchasing more than 20 titles (Jiang and Xie 2003, p. 55). *Modern Maturity*, the magazine with the largest circulation in the USA, employed a total of 62 staff, while *Story-telling Session*, the magazine with the largest circulation of 4.13 million in China in 1998, employed a total of 95 staff, about 1.5 times that of *Modern Maturity*, but with only a fifth of its circulation. Labor productivity in China's cultural industries is clearly much lower than that in the developed countries, and consequently China's cultural industry can only create less value. The small monetary value generated by magazine circulation in China is testimony to this point.

Let's perform a further analysis by taking labor productivity in education as an example. One of the best indexes of labor productivity in education is the ratio of teachers to students. This index may not precisely express the level of labor productivity of each country due to the variance in each country's real situation.

**Table 7.6 Ratio of primary school and high school
teachers to students in China, France, and Japan (%)**

Country	Year	Primary school	Junior school	High school
		Student–teacher ratio	Student–teacher ratio	Student–teacher ratio
China	2002	21.4	19.2	17.8
France	1990	16.1	13	13
Japan	1990	21.1	15.6	12.7

Source of data: Refer to Table 7.1.

As Table 7.6 suggests, there are significantly more students per teacher in China than in other countries. In other words, the ratio of input to output in China is rather low. When non-instructional staff are taken into consideration, the output is even lower. All these facts suggest that the labor productivity of China's education is low, and there is still a large gap between China and the developed countries.

Analysis of output by amount of value

For a comparative study of country outputs, we measure output in constant local currency. The output index of the cultural industries of each country is then an index of the value we wish to examine.

**Table 7.7 Index of output of the cultural
sector in selected major countries**

Country \ Time	1998	1999	2000	2001
China	1,824	2,098	2,391	2,769
USA	3,924	4,266	4,617	4,940
UK	600	625	665	718
France	567	541	595	659
Japan	196,017	203,819	218,314	228,390

Unit: 100s of millions of the monetary unit of the country

Sources of data: refer to Table 7.1.

170

Table 7.7 suggests that since 1998, laborers in the cultural industries of all countries have created growing amounts of value, particularly in China. Not only have the absolute amounts of value increased significantly, but annual percentage growth is high, reaching 15.8% in 2001 for China. Growth rates in other countries are equally significant. Moreover, the share of the cultural industries in output is rising in general.

The definition of the cultural sector also varies. The US definition covers culture and the arts (including performance art and museums), show business, publishing, and music and the recording industry. This is clearly much stricter than China's definition. The definition of the UK's creative industries is conceptually broader[3] including publishing, music, performance art, film, television and radio, software, games, advertising, architecture, art design, artwork, antiques, handicrafts, and fashion. The definition of the cultural sector used by France and Japan also varies. It is necessary to take these different definitions into consideration before a serious study on value creation by labor can be conducted.

Here, we single out the cultural sectors of the USA and the UK for further investigation.

According to a report released by American Cultural Institutions dealing with the impact of Cultural Consumption on the Economy, by June 10, 2002, US non-profit cultural institutions had created a $134 billion market for the American economy, of which the market directly created by US cultural institutions was $53.2 billion and the market of tied-in products was $80.8 billion (Jiang and Xie 2003, p. 56).

The structure of the cultural product market lends itself to oligopoly, and US show business is no exception. The US show business market has been carved up by Disney, Sony, MGM, Paramount, Fox, Universal, and Time-Warner. In 2000, US box office receipts reached a record high, totaling $7.7 billion. US show business also occupies a very dominant position in the global market. America's television programs run in more than 125 countries and regions. In the European market, US video products such as films

---

3   Editor's note: the UK definition, also in use in many other countries, captures those industries which make intensive use of the creative workforce. See Bakhshi et al. (2013)

accounted for 70%. It is estimated that US audio and video products make up 57.6% of the world market.

The USA has highly developed cultural industries, and the market for cultural products has always played a very important role in America's economic development. As early as in 1977, the net earnings of the US cultural industries totaled $55 billion. This accounted for 2.8% of US GDP, and the sector was ranked second among all US economic sectors, following medical services. According to the latest report on the copyright industry entitled *Copyright Industry in the American Economy* (most US cultural products are copyrighted), the value created by the US "core" copyright industry jumped from $96.4 billion in 1977 to $226.5 billion in 1992. By 2000, the gross product produced by the US copyright industries totaled $457.2 billion, accounting for 4.9% of US GDP in 1999. Since 1977, the growth rate of the US copyright industries has been twice that of the economy as a whole (Hu 2002, pp. 67–8).

At the same time, the export of US cultural products has increased dramatically. After 1995, the export of US cultural products achieved double-digit growth. In 1997, the volume of US cultural product exports totaled $66.85 billion, taking first place in terms of export volume. During the same period, the volume of export of autos and auto spare parts was only $58.34 billion.

The UK boasts a market economy with a very long history. As an integral part of the market economy, its cultural sector has developed into a full-blown industry. As early as in 1982, its output totaled £5.976 billion, accounting for 2.6% of UK GDP and employing a total of 628,000 people. Among its subsectors, literature publishing had the highest output, reaching £4.5 billion, while broadcasting, film and video, audio, music, and drama followed suit with outputs of £644 million, £333 million, £305 million, £173 million, and £67 million respectively. In the music industry, the income of musicians totaled £45 million and the income of composers £22 million. In 1995, the output of the cultural industries accounted for 4% of the UK's GNP, surpassing any type of the UK's traditional manufacturing industry.

8
Value creation by labor in the service industries

Marx studied UK manufacturing industries, at that time the most representative of world capitalist development, unveiling the general law of the development of capitalist societies more than 150 years ago. The economic and industrial structures of the capitalist countries have evolved dramatically; by the early 1990s, the share of the service industries in GNP had risen from 20–30% in the developed countries over a century ago, to 60–70% in those countries, 50% in the semi-developed countries and 34% in China. Trade in services has risen to 25% of the global trade volume and is expected to continue growing.

Since the service industries exert great influence over a country's economic development and job market, we should devote increased effort to studying them from the perspective of economic theory. This is a complicated undertaking, because research into the theoretical aspects of the service economy still falls short of expectations, accompanied by wide and deep-rooted differences of opinion, in all schools of thought. This is because of the particularity of the service industries, the changes they are undergoing, and the growing universality of their scope.

Historical review of theories of the service economy

We shall now address the two main bodies of theory relating to the service economy: Marx's, and those of Western scholars. Because of the differences in their research goals and subjects of study, they differ widely.

Marx's theory of services

As noted, Marx made material goods production his main research area in his studies of the socioeconomic problems of capitalist societies in *Capital*, singling out the British textile industry for special treatment. He pointed out that the production of wealth by capitalist societies was characterized by large stocks of self-evidently tangible commodities. These could be accumulated over a long period of time, they could exist in the absence of producers and consumers, and they were transportable.

Products can be divided into material goods such as clothes, automobiles, and planes which exist independent of other factors, and non-material goods such as transport and communication, which exist in the form of living labor from which they cannot be separated. As Marx wrote, "in addition to the mining industry, agriculture and processing industries, we also have the fourth area of material goods production .... which was transport" (Marx and Engels 1972c, p. 444).

This suggests that transport can be classified in the same area as mining, agriculture, and processing whose purpose is to extract materials from nature. It does not actually produce or provide material goods, but creates products in the shape of living labor, which provide the intangible use value of changing the spatial location of material goods, so that these can be delivered to consumers as consumer goods in a real sense.

As we have noted, there are two types of non-material goods. The first consists of things like books or audiovisual products, which can exist in the absence of producers and consumers. The second take the form of living labor. These goods include live concerts and lectures. Both can be produced as commodities and become products of social labor by entering the exchange system. Marx argued that it was unscientific to define productive labor as that engaged in material production, an idea which he considered a one-sided outcome of Smith's outlook.

Table 8.1 provides a general classification of production based on the above analysis.

Table 8.1 general classification of production by type of good and type of labor

	Production of material goods	Production of non-material goods
Material production by labor	Mining (oil, natural gas, coal, iron) Agriculture (cropping, forestry, husbandry, fishing) Processing industries (textile, metallurgy, food, clothes)	Painting Sculpture Publishing (natural and social sciences, literature and artistic creation)
Non-material production (service) in the form of living labor	Transport Telecommunication Architecture Sewing Repairing Dining	Entertainment (dancing, music, drama) Scientific research, education Medical services Information and consulting

The concept of service in economics

The term "service" has wide implications. In economics, it usually refers to the work done in selling and purchasing commodities. More generally, it refers to the use value of a particular type of labor, just as material goods have their own special use value. However, it is called a service because its result is not a material good, but the living labor itself.

This implies that the service provided by labor is no different than, for example, that provided by a machine, such as a clock (Luo 1990, p. 264). We conclude that service is a particular type of use value, like that provided by other material goods, but taking the form of living labor. Yet if the result is provided without the presence of living labor, for example, as a book, it could be argued that only a material good, not a service, is provided.

Thus, the normal economic definition of a service is not without contradiction. How might we respond? We begin from the following two points. First, the party providing services and the party receiving services are related through exchange. Second, a service is also a type of commodity not qualitatively different from material goods. The difference lies only in form. Both types of commodity have use value. However, that of a service is given by the character of the living labor involved, not its material form. A book, for example, has the same content whether it is printed on paper or delivered electronically as an e-book.

We now attempt to clarify these points and resolve these difficulties through a more comprehensive analysis of the concept of "service" and its relation to living labor.

Pure services and non-pure services

The products of labor take two forms: tangible and intangible goods or services. There are two types of the latter. The first is use value in the form of labor that fades away the moment it is provided. For example, suppose a concert is given in Beijing by three well-known tenors. To hear their beautiful singing, customers pay a high price for a ticket; the three tenors sing and they enjoy it. Their enjoyment stops once the singing is over. Since such use value can only be provided for customers in the form of living labor, Marx termed it a "pure service." But a customer may also choose to purchase a use value directly in the market, or cause it to be produced by purchasing living labor. For example, he might order a suit by choosing cloth and inviting a tailor to make it up into a suit, instead of buying it in the market. Marx treated the latter as an "impure service" in which the living labor used to create use value does not itself necessarily constitute the use value.

Sole-purpose service and not-sole-purpose service

A second distinction concerns whether purchase is for the consumers' direct use or for resale. In the case of the tenors, the consumers purchase living labor from a service provider and consume it as pure use value. They do not intend to resell it or its product. A second example is when a family prepares some cloth and invites a tailor to make clothes out of it for family members. These are for family use, not for sale.

A second type of service delivery takes place when the living labor of service providers is used to produce commodities subsequently sold in the market, not for personal consumption. The production and sale of beautiful writing by an individual calligrapher belonged to this latter type of service. The same applies if a private school employs teachers to give lectures to paying students.

The above distinctions have important economic implications. The first distinction defines two forms of services related to living labor; the service is directly purchased as labor but may be used to produce material as well as intangible goods. Intangible goods are always services, but not all services are intangible. Intangibility is a necessary but not sufficient condition.

This distinction has caused economists great difficulty in analyzing the economic nature of services. They regard the precise definition of services or their scope as an impossible mission. Take for example a consulting firm that employs both a team of economists and a team of computer scientists, and which provides econometric consultation and sometimes software services related to econometric analysis. From the perspective of the labor process, the two types of service are more or less the same, since they consume the living labor of economists and computer scientists. But from the perspective of the outcome of this labor, the two types of service are different. One is a pure service (consulting) and another (software products) is not. They belong to different statistical categories.

This distinction is more significant as it relates to productive and non-productive service. Pure service is treated, in economics, as a non-productive service which does not create value. Not-sole-purpose service is treated as productive, creating the value of service products.

In capitalist society, there are some independent producers who are employed by public institutions, or as individuals. As capitalism and S&T develops, it takes over the production of ever more commodities. Like a shining sun it obscured all the obstacles to its progress and becomes the master of social production. In the service sector, employed labor comes to comprise an overwhelming percentage of all service labor.

Capital is actually value capable of yielding surplus value. As we have noted, to make capital expand, the capitalist needs labor power, which is combined with elements of production to produces commodities whose value is greater than the sum of the expenditures. Each production cycle follows the previous one, as shown in Figure 8.1.

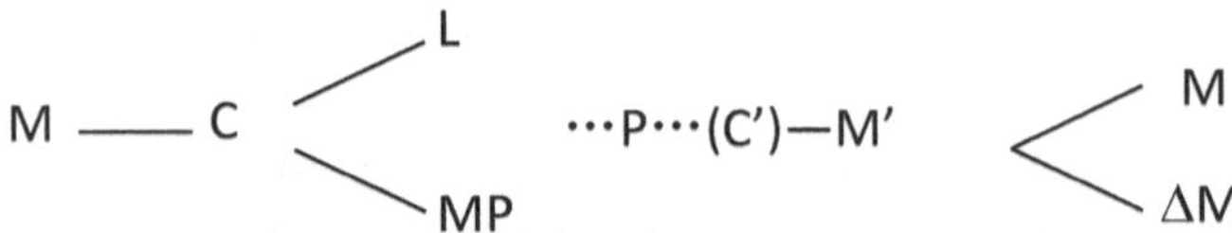

Figure 8.1 The circuit of capital

In the above equation, M stands for the money capital advanced by capitalists, C' for material goods produced by service labor, L for labor power, and MP for elements of production. P is the process of production. C' stands for capital goods produced by service labor. M' stands for the sum of values after the goods have been sold. ΔM represents surplus value. What really concerns capitalists is to make their capital expand; the different lines of commodities are not that important from their perspective. However, when providing the use value of services, the form of commodities assumes two types: pure services like transport, artistic performance, and processing for customers, and material goods produced by service labor, which we might call a replacement for pure service. The replacement could for example be the clothes produced by a tailor hired by a capitalist.

In addition to the services provided by employed labor, there are also a small number of independent producers in capitalist societies. These independent producers normally command few elements of production. Laborers in the repair and assembly industry, for example, rely on their technical skills to provide services using a limited number of instruments or tools, often providing door-to-door services. Clearly, such economic relations have nothing in common with exchange between capital and labor. Although they provide services, belong to the category of productive laborers, and create value, they cannot be regarded as capitalist commodity producers. They are thus neither productive nor non-productive laborers.

Individuals, families, and some public institutions also employ workers to provide various services in both pre-industrial and contemporary societies,

178

providing them with income. However, these funds are either private personal income or, with public institutions, derived from the redistribution of national income. Their labor is consumed as pure use value, providing pure services, not commodities. Indeed, they even receive commodities from the buyers (Marx and Engels 1972c, p. 151). They are thus non-productive.

For all these reasons it would be unscientific simply to divide service-providing labor into productive and non-productive, and irrational to draw a distinction between labor producing services, and labor producing, or directly engaged in producing, material goods.

Western theories of the service economy

As discussed above, research into the economic aspect of service production is complicated by the particularities inherent in the concept of "service" which, just like the term "value," has become a phrase in common popular use. It was not originally an economic term in a strict sense, even though it is widely employed in economics. In fact, Western academic economics has no generally agreed definition of service. In the literature we find three meanings of the word.

(1) If an individual or business provides assistance or use value contributing to the welfare of a recipient, it is said to provide a service.

(2) A service is an intangible good for exchange with a certain amount of exchange value, and its use value is instantaneous (for instance, entertainment), reusable (information), or variable (specialized consulting).

(3) Service is the result of purposeful activities of an individual or a business, which may or may not receive a reward.

Thus the concept has been rather ambiguous and general, and consequently lacking in academic rigor.

The earliest scholar of the issue was Say (2001), who pointed out in *A Treatise on Political Economy* that intangible goods (services) were also the fruits of human labor and a result of capital. He thus developed a deeper understanding of wealth than Adam Smith – who defined wealth as tangible or materialized goods – dividing such goods into several categories.

The classical economist Bastiat argued, in his *Economic Harmonies*, that labor and service involve effort and provide satisfaction. They have to be transferable, because otherwise they cannot be provided. However, the proportionality between value and effort has never been evaluated (Bastiat 1996, pp. 76–160). Bastiat further held that capital and labor provide services for each other. To evaluate a service, he suggested two standards: the service provider's effort and level of stress suffered, and the recipient's relief from stress.

Marx leveled severe criticism at Bastiat's economics. In his work, "service" can be used in two ways. It can refer to a particular type of use value – the general usage of the term – or have the specific meaning of the multiplication of capital. The latter focuses on the following point: if labor exchanges with capital rather than income, then it provides services with the special role of creating surplus value (profit) for capital. Marx termed this the service provided by laborers employed by capital for capitalists, and distinguished it from service in a general sense:

> *Service is in general only an expression for the particular use value of labor, in so far as this is useful not as a material object but as an activity. There are all entirely indifferent forms of the same relation, whereas in capitalist production the do ut facias expresses a very specific relation between objective wealth and living labor. Hence because the specific relation of labor and capital is not contained at all in this buying of services, being either completely extinguished or not present at all, it is naturally the favorite way for Say, Bastiat and their associates to express the relation of capital and labor. (Marx and Engels 1972c, p. 435)*

Fuchs (1968) was the first to apply classical analysis to the service economy of post-Second-World-War America. He argued that a service is perishable at the time it is produced or created. A service is provided in the presence of a customer. It cannot be transported, stored, or accumulated, thus it lacks substantiality. Although this definition is characteristic-oriented, it fails to state which characteristics of a service are in fact essential.

The marketing guru Kotler (2007) defined a service in *Marketing Management* as follows: "A service is any act or performance that one party can offer to another that is essentially intangible and does not result in the ownership of anything. Its production may or may not be tied to a material product." This definition has limitations: intangibility being a necessary but not a sufficient condition for a service, it concerns only the form, not the content. The provider of service labor temporarily cedes the rights to that labor to the recipient of the service.

Although labor in this form does not result in a material object, the use value it provides does not differ essentially from that provided by a material object. It does not follow that transfer of ownership is only secured by the possession of material objects: consuming the use value provided by living labor also involves transfer of ownership.

The economist Hill (1997) defined service as a change in the condition of a person, or of a good belonging to some economic unit, brought about by the activity of some other economic unit. Defining a service in terms of its outcome, he does not break free from the shackles of commodity definition, but admits it to be the result of labor, distinguishing his definition from other vulgar economic concepts.

> *A service is an activity such that the activities of a producer may change the condition of some economic units. This change could be realized by the changes in the material condition of goods owned by a consumer unit. On the other hand, this change may affect a person or a group of persons' material or mental conditions. Whatever condition, the notable feature of service production was that producers did not add the value to the goods or himself, but added the value to the goods of an economic unit ....*

> *A service should be provided for an economic unit and this point was inherent in the concept of a service. Service production stood in sharp contrast to the production of material goods. In the production of material goods, a producer may not be fully aware of the end users. A peasant may grow crops in the complete absence of the landlord. But a teacher could not exercise teaching without the presence of pupils. As for a service, the actual production process must be in contact with an economic unity so as to make the service transacted. (Hill 1977, pp. 315–38)*

A common point in service production is that service must be delivered and consumed at the time it is created, sharply distinguishing it from other types of production. In the production of material goods, there is no such limitation. It suggests that a service cannot be added to the producer's stock of completed goods (Hill 1977, pp. 315–38).

The economist M. Sokolov (1985), of the former Soviet Union, defines service in his *Non-Productive Economics* such that labor and service have dual implications. "First, labor and service could be understood as a type of particular use value produced by the consumed labor; Second, if labor was to be exchanged with income, then labor and service could be understood as a form of non-productive labor"(Sokolov 1985, p. 221).

The New Palgrave Dictionary of Economics (NPDE 4, p. 314) states that:

> *In everyday language, we make a clear distinction between goods and services. When we refer to services, we tend to think of services rendered to people (classic examples are Fourastie's much cherished hairdresser, Baumol's singer and Pigou's valet. A more recent use of "services", namely, business services, refers to the process of externalizing parts of R&D, or management functions. Services are commonly seen as extending to activities like retailing, banking, insurance and non-market activities linked to public and private administration It is, moreover, current practice to include transport and telecommunications within this already vast set of activities …. what is striking is the contrast between the relative simplicity of current usage and the difficulties encountered in defining services within an economic analysis.*

Some further definitions in Western textbooks (e.g. Fitzsimmonds and Fitzsimmonds 2006, pp. 3–4) are that a service consists of action, procedure, and performance, or that it is an activity, or series of activities, of a more or less intangible nature that normally, but not necessarily, takes place in interactions between customer and service employees and/or material resources or goods and/or systems of the service provider, which are provided as solutions to customer problems.

Most authorities consider the service sector to include all economic activities whose output is not a material product or construction, which is generally consumed at the time it is created, and in which value is added. A service emphasizes the intangible interaction between a customer and its providers. It is also argued that a precise definition should distinguish goods from services on the basis of their attributes. A good is a tangible material object or product that can be created and transferred; it has an existence over time and thus can be created and used later. A service is intangible and perishable. It is an occurrence or process that is created and used almost at the same time. Service is also defined as an experience in which a customer acts as a co-producer, and which perishes with time.

There are thus countless definitions of service. However, a common thread is their emphasis on intangibility and synchronicity between production and consumption.

The concept of tertiary industry

In the absence of a consensus even on the definition of services, any study of theories about them is fraught with difficulties. But there is a practical question also: how does the system serve statistical purposes?

Most economic theory recognizes a basic classification of business establishments into three broad categories, expressing the idea that industries sharing similar characteristics should be grouped into broad "sectors": primary, secondary, and tertiary. There are three general approaches, described below. As we shall see, services are loosely identified with the tertiary sector, but the identification is not rigorous.

The idea of a three-sector classification first appeared in *The Clash of Progress and Security* by A. Fisher (1939), a British economist and professor at the University of Otago, New Zealand. Shortly after, the British economist Colin Clark (1940) further elaborated this idea in his *Conditions of Economic Progress*. This classification, and its use in analyzing the economic development of Western countries, found gradual acceptance in Western economic circles and statistical agencies. Nowadays the national economic statistics of the vast majority of countries around the world are based on this basic classification, notwithstanding variations in economic level and structure.

However, though it may serve to outline the developmental stages of different industries in the national economy, it is not a precise classification in the economic sense, and gives rise to many shortcomings in economic statistics. It also may not help precisely predict the economic level and structure of a country or, on a more general level, facilitate multi-country studies.

The second broad approach is found in the International Standard Industrial Classification of All Economic Activities (ISIC) developed by the United Nations and used all over the world, being subsumed under the system of national accounts (SNA). ISIC has gone through four editions, wielding enormous influence on the classification of business establishments of Western countries. Australia, New Zealand, the EU countries, and Japan developed classifications based on ISIC.

The third broad approach, known as the North American Industrial Classification System (NAICS), is based on ISIC. One of its unique points is its capacity to predict new trends of economic development in a timely manner, as it closely monitors the development of emerging industries. It has the potential to be a new standard.

However, economists still cannot agree on the classification of business establishments. Table 8.2 is a brief list of the classification of business establishments by some economists, taken from Huang (2000, p. 65).

Table 8.2 shows that the concept of tertiary industry is not conceptually the same as service industry. The two concepts are mutually related but different from each other. Clark stopped speaking of "tertiary industry" after 1941, and began to use "service industry" instead. His definition is quite close to Marx's concept of service.

Moreover, while the economists mainly subsume government agencies under tertiary industry or service industry, Kuznets (1999) subsumes transportation and telecommunications under the category of industry, which is consistent with the approach of the classical economists. Marx also took transportation as productive. In terms of the form of labor, however, transportation and telecommunication belong to the service industry.

Table 8.2 Different classifications of business establishments

Sector	Fisher (1939)	Clark (1941)	Clark (1954)	Fourastie (1959)	Kuznets (1957)	Kuznets (1957)
Manufacturing	Secondary Industry	Secondary Industry	Industry	Secondary Industry	Industry	Industry
Architecture	Secondary Industry	Secondary Industry	Service Industry	Secondary Industry	Industry	Industry
Public facilities	Secondary Industry	Secondary Industry	Service Industry	Secondary Industry	Industry	Industry
Transportation	Tertiary Industry	Tertiary Industry	Service Industry	Tertiary Industry	Service Industry	Industry
Telecommunications	Tertiary Industry	Tertiary Industry	Service Industry	Tertiary Industry	Service Industry	Industry
Trade	Tertiary Industry	Tertiary Industry	Service Industry	Tertiary Industry	Service Industry	Service Industry
Service sector	Tertiary Industry	Tertiary Industry	Service Industry	Tertiary Industry	Service Industry	Service Industry
Government Agencies	Tertiary Industry	Tertiary Industry	Service Industry	Tertiary Industry	Service Industry	Service Industry

What type of industry might the concept "tertiary" really refer to? Generally, it is held to include such industries as the following:

- architecture
- transportation
- urban public utilities
- consulting
- entertainment, for example drama and music
- education and public health
- repairing, washing and dyeing
- dining and hotel services
- hairdressing, bathing, photography, and tourism
- commerce, leasing, finance, and insurance
- governmental agencies including defense.

Thus, the concept is not really based on any underlying similarity between these industries. It is defined by elimination, creating a hodge-podge of all business establishments outside mining, agriculture, and manufacturing. In contrast, the concept of service industry is conceptually clear and scientific.

The two concepts are thus different. Tertiary industry is defined by elimination while service industries are normally defined by the form of the labor they employ. Being based on production, a characteristic of the activity of living labor, the second definition is less ambiguous. Tertiary industry is further based on the concept of a supply chain. It implies that economic development normally follows the path from low-level industries to high-level industries, the responsibility of low-level industries being to provide the raw materials for high-level industries. The words "primary" and "tertiary" themselves illustrate this point. The concept of service industry is however based on the characteristics of production and the needs of each business establishment. Finally, the economic implications of the tertiary concept are more related to the domestic economy of a particular country, while those of the service concept are more connected with internal and external markets.

We are now in a position further to subdivide the scope of service industry in social productive systems, as shown in Figure 8.2.

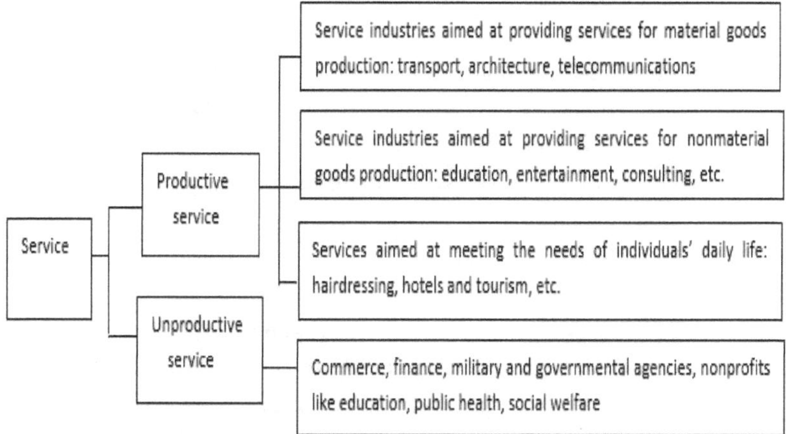

Figure 8.2 Classification of service labor

China's statistical system

We now turn to China's own system for reporting on the service industries. Does its classification system serve economic statistics efficiently?

China applied the Material Product System (MPS) from 1949 until April 1985, when the State Council agreed the wide distribution of its Report on Compiling Statistics on the Tertiary Industry, marking the beginning of the adoption of SNA. This report subdivided China's business establishments as follows:

- primary industries: agriculture (forestry, husbandry and fishing industry)
- secondary industries: industry (including mining, manufacturing, running water provision, power, gas, and architecture)
- tertiary industries: all other industries.

Tertiary industry was further divided into transport and services, covering four areas:

- logistics: this area includes transport, telecommunications, dining, supply and storage
- services to production and consumers, including finance, insurance, material goods census, real estate, public services, civilian services,

187

tourism, consulting and information services, as well as technological services of various kinds

- education and public welfare, including education, culture, broadcasting, scientific research, public health, sports, and social welfare
- services for social needs, including governmental agencies, the Communist Party of China (CPC) and various social organizations, military, and police.

The service industries in China contain hundreds of industries, a full list being beyond our scope. The following is an indicative summary:

- agriculture, forestry, husbandry, fishing, mining, hydraulic systems, transport, storage as well as telecommunications (including railroad, expressways, waterways and air transport, and support industries such as storage)
- wholesale, retail and catering (including food and beverages, wholesale household goods, power and materials, wholesale mechanical and electronic products, retailing, and agencies)
- finance, insurance and real estate (including development and management)
- social services (including public services, residential service, hotels, leasing, tourism, entertainment, information and consulting applied computer services)
- public health and social welfare, education, culture, arts and broadcasting (including colleges and universities, primary and high schools, broadcasting, film, and so on)
- scientific research and technological services (including natural science research, social science research, multidisciplinary research, meteorology, seismology, field surveys, quality control, oceanography, environmental protection, technology diffusion)
- government agencies, CPC, and social organizations.

Value creation by labor in service industries

Capitalist development has brought about a dramatic transformation of the economic structure of all major market economies, of which a notable feature is the dramatic increase in the share of the service industries in the economy, notably output and employment. This transformation began to attract economists' attention some time ago. Fisher (1939) was the first to attempt an in-depth analysis of the history of economic development of the major market economies, which gave rise to his well-known thesis of three stages in the evolution of economic structure.

Clark then conducted a longitudinal study on industrial outputs and labor inputs, advancing the thesis that the agricultural labor force was decreasing while that in manufacturing and services was increasing. Clark's theory was consistent with William Petty's central ideas, and became known as the Petty–Clark law, delineating the relationship between economic growth and the evolution of economic structure. The experience of several countries at different stages of economic development has validated the Petty–Clark law.

In the 21st century, service industries in the developed countries reached 70% of GDP, as the law suggests. China also conforms to the law. By 2001, its service industries accounted for 33.6% of GDP, becoming one of the key sectors and playing an extremely important role in Chinese development. This makes an in-depth study of economic theories related to service industry an imperative. Specifically, breakthroughs are needed on such important theoretical issues as the quality of service products, the nature of service production, value creation in services, and their relation to economic growth.

In the first chapter we developed the concept of service, and established the scientific character of Marx's definition. A service is a particular form of the use value of labor power. Service is in general only an expression for the particular use value of labour, in so far as this is useful not as a material object but as an activity (Marx and Engels 1994, p. 451).

Service *per se* does not produce a useful effect in the same way as a material product, but it does produce a useful effect as an immaterial product, namely living labor.

Based on this definition, we hold that service labor should include not only services provided for material production, such as telecommunications and sewing, and the services entering cultural production such as performance and painting, but also service labor that circulates commodities and currencies, and services offered by governmental agencies. However, it should not include materialized services functioning as inputs to material production, specifically cultural products in materialized form. Since service labor can be divided into absolute and non-absolute service labor, we also argue that not all service labor creates value. Military and government agencies do not create value. Only productive service labor consumed by individuals or serving as an input into material products (including cultural products) creates value. Our study is confined to productive service labor.

Similarities and dissimilarities between service production and material product production

In material production, with given resources and technologies, producers may turn the subject of labor into real material products with a definite quantity of use value. Therefore, the living labor of laborers is expressed in this use value. To a large extent, these material products and their use value are stripped of the characteristics of their producers and consumers. The former can sell them right away, or keep them for some time. The latter can, correspondingly, start consuming straight after purchase, or delay. They can resell their purchase at a higher or lower price, or send it to other people. Production, exchange, and consumption thus constitute the whole complex cycle. In this chapter, we take the production, exchange, and consumption of material products as points of reference for an in-depth study of the characteristics of the production, exchange, and consumption of services.

The synchronicity of service production and consumption

The production of material goods is normally undertaken in the absence of any potential consumer. In services, however, production and consumption are not so completely independent, and happen more or less simultaneously. Consumption normally terminates very shortly after production is over. This also makes service labor devoid of an independent exchange process. Under normal circumstances, exchange precedes production, the completely opposite of the exchange of material commodities.

190

The outcome of production

A pure, or absolute, service creates no material product. For example, going to a concert hall to enjoy a singer consumes a type of service. But if the labor activity is not an absolute service, as when a software engineer develops a package of management software, the outcome is an alienable product, in contrast with a pure service. However, if the software engineer is invited to provide a consulting service for a consumer, their labor is provided as a pure service. It can be concluded that a pure service[1] may not be used for exchange purposes, as may a service which results in an alienable product. Such a characteristic raises two important questions on how to measure service labor, and how to accumulate its effects.

The first question is very important. Most services cannot be further subdivided, so that there is no obvious unit that can be used for measurement. In some industries, the outcome of the labor provides a measure of the service it produces. For example, the amount of goods carried by the transport industry can be used to compute a rough measure of the output of transport labor. In most cases, this is uncontroversial.

A second characteristic of service labor is also very peculiar. Since its outcome is not material, for the most part it cannot be accumulated. Yet some forms, such as education, produce outcomes which can be accumulated as human capital (Hill 1997). It can thus have a lasting impact.

Individualization

Material production is an independent process undertaken in the absence of consumers. This is the reverse for pure services. Because production and consumption are synchronized, consumers exert an influence on

---

1   Translating editor's footnote: I have used the words "pure" and "impure" to distinguish what in the original are referred to as productive and unproductive service labor. This is not the same as the Marxist distinction, which the text deals with in earlier chapters, between labor that is productive of surplus value (exchanged against capital) and labor that is not productive of surplus value (exchanged against revenue). I have introduced the pure–impure distinction to avoid any confusion, to refer to whether the labor results in a separable, alienable product that can be stored and transferred in the manner of a material product, which is the clear intention of the writers.

the production of a pure service. The assessment of its quality depends on both subjective and objective factors of both the providers of the service and its consumers. But service quality is highly subjective, and varies from consumer to consumer. Factors include the quality of the environment when the service is provided, the conditions of the facilities, the appearance and well-rounded background of service providers, and their willingness to serve consumers.

As a result, the most important difference between pure labor and non-pure labor is that consumers have the opportunity to participate in the pure service process. A prime example is education. As a Chinese saying goes, "teaching students in accordance with their aptitude." In other words, there is no bad student, but there are bad teachers.

The use value and value of services

It is generally accepted that the value of a material product has a dual character. If it is a commodity, it has use value and value. The first refers to its usefulness, and determines what kind of object is functioning as a commodity. If it has no use, it ceases to be a commodity. This makes the commodity itself a use value. As Marx once argued, a commodity, in the first place, is an object independent of a subject, which is capable of meeting people's needs.

> *A commodity is, in the first place, an object outside us, a thing that by its properties satisfies human wants of some sort or another. The nature of such wants, whether, for instance, they spring from the stomach or from fancy, makes no difference ... . The utility of a thing makes it a use value. (Marx 1965, p. 27)*

Although Marx's comment concerns material production, it has important implications for our understanding of the nature of service labor. As we have noted, for Marx a service only expresses a peculiar use value of labor. Therefore, we argue, service also possesses the attribute of use value. However, a service is not useful as a material object but as living labor. Its nature lies in the process that supplies it, in contrast to the use value of an immaterial object.

192

A service must have some use value, just like a material product. This fact presents itself as follows:

It meets people's material and spiritual needs. Business establishments produce both material products like grain and autos, and immaterial products like transport and education. Both are indispensable for the normal running of a society, and both have use value. Under certain circumstances, they are mutually substitutable.

The use values of services are part of social wealth. In capitalist society, social wealth is exhibited as an accumulation of products. However, as it develops, the proportion of services in output rises steadily and becomes more diverse. New services become available and existing ones improve, significantly increasing the use values at society's disposal.

Under the socialist market economy, services are bearers of exchange value, just as material products are. A service *per se,* a process in which living labor is the input, is actually a kind of activity, notwithstanding it cannot be turned into a material object.

Services, if provided as commodities, also have value. This is because:

Under the socialist market economy, there are different productive entities which are independent producers within the social division of labor. To convert individual labor into a part of social labor, it has to go to the market to enter the exchange process.

When an individual manufacturer produces a service, it consumes human labor in a general sense, just as human labor is consumed when manufacturing a product. The two types of labor are both general human labor.

Each type of service has a different use value. Though they consume different concrete human labor, these different use values, by entering exchange, finally turn into social values. Therefore, the source of their value is none other than abstract human labor, which forms their value. Abstract human labor is thus the essential characteristic of their value.

So how can we determine the amount of the value of a service? For a material product this is measured by the amount of labor required to produce it. But as noted earlier, the synchronicity of the production and consumption of service labor suggests that to a large extent, consumers participate in service production. As a result, the quality of the service becomes important, distinguishing it from material product production. The creation of value in service depends on both the service provider and consumer.

Therefore, the socially necessary labor time of a productive service is the average level of labor time a service provider needs in order to produce it. This comprises the following:

Constant capital, being the value of materials consumed in service production. This creates no new value but is transferred to the service product by the living labor of the service producers.

Variable capital, being the value of labor the service laborer contributes. Laborers perform two functions: they compensate for the lost value of constant capital consumed in production, and create new value which exceeds the value they consume in reproducing their labor power.

Surplus value is created by this surplus labor and appropriated by the capitalist.

Three misunderstandings about value creation by service labor

Service is a type of immaterial product. It is widely believed that because a service is intangible, it cannot be presented to consumers in materialized form. It is therefore supposed that "being immaterial" is the defining characteristic of a service. But actually, this distinction is coterminous with Adam Smith's concept of productive labor. We argue instead that "being immaterial" is a necessary but not sufficient condition for being a service. What is essential about a service is that it should be useful only as living labor. This is the central premise of our own distinction between material products and services.

For example, if a software company posts a product on the internet for customers to download, is this a material product or a service? This question admits of different answers. If we hold fast to the notion of "immaterial product" then the software company sells a type of service, since its product is intangible. But if the usefulness of service labor is taken to be the defining characteristic of a service, then the downloadable product is a real product, not a service. But if the software company provides its customers with technical consulting, this is a service.

The second misconception concerns whether service labor creates value. In fact, not all service labor creates value. Two schools of thought are in play. The first argues that only those services that are aimed at producing material products create value. Pure services then do not create value, and merely realize or distribute value. The second school believes that all types of labor create value, not only in material goods production but in cultural production. From this standpoint even governmental agencies, the military, and the police system may create value. We consider both viewpoints to be one-sided. Not all service labor creates value; the services provided by the military and governmental agencies do not create value. But pure service that provides a use to private consumers or business creates value, whether or not it leads to a material product.

Services contradicting the law of a society or social morality do not create value. In any society, there are organizations whose services contradict law and social morality, on which the authorities should crack down hard. Since China practices a system of socialist market economy, it should outlaw any service contradicting its law and social morality. For example, theft does not create value (even when organized as a business with constant capital such as firearms.)

Studies of labor productivity in the service industries

In the early years of human society, human beings lacked means of production; all forms of labor were a test of material human strength. With the accumulation of productive experience and means of production, the efficiency of labor has risen, helping to liberate human beings from the shackles of manual labor. With the advent of capitalism, advances in S&T further upgraded the means of production, and released energy to expand production massively. The capitalist economies thus could create and accumulate more social wealth in less than 100 years than in any previous period in history.

Managing production on an appropriate scale, in the case of material products, involves subdividing them into basic units, with each basic unit homogeneous in terms of use value. Subdivision is the basis of statistical analysis and hence management. The value of each basic unit can however be aggregated with that of another, as in measuring the output of a broad sector.

Things are in general different in the service industries. Since a service is a process of living labor input, it is futile to try to subdivide living labor. Consequently, aggregation is impossible and as a result, a basic condition for management of service production on an appropriate scale is not satisfied.

Nevertheless, with the development of S&T some service industries, characterized by a low level of individuality, do use modern technology to provide subdivided packages of service whose values can be aggregated. Thus, the transport and telecommunication industries can be managed on an appropriate scale.

The mode of production of each of the many service industries varies, so that some provide standardized services while others do not. In consequence, the composition of their capital structure also varies. Standardized services make it easier to replace manual labor with advanced means of production (for example, machines), making it more likely that their industries will become capital-intensive service industries in which labor productivity is rising.

However, in less standardized service industries, because of their high level of individualization, production by its nature is not possible in the absence of consumers, making it more difficult to replace manual labor with machines. In consequence, it may be harder to raise labor productivity. A prime example is the medical profession. Although modern medical technologies help with diagnosis, the diagnostic process itself cannot continue in the absence of patients.

These differences between service and material production create theoretical obstacles to measuring the output of the service industries, and consequently, increases in labor productivity. We now turn to this issue.

Western studies

One of the findings of Western economic and statistical studies is that the rate of productivity increase in services has been lower than in manufacturing. Yet the percentage of services in output has been increasing steadily. The end result is a tendency for the overall growth rate of productivity in the Western economies to slow down.

Fuchs (1968, 1987) was the earliest economist to raise the issue of service productivity, arguing that it was one of the main reasons for rising employment in the service industries. He made three points. First, since the income elasticity of service demand is greater than 1, the share of services in output will grow with income. Second, the externalization of services is developing. Improved technology and rising incomes lead households and businesses to seek services from the market instead of providing them. Last but not least, the relatively low productivity of services makes their average cost higher than elsewhere.

196

Research on labor productivity in the service industries helps explain a puzzle. In theory, we have shown it is hard to raise labor productivity in industries providing non-standardized services. But empirically, there is strong evidence that such a phenomenon exists. So we introduced the human capital variable, and found that the growth of labor productivity is positively related to its growth rate and output elasticity.

We cannot however rule out of court the idea that labor productivity grows rather slowly in the service industries, because the sector as a whole is a mix of labor and capital-intensive industries, and includes many knowledge-based service industries. Policy makers need a more precise understanding of how the service industries are developing, fostering the education and training sectors to increase the human capital of laborers and promote the development of knowledge-based service industries. This would improve the labor productivity of the service industries and allow the service industries to create more social wealth.

Empirical studies on how value is created in service industries

The path of economic development of every country suggests that service industries are assuming a more and more important role in its economic landscape, especially in the 21st century. Generally speaking, they employ the largest number of laborers and their output takes up the largest percentage of a country's GDP. It is not surprising that they are increasingly believed to be the mainstay of a modern national economy.

Taking the USA as an example, we found that 75% of its GNP was produced by the service sector, and 76% of US laborers were employed in service industries. Considering this prominent position, this is clearly an area of scholarship that deserves in-depth study. As the importance of the service industries rises, it is imperative to clarify the issues concerning value creation by labor in these industries, and we therefore undertook empirical studies to shed light on this.

The service sector is composed of a large number of organizations, and contains both capital and labor-intensive industries. In the initial stage of industrialization of a country, most service industries are labor intensive, and capital-intensive industries are few and far between.

The authors attempted to illustrate this point by citing the structure of British labor power. Based on Table 8.3, we found that the service sector for persons took up a greater percentage of the entire sector over time. This suggests that the British service sector was basically labor-intensity-oriented in its early years.

Table 8.3 Labor structure in the UK service industries
(% of costs attributable to labor)

Year	Production sector		Service sector			
	Agriculture	Industry	Transport	Services for persons	Public services	Total
1801	35.9	29.7	11.2	11.5	11.8	34.5
1831	24.6	40.8	12.4	12.6	9.5	34.5
1861	18.7	43.6	16.6	14.3	6.9	37.5
1891	10.5	43.9	22.6	15.8	7.1	45.5

Source: Table 75 of Huang (2000, p. 262).

The preceding arguments underline how important it is to study both the theoretical analysis of service industries and their empirical development. In the early stages of industrialization, most service industries are labor-intensive, a point illustrated by a glance at the British labor force statistics, shown in Table 8.3. Services to persons took up a greater percentage of the labor force in the 19th century, and it was only in the post-industrial age that the capital-intensive service industries started to blossom. Even so, some labor-intensive service industries remain.

We chose labor costs in the service industries as an indicator instead of labor time input, because data on the latter are hard to obtain.[2]

We now present a detailed contemporary empirical study, composed of two parts. The first is a comparative study of value creation by labor in the US and Chinese service industries. Since the USA is a well-developed market economy, human capital is more concentrated in its service industries than in China. If human capital increases earnings, we should expect the value added per worker in US service industries to be higher than in China.

---

2   When the sector is labor-intensity oriented, we can deduce the input of labor time by multiplying the number of employees by the legally prescribed working hours. To avoid more conversions, it is possible to replace labor time input by the number of jobs.

The second part is a comparative study of the structure of US and Chinese service industries. Its purpose is how labor inputs affect value creation in each industry, and bring to light the law of the development of developed-country services, hopefully providing meaningful information for China's policy makers.

Table 8.4 Employment and total output of service industries in the USA and China

Country / Index / Year	China			US		
	Number of employees by service industry x 10,000	Growth rate of employment in service industry (%)	Total output of service industry (Unit: ¥100 million)[a]	Number of employees by service industry x 10,000	Growth rate of employment in service industry (%)	Total output of service industry x $100 million[b]
1985	8,359	——	2,556.20	7,500.70	——	22,395
1986	8,811	5.41	2,945.60	7,711.80	2.81	24,803
1987	8,850	9.48	3,505.60	7,983.20	3.52	25,816
1988	9,949	19.15	4,510.10	8,196.60	2.67	27,896
1989	10,147	1.99	5,403.20	8,391.30	2.38	30,325
1990	10,533	3.8	5,813.50	8,504.90	1.35	32,940
1991	11,015	4.58	7,227.00	8,523.20	0.22	33,961
1992	11,742	6.6	9,138.60	8,818.70	3.47	36,132
1993	12,737	8.47	11,323.80	8,860.20	0.47	38,745
1994	14,123	10.88	14,930.30	8,961	1.13	41,190
1995	15,055	6.6	17,947.20	9,100.90	1.56	43,712
1996	17,927	19.07	20,427.50	9,261.90	1.76	46,383
1997	18,432	2.82	23,028.70	9,475.50	2.3	49,278
1998	18,860	2.32	26,104.30	9,658.70	1.93	59,470
1999	19,205	1.83	27,037.70	9,898.30	2.48	56,446
2000	19,823	3.22	29,978.70	10,041.10	1.44	58,928
2001	20228	2.04	32254.3	10187.3	1.46	63038

Notes: We did not convert Chinese output to US$ because of the dramatic fluctuations in the exchange rate between 1985 and 2001, shown in Table 8.5. US statistical indicators do not include government services. The figures were based on the indices of the same year. As the data for the USA were not complete, some figures were deduced by employing the percentage of the service industry in GDP and the percentage of service industry in the tertiary sector.

Source: China Statistics Yearbook and World Statistics Yearbook, issues for 1996–2001.

Table 8.5 Exchange rates for selected years

Year	1985	1988	1990	1991	1994	2001
US$ and RMB exchange rate	2.93	3.72	4.78	5.32	8.62	8.28

Source of data: China Foreign Economic Statistical Yearbook (2002), China Statistical Press.

The regression model

Certain factors dominate the path of economic development even though each factor plays a different role. We focus on the relationship over time between the output of the service, industries, which we shall call Y, and the number of laborers employed there, which we shall call X. This can be represented as a linear function, for simplicity. If more factors are taken into consideration, the analysis gets more difficult. Our simple model singles out the main factors that impact the development of service industries, using a one-dimensional linear regression equation to test our hypotheses. The sampling frame for China and the USA was between 1985 and 2001.

We represent the relation by the equation

$$Y = a + bX. \qquad\qquad 8.1$$

China

For China's service industry, equation 8.1 can be estimated as:

$$Y = -17,904.36 + 2.331X \qquad\qquad 8.2$$
$$(-14.138) \quad (6.658)$$

$R^2 = 0.989$;

$R = 0.990$;

$F = 710.634$

Table 8.6 shows the residuals of this regression.

200

Table 8.6: Predicted and actual value of China's service industry output

Year	Actual value Y_i	Estimated value Y_i^*	Residual e_i	Degree of dispersion d $(d=e_i/Y_i^*)$
1985	2,556.20	1,580.50	-975.7	-0.62
1986	2,945.60	2,630.10	-315.5	-0.12
1987	3,505.60	2,725.00	-780.6	-0.27
1988	4,510.10	5,286.70	776.6	0.15
1989	5,403.20	5,748.30	345.1	0.06
1990	5,813.50	6,648.10	834.6	0.13
1991	7,227.00	7,771.60	544.6	0.07
1992	9,138.60	9,466.20	327.6	0.03
1993	11,323.80	11,785.60	461.2	0.04
1994	14,930.00	15,016.40	86.4	0.05
1995	17,947.20	17,188.80	-758.4	-0.04
1996	20,427.50	23,864.80	3,437.30	0.14
1997	23,028.70	25,060.60	2,031.90	0.08
1998	26,104.30	26,058.30	-46	-0.001
1999	27,037.70	26,862.50	-175.2	-0.006
2000	29,978.70	28,303.10	-1,675.60	-0.06
2001	32,254.30	29,747.10	-3,007.20	-0.1

The equation thus explains 98.9% of the total variance of the sample. The t-test value ta0 is -14.138 and ta1 is 26.658. showing the results to be statistically significant with a p-value below .05. The degrees of freedom are 1 and 15, respectively. The F-distribution is F0.05 (1,15)=4.54, and is also valid. The results thus suggest that the number of people employed by China's service industry explains most of the variation in its total output. The relation is positive.

USA

$$Y= -98516.57 +15.623X$$
$$(-19.22) \quad (27.19)$$

$R^2 = 0.98;$

$R = 0.99;$

$F = 739.28$

The residuals are presented in Table 8.7.

Table 8.7: Predicted and actual values of the output of the USA's service industries

Year	Actual value Y_i	Estimated value Y_i^*	Residual e_i	Degree of dispersion d $(d=e_i/Y_i^*)$
1985	22,395	18,667	-3,728	-0.2
1986	24,803	21,965	-2,838	-0.13
1987	25,816	26,205	389	0.01
1988	27,896	29,538	1,642	0.05
1989	30,325	32,580	2,255	0.07
1990	32,940	34,355	1,415	0.04
1991	33,961	34,641	680	0.02
1992	36,132	39,258	3,126	0.08
1993	38,745	39,906	1,161	0.03
1994	41,190	41,481	291	0.01
1995	43,712	43,667	-45	-0.001
1996	46,383	46,182	-201	-0.004
1997	49,278	49,519	241	0.005
1998	53,470	52,381	-1,008	-0.02
1999	56,446	56,125	-321	-0.006
2000	58,928	58,355	-573	-0.01
2001	63,038	60,639	-2,398	-0.04

This result is equally significant. Employment explains 98% of total variance, with a correlation coefficient of 0.99. t_{a0} is -19.22 and t_{a1} is 27.19, yielding a p-value also below 0.05. The degrees of freedom are 1 and 15, respectively.

Comments

The independent variable in the Chinese regression has greater explanatory power than in the US regression, reflected in the variance explained by the independent variables of each regression model. This might suggest that the proportion of the increase in China's output of service industries owes more to the increase in the number of people employed by this particular industry than in the USA: that is, labor intensity plays a greater role in the development of China's service industry than the human capital factor.

However, the dispersion in the Chinese regression is greater than in the American regression, which suggests the number of laborers may have less impact on output in the USA. As previous chapters have shown, for example the export rankings of specialized services such as accounting and technology, and also audiovisual products, suggest that US service industries are generally human capital-intensive.

Employment in China's service industries has grown continuously since 1985 at an average rate of 5.7% annually, absorbing an increasing number of laborers. The sector has become an important component of China's economy, creating large amounts of value. In contrast, the US service industries are well developed. Although output is increasing, employment is growing more slowly, at an average annual rate of 2%. This suggests that most US service organizations have transformed into knowledge-based service organizations; their value-creating capacity depends on the human capital factor rather than the sheer number of laborers. This confirms Marx's argument that complex labor is an aggregate of simple labor.

We now move on to explore these issues from the standpoint of the service industries' internal structure. Tables 8.8 and 8.9 present data on the structural evolution of the US and Chinese service industries respectively. In these tables, each figure is a percentage of the total in the relevant major category. Thus, the figure for telecommunications in China in 1993 tells us it accounted for 44.9% of its general type of service industry, which was transport, telecommunications and storage systems, etc.

Table 8.8 Structural change in the US service industries between 1970 and 1993

	Value added (current $)						Employment					
	1970	1975	1980	1985	1990	1993	1970	1975	1980	1985	1990	1993
Telecommunications	37.3	40.3	40	45.3	45.9	44.9	29	30.1	30.3	29.5	26.5	25.3
Finance	13.2	12.2	14.2	17.2	16.6	18.8	27.7	27.2	25.4	24	21.4	20.2
Insurance	9	8	9	6	7	8	21.6	19.9	17.9	15.3	14.4	13.7
Real estate	58.1	57	52.4	49.2	45.7	42.8	10.8	11	10.4	9.5	8.8	8.3
Service management	19.6	21.8	23.9	26.9	29.9	29.6	39.8	41.7	46.1	51.1	55.2	57.6
Social and community services	61.8	66.8	68.2	68.8	70.6	71.8	62.7	70.7	71.8	72.2	73.1	74.2
Individual and household services	29	24.9	22.8	22.2	19.1	17.3	31	22.8	21.2	21.2	19.3	18.1

Source: Huang (2000, p. 287).

Table 8.9 Structural change in China's service industries

Unit: percentage

	Percent of total value added (based on current price)						Percentage of employment					
	1995	1996	1997	1998	1999	2000	1995	1996	1997	1998	1999	2000
Telecommunications	17	17.1	16.5	16.4	16.5	18.1	11.5	11.2	11.1	10.6	10.5	10.2
Finance	19.4	19.7	19.7	18.6	17.9	17.5	1.61	1.63	1.68	1.66	1.7	1.65
Education, culture and broadcasting	6.3	6.6	6.8	7.2	7.8	8	8.74	8.43	8.44	8.34	8.16	7.89
S & T research and technological support	1.5	1.6	1.9	1.9	2.1	2.1	1.07	1.02	1.01	1	0.9	0.87
Social and community services	8.6	8.4	9.5	10.5	10.7	10.9	4.16	4.17	4.39	4.6	4.8	4.65

Source: China Statistics Yearbook, issue 1996–2001.

Table 8.8 shows that the internal structure of the US service sector changed significantly in the two decades to 1993. Telecommunications grew from 37.3% of the secondary service sector in 1970 to 44.9% in 1993, an annual change of nearly 8%. However, growth reached a plateau in the 1990s, and the number of people employed by this industry then started to decline. This trend supports the hypothesis that telecommunication and transport share similar economic characteristics, having a greater potential to improve labor productivity through technological progress. It further supports the argument that although the human capital factor is in the ascendant, it may still create greater value than before with fewer laborers.

The second important change is that the total output of management and social services such as educational and medical services has risen continuously, at annual rates as high as 10%. The number of people employed by these industries is also increasing. This suggests that those service industries that provide individualized services for the public will inevitably suffer a slower rate of growth in labor productivity. Most of the increments in value added come from the increasing number of people employed in these service industries.

The third important change is that the output and the number of people employed by the insurance industry and real estate was declining. This suggests that the decreasing transaction costs of these industries may benefit the overall economy.

Finally, the percentage of value added compared with output in personal and household services, as well as the number of people employed by these industries, saw a significant decline. This suggests that these services are increasingly being replaced by other commodities, and run the risk of being eliminated eventually.

Table 8.9 illustrates the equally important changes under way in China's service industries. As China's economy grew, its most important basic industry – telecommunications – was developing more rapidly. By 2000, its value added accounted for 18.1% of the corresponding service sector, an annual growth of 1.3% since 1995. More importantly, these industries create large amounts of value for the whole society, while the number of people they employed gradually declined. This trend is consistent with that of the USA, and suggests that under the influence of modern technologies, the transport and telecommunications industries are very likely to increase their use of human capital, and consequently create more value with less labor input.

Employment in the finance and social service industries was steady, while the number of service industries providing miscellaneous services was rising. This suggests that as society develops, the service industries are becoming more externalized.

Employment in education, culture, and broadcasting, as well in S&T industries, continued to decline while their value added grew, suggesting they were making more intensive use of human capital.

The similarities between the structure of Chinese and US service industries are thus that the transport industry is developing rapidly while employment declines relatively, while transaction-based service industries like finance are declining. The difference is that the value added by China's service sector is growing much more rapidly. The service demands of business establishments have been rising rapidly while the number of laborers employed by China's education and S&T industries is declining. This suggests the decline of laborers in human capital intensive industries makes value creation more difficult.

9
Value creation by labor, science and technology, and management

This chapter deals with intensity of labor, and specifically the theory and practice of value creation by labor in science and technology (S&T) and management. This is not in general an independent form of labor, functioning in parallel with labor of material production, but is a form taken by labor inside the fields of material or service production. This chapter separates out this form of labor for independent study, to deepen the recognition of this topic.

Deng Xiaoping's well-known argument that S&T are primary productive forces has been repeatedly tested and has proven an indisputable truth. Indeed, it is universally acknowledged that S&T is the foremost factor in promoting socioeconomic development. Advances due to S&T are also transforming traditional beliefs and values, culture and moral standards. In short, its development is the engine of economic growth throughout the world.

Consider the following examples. At the turn of the 20th century, advances in S&T contributed about 10–15% of economic growth to some developed countries; this rose to 40% in the mid-20th century and by the 1970s, to 60–70%. Nobel Prize winner Robert Solow (1991) has suggested that the long-run engine of economic growth is not capital and labor, but S&T. In some OECD countries, the total output of the information industry, telecommunications, PC and software industry amounts to a large proportion of GDP, suggesting that these industries are the major driving force of their growth.

For these reasons, many countries believe that a public understanding of the role of science is the linchpin of success in future economic competition. If China feels obliged to take a place in the world's economic landscape and maintain its economic growth, or even to reduce the gap in between it and the West, it will need S&T to promote development. For this reason, we now study its role in value creation.

Classifications and characteristics of S&T labor

DEFINITIONS

What is science? According to the Sea of Words (Cihai 1980, p. 1746), science is the system of knowledge dealing with nature, society, and thought. Darwin, possibly the first scientist to define the concept of science, argued it was an activity "grouping facts so that general laws or conclusions may be drawn from them" (quoted in Franz 1957, p. 157). There are many other definitions. We shall define science as a dynamic system comprised of knowledge, the activities that generate it, scientific methodology, and the social organisms and culture that organize it.

This concept of science leads to two conclusions. First, science is a set of knowledge systems that people can use to understand and transform the objective world. At this level, a knowledge system is generally referred to as science, scientific knowledge, or scientific findings. But science is also a type of labor whose purpose is to know and transform the world. The knowledge system can in this sense be described as a kind of R&D activity.

If that is science, what is technology? Cihai offers two interpretations, strict and broad. The first refers to craftsmanship derived from production that applies theories of natural science. The latter extends to the means of production and machinery.

Diderot, the first scholar to offer a definition of technology, proposed it was a system in which productive tools were jointly made for a specific purpose. We shall treat it as the aggregate of many different means and methods for producing material goods in accordance with practical experience or scientific theories.

This definition has two consequences. Technology is a set of rules and methods used to devise and produce material goods. Its development is based upon practical experience or scientific theories. This includes productive technology, management technology, and technological achievement. But it is also a type of social activity: specifically, R&D.

These are two different ideas whose evolution arises from the relation between social practice and understanding, which is an economic relation. Science deals with understanding: it concerns an objective world, independent of human beings, how this evolves and why. Technology is practice-oriented, dealing with what people may do to provide what they need. But these ideas are related. In social practice, the desire to increase labor productivity creates a demand for new technologies.

In the early stages of the industrial revolution, productive practice dominated over scientific concepts or principles. James Watt's steam engine was not based on any specific scientific theory, but improved on earlier inventions based on practical experience. Theories arose later. By 1879, Diesel invented a petrol engine based on both theory and practical experience. Such processes exhibit the interaction between science and technology. Historically, technology drove advances more than science. Beginning early in the 20th century, the converse has figured ever more prominently.

Classifications of S&T labor

Standards for classifying S&T labor vary. We apply two standards. The first set of characteristics are those used by the practitioners themselves:

Research and Development (R&D) refers to systematic innovative work aimed at increasing human and social knowledge and applying it to real-life situations.

Science and Technology Education and Training (STET) refers to work that provides higher education and life-long training for scientists and engineers, either to qualify for degrees and diplomas, or in graduate education, or in other areas of higher education.

Science and Technology Services (STS) refers to work aimed at promoting scientific research and experimentation, and spreading and applying scientific knowledge (Sun et al. 1995, p. 6).

A second classification corresponds to the result of the activities undertaken:

Basic research explores the laws of development of nature, human society and the human mind; it spawns new inventions and makes new discoveries, accumulates scientific knowledge, and develops new theories to understand and transform the world. It is arduous and characterized by low success rates: 5–10% with final commercialization at 2–3%.

Applied research devises new methods, technologies, and materials using the relevant findings of basic research and general scientific knowledge. It is a bridge between basic research and R&D, whose characteristic is its purposefulness. Its success rate is 50–60%, and the odds of commercialization are greater than for basic research.

Developmental research applies the findings of applied research to new products, or improves old products and craftsmanship, relying on design and technical work. More often than not, it has a clear purpose and its success rate is well above 90%, with the highest likelihood of its being commercialized.

Labor in S&T is not limited to business establishments. It also includes those working in other research institutions, education and training institutions, and all labor aimed at spreading scientific knowledge and providing technological services.

Characteristics of S&T labor

There are both similarities and dissimilarities between S&T labor and productive labor in general. Its general characteristics relate to those of social production, which always takes place under definite relations of production. In a commodity-based economy, the means of production belong to individual owners, each producing use value. Private and social labor are both integrative and diametrically opposed. Their outcome is the product; since the commodity is a unity of use value and value, labor is dual, being abstract and concrete.

The study of these two aspects of S&T labor requires a variety of theories. As a type of concrete labor, S&T labor develops or upgrades technologies and research facilities. But if its particular characteristics are not considered, it is no different from general abstract productive labor, being merely the undifferentiated labor, inherent in the product, that forms its value. S&T labor is a unity of these two aspects. Its individualized characteristics are:

Creativity: Its goals and its nature dictate that creativity is a primary characteristic of scientific labor. It is consequently largely the result of mental power. Its primary goal is to probe the unknown universe, or create new systems of knowledge, or devise new types of craft or new inventions. The creativity of scientific labor rules out being replicated. Replication is diametrically opposed to creativity and inventiveness, being absolutely and in no sense the same. Creativity runs through the whole process of any scientific exploration. It is no exaggeration to say that creativity is the primary characteristic of scientific labor.

Exploratory character: While creativity is the basic characteristic of scientific labor, the desire to create motivates humans to explore the unknown world. Its complexity makes this an arduous and long-term process fraught with uncertainty. Scientific exploration requires the enterprising mind of the scientist, constant adaptation of research strategies, a readiness to find and use new trends in science, and a mindset that can accept failure. These comprise a coherent whole.

Inheritance: Humans constantly accumulate experience about how to know and transform their world. This great wealth is part of the development of human civilization. Neither scientific knowledge nor invention are plucked out of thin air, they build on previous research findings. As Newton once suggested, we all stand on the shoulders of giants.

Uncertainty: General labor engages in production with a defined time span by following rigid rules and standard procedures. Exceptions are rare. But the inherently complex nature of S&T labor means it is fraught with uncertainties. First, the amount of time it requires is uncertain. The normal time span for R&D projects lies between a couple of years and several decades. In basic research, several generations may be needed, and sometimes nothing is achieved even after several generations' effort. Second, the outcome is uncertain. Being creative and exploratory, this type of labor is fraught with complexities. The outcome may be inconsistent with expectations, falling short of them or indeed producing nothing. But new opportunities may also occur leading to an unexpected but spectacular success. Not surprisingly, scholars have found it difficult to measure the outcome of S&T labor in terms of scientific achievement. We argue for a complete and complex evaluative system to measure such contributions precisely.

Scientific labor has additional characteristics such as continuity, changing locations, long duration, and the unitary nature of modern S&T. These however may not be essential to the definition of scientific labor.

Value creation by S&T labor: a theoretical framework

We now turn to theoretical analysis, looking at the following questions. Why do we say S&T labor creates value, and does it create more than general labor? How can we estimate how much value it creates, and how does this differ from other forms of labor? How is this value realized?

The nature of the value created by S&T labor

Mental labor is one of the bases of commodity value

People cannot engage in politics, art and so on, unless they their material needs for eating, drinking, clothing, and accommodation are met, making material production the most important requirement of human development. Low productivity, and the underdevelopment of S&T, meant that for much of history social labor could only meet people's basic needs. Production was mainly physical well into the industrial age, when machinery was in widespread use.

In this phase, the human is subordinated to the machine. Because of the high organic composition of capital, workers had no choice but to adapt to the technological structure of machinery. In capitalist societies, as the market extended, the social division of labor became increasingly specialized, and concrete labors differed increasingly from each other.

> *Productive activity, if we leave out of sight its special form, viz., the useful character of the labour, is nothing but the expenditure of human labour power. Tailoring and weaving, though qualitatively different productive activities, are each a productive expenditure of human brains, nerves, and muscles, and in this sense are human labour. (Marx 1965, pp. 31–2)*

214

Marx put the brain first in the list of labor power's organs, because all other productive activities are under its guidance. in contrasting an architect with bees, he argues, "No matter how inferior the architect, he builds a future house in his brain before it is actually built; bees however build their nests out of instinct" (Marx 1965, p. 111).

As modern S&T developed, the organic composition of capital rose; great changes took place in the mode of production, and the amount of physical labor power directly serving the machines decreased, so that the subordination of human to machinery was replaced more and more by personal initiative, and mental labor gradually acquired the dominant role in production.

The main feature of S&T labor is that it is mainly mental. It takes a relatively long time to train and educate S&T workers. They cannot take on sophisticated S&T work without definite theoretical knowledge as well as practical ability. Moreover, though some means of production are materialized, like instruments or books, others are spiritual, such as the knowledge and experience of previous generations. In both cases only workers with a certain intellectual level of formation can use them. Finally, the object of S&T labor is the exploratory study of nature, society, and thought. Unlike digging coal in open air, this cannot be done with purely physical labor, but requires abstract logical thought. Thus, S&T labor is the sum of physical force and intelligence, and overall is mainly intellectual.

Value always arises from a combination of physical with mental labor. In the era of knowledge-based economy, mental labor is the main form, and so the value of the product will be measured by the cost of mental labor, over a definite period of time. In the primary stage of socialism, since productivity remains underdeveloped, some physical labor will persist. However, as technology progresses, the proportion of mental labor will rise, and it will become the main form of labor in value creation.

Complex S&T labor can create greater value

In Marx's theory, the magnitude of value is given by the time worked by average simple labor owned by the organism of every ordinary person without no special characteristics. However, with the progress of S&T, the form of labor has developed, and mental labor has become more significant. If we do not take into account complexity, and treat all labor power as simple labor power, we will be unable to recognize the contribution of mental labor to value in the socialist market economy. It is thus insufficient to show that mental labor creates value; we must also elaborate theoretically that complex mental labor creates greater value than simple labor.

Marx fully recognized the relationship between complex and simple labor. He held that simple labor was a historical category; moreover, complex labor should be regarded as a labor promising greater value. "Skilled labour counts only as simple labour intensified, or rather, as multiplied simple labour, a given quantity of skilled being considered equal to a greater quantity of simple labour" (Marx 1965, p. 32).

Simple labor power is that common to the organism of every ordinary person, and complex labor surpasses average simple labor power. It is molded mainly by education, training, and the accumulation of experience, and contains only a small amount of talent. Talent is a kind of accidental phenomenon, which cannot be controlled by human beings and is not the subject of economic study. There are different degrees of complexity of labor, and the criterion that distinguishes them is their knowledge content. The greater the knowledge content, the more complex the labor. Since S&T labor requires a lot of knowledge, it is complex. S&T labor is also highly innovative; creativity is its essence. Since such ability is not within the common thinking ability of average people, this creative labor is rare and precious. Creative labor is not the same as repetitive complex labor. It requires S&T laborers to grasp deeper and more extensive knowledge and to understand its structure, depending on unique thinking processes. It is thus a more sophisticated complex labor. It cannot simply be equated to a multiple of simple labor, and can create much greater value than simple labor could in the same time.

It also takes time and expense to acquire the ability needed to undertake complex labor, so the value of the labor itself will be larger. "This power being higher value, its consumption is labour of a higher class, labour that creates in equal times proportionally higher values than unskilled labour does" (Marx 1965, p. 138). According to statistical data from the US Department of Commerce, manufacturing employment in 1992 was lower than in 1970, but the value of output nearly doubled. This arose from the application of

S&T and improvement in the quality of the work force as a result of the mental labor of R&D. This success is due to complex labor. Since the Second World War especially, countries have trained teams of specialized talents to produce a high-quality workforce engaged in high-level work because they did not begrudge the money spent on education. Thus, though living labor decreases relatively or even absolutely, it can create greater value.

Abstract labor creates the value of the commodity

There are various concrete forms of S&T labor whose products appear as the result of all manner of mental work. From the perspective of the product there are both tangible and intangible S&T achievements. The former include new materials and instruments, while the latter include recipes, patents, and technical know-how. Setting aside all these concrete features, only one thing remains, which is the productive consumption of brains, muscles, nerves, hands, and so on, that is a mere coagulation of indistinguishable labor. These products only show that their production costs human labor power and accumulates human labor. As abstract human labor, it forms the value of a commodity.

The use value and exchange value created by S&T labor

From the perspective of social use value, there is no difference between a material product and the results of S&T labor. They both meet a definite need and are products of concrete labor, constituting the content of social wealth. But there are also differences. First, they meet different needs. Material products meet main material or natural, physical needs, while technological products satisfy the demands of cognition and production. Technological products, for the most part, can only create actual social wealth with the help of a productive process, although this resembles those objects of labor that require reworking. As concrete labor, S&T labor produces and reproduces various use values, and in this sense is a special kind human labor for a special purpose; as such, it creates use value.

Second, the forms of existence of the two types of product differ. Material products are external objects independent of producers and customers. They are endowed with certain physical features and their use value is tangible and non-ideal; however, except for a small portion that are tangible, technological products do not present themselves in the form of a special use value materialized in an object. They are characteristically non-material and ideal, such as scientific theories, design proposals, and so on. Though they may depend on some physical medium, the use value is not the medium, but the concept or knowledge attached to it.

In the modern market economy, there is still a contradiction between private and social labor. Private labor can only externalize itself in social products through market exchange. S&T labor is no exception, especially in developed capitalist countries where it constitutes a large part of social labor as a whole. In the market, what people exchange is their labor, which manifests itself in value; in a monetary economy, value is embodied in a certain amount of money, as price, its monetary form. Since S&T labor realizes its value in a modern market economy, its products have exchange value and a market price.

Duality of the value of labor in S&T: self-value and transformation value

We know that many products of scientific labor are non- material and ideal. The core of its outcome is the system of knowledge to which it gives rise. However, this is only potential productivity which cannot yield benefits unless it is transformed into direct productivity by being applied in a productive process. This gives rise to two forms of the value produced by S&T labor: self-value and transformation value.

The self-value of the products of S&T labor is their internal scientific value, namely logic, truth, creativity, and availability. The degree of this self-value is determined by its scientific validity. The transformation value of S&T products consists of demonstrations of their self-value in actual applications, and is embodied in its economic effect on productivity and social function. If an S&T product cannot be transformed in this way, the labor cannot be recognized by the society, and should be considered as invalid labor. The transformation process transfers S&T products to machinery, productive approaches, chemical processes, and so on.

Self-value and transformation value are a unity of opposites: self-value is the basis of transformation value; transformation value is the embodiment of self-value. Since the realization of value is complex, we discuss it in the third part of this section. At this point we note that self-value and

218

transformation value are not necessarily proportional to each other because the value of S&T labor is realized in a different way from that embodied in material products.

S&T itself does not create value

Earlier, we explained that the concept of S&T has two connotations. Science is not only a system of knowledge, but also a human activity; technology is both the sum of a series of principles and approaches, and an R&D activity. For this reason, we must distinguish between the concepts of S&T themselves, and S&T labor as such. The former exists as a system of knowledge: the latter refers to the living labor of S&T workers.

Marx articulated two layers of the role that S&T plays in productivity. First, its products constitute a common social productivity in the shape of knowledge formation; second, in the form of fixed capital, S&T products are applied to specific productive processes where they directly raise productivity. The accumulation of knowledge and skills, and the general productivity of social wisdom, are opposite to labor and absorbed into capital. Hence, they present as an attribute of capital, or more accurately speaking, of fixed capital, provided that fixed capital takes part in the productive process as a real means of production. S&T has undergone a certain level of development, and its function in industrial production has become increasingly apparent. But why did Marx not say that S&T itself could create value? Because the factors determining labor productivity and value are different, we must make a strict distinction. Multiple factors determine labor productivity, including the laborers' average skill level, the development of science and its application in techniques, the ways productive process are combined socially, the scale and efficiency of the means of production, and natural conditions; but only one factor determines value: abstract labor. S&T are primary productive forces in modern productive activities, and their status and function are increasingly significant, but they still cannot create new value without living labor.

The application of S&T raises human labor to a higher power. The reason it creates more use value and more value is that it raises the productivity of laborers, increasing the complexity of living labor. This relationship is the key to understanding all other issues. It is human living labor that creates value, not S&T itself. From a broad cultural perspective, only laborers can be the subjects that create use value and value. There is not an atom of use value in commodity exchange. No matter how advanced the new technology is, though it can raise labor productivity dramatically, it is still a means of production. S&T itself is a materialized system of knowledge, but it is not value. No matter how automatic a machine may be, it cannot function without human operations, and its value is transferred gradually to new products by living labor. The intermediate link between advanced S&T and both use value and value is the improvement of living labor productivity. Logically, if we say S&T can also create value, we deny the significance of living labor with different productivities in value creation.

The above does not deny the important role that S&T plays in value creation. Its application in production is the premise for creating more use value and the necessary condition for creating more value. In modern production, the role of S&T is more prominent and crucial than ever before. However, as a factor of production, its properties have not changed; therefore, it cannot be the source of value creation. Indeed, since S&T is often embedded in advanced machinery, if it could create value, then the logic conclusion would be that advanced machinery can also create value.

10
The magnitude of value created by S&T labor

Introduction

We know that labor in S&T is high-level and complex, and can create great value. But though the market reflects this value to some degree it does not do so not comprehensively, so the issue of how to evaluate S&T labor properly remains. There exist S&T institutions which pass professional judgments on scientific and technical laborers and their work, abiding by definite principles, processes and standards. We too should adhere to a number of principles:

(1) The principle of independence, objectivity and justice. This cardinal principle requires evaluative institutions or personnel to be free of external administrative disturbance during evaluation, which should be based on objective facts, not personal preferences.

(2) The principle of scientific standards. The process of evaluation should have a scientific basis, and its indexes and results should be comparable.

(3) The principle of feasibility. The information collected during a definite time period should match the fee paid and should strike a balance between scientific norms and feasibility.

S&T labor is mainly mental, although it combines physical and mental activities. Evaluation calls for a comprehensive inspection of the outcomes, abilities and condition of S&T personnel. Each type of S&T labor is concrete in some field and requires a specific evaluative system, so no system should be absolute.

Basic research, applied research, and development should be treated differently. The international community has standard practices, for example measuring basic researchers by published theses; applied researchers by patents or technical level; or development researchers by the direct or potential economic or social benefits they create. Sekimototadahiro, NEC Corporation's top advisor, proposed a standard known as "3P" to evaluate personnel at the 1999 China Youth Technology Forum. For those in basic research working for "the day after tomorrow," publications are the main standard; for development staff working for "tomorrow," patents are the criterion; while for personnel in applied research, which is for "today," performance is the standard (Deng and Wang 2002, p. 205).

A variety of criteria may thus be applied. For the purpose of analysis, we will take applied research as an example, because all staff in this area require definite S&T theoretical knowledge. The value of the results can be realized in exchange, and reflects the underlying labor value.

Because of the creative nature of S&T labor, the measurement of its value is difficult and sophisticated. The features of the S&T products require us to take into account the social need for the knowledge products created (He 1999, p. 79)· We must also distinguish between the labor time needed to produce scientific knowledge and that required to reproduce it.

S&T labor has particularities which we can describe as vertical and horizontal. Vertical S&T labor refers to its continuity. A discovery or invention results from the efforts of several generations. For example, Daguerre's camera was invented in 1838, as long as 38 years after the discovery of the first photographic plate. Yet the patent could only be granted to the inventor, even though the invention arose because he had absorbed the productive achievements of past generations. Socially necessary labor time, calculated as the inventor's time alone, underestimates the full value of S&T labor. Horizontal S&T labor refers to cooperation. Especially nowadays, S&T is the collective work of a technical community, and the individual rarely achieves significant breakthroughs. The magnitude of value must take into account the total of this cooperative labor time. In Marx's opinion the evaluation of science, which is the result of mental labor, is generally lower than its value, because the labor time necessary to reproduce scientific knowledge is lower than that needed to produce it for the first time. For example, a student can grasp the binomial theorem in an hour.

A third difficulty is that in the product value C+V+S, part of the constant capital C is formed by the accumulation of information and knowledge, while the other part comprises the consumption of materials whose turnover time is easy to identify; the value V+S transferred by the former may be perpetual, or one-off. How then can we determine the value of S&T products? There are four opinions in academic circles.

First, the value of an S&T product is determined by the individual time that produces it. He Yuchang (1999) considers that the measurement of creative labor must be connected to the social need for the knowledge products created, and that during measurement, socially necessary labor time cannot be the standard; creative mental labor can only be estimated as individual labor time. This is because the labor of an inventor of an S&T product is recognized as effective by society, so their individual labor time basically equals the socially necessary labor time; individual value is consequently also social value (Zong 1986).

Second, the value magnitudes of S&T products are determined by socially necessary labor time rather than by complex labor: that is, the labor time necessarily consumed by more sophisticated labor. The commodity value of products employing the same technology is determined by the average socially necessary labor time expended in researching and applying the technology to produce these products (Lu 2002, p. 41). This is the opinion of Rojneva, a Soviet economist. She argues that the R&D process has two components: similar or repeated basic operations and independent creative labor. She estimates the former to be two-thirds of the total. The value of creative labor can be estimated by experts (Lu 1985). This viewpoint applies Marx's concept of the value magnitudes of material commodities to the determination of the value magnitudes of S&T products, but ignores the specific features of these products. Further, the estimate that "basic operations" constitute two-thirds of the whole lacks a scientific foundation; finally, assessing the value of creative labor by experts is not accurate and ignores the essence of market exchange.

Third, the value contribution of S&T labor is measured by the social labor that is saved in production. People who hold this view consider that the saved social labor is a standard to evaluate the value magnitudes of technological products (Zhang 1987, pp. 39–41). However, according to Marx's value theory, the value of a commodity already exists when the product is created, and it acquires the currency form through market exchange. The view that labor in S&T products is saved labor is a kind of subsequent ratification, which is not correct. Moreover, while for common technological products the labor saved can be calculated, for some fundamental S&T products, this is difficult.

Fourth and finally, products of S&T labor have no value but only price. People who believe this hold the view that technological innovations, art creations, and so on have a price but no value. That is to say, their prices are not based on their values; the production and exchange of this kind of commodity are not established by commodity production or the law of value (Ding 2002, p. 53). A scientist's discovery (Meng 1999, p. 232), for example, cannot be measured in terms of abstract labor, because this labor is not uniform. The exchange value of S&T products is the social shell of value which will eventually be filled by social abstract labor. We disagree with this, because S&T labor is part of total social labor, and as such is the undifferentiated labor of scientific workers, which means its products must have features of value. We cannot deny the attribute of value to a product just because it is hard to measure.

Actually because of the special characteristics of S&T labor and its products, the value it contributes can only be estimated approximately. Indeed, because of the complexity of modern production it is in any case difficult to calculate accurately the average quantity of labor which is found in material products. Marx (Marx and Engels 1972d, p. 202) notes that though in certain productive conditions, people can know exactly how many workers are needed to make a desk and the amount of the labor needed to create a product, this is not always the case for non-material products because, like the result itself, the quantity of labor required to achieve the result comes from speculation.

This thesis is relevant to the value of S&T labor today. Our own view is that the value magnitude of an S&T product is determined differently from that of a material product; not by average socially necessary labor time, but the individual labor time that creates it for the first time. Our reasoning is as follows. S&T labor is typically mental labor which is creative and complex and so lacks uniformity. However, this in itself does prevent it being abstract. Scientific products also contain undifferentiated human labor – that is, abstract labor. However, we cannot ascertain the magnitude of their value by studying average labor time, but must connect it to social needs for knowledge. Marx noted that socially necessary labor time is limited by the proportion used in each specific branch of industry. This limitation is just a demonstration of the further development of the whole law of value, though necessary labor has another meaning here.

From the standpoint of social production as a whole, S&T labor is a definite portion of total social labor. It is also necessary in another sense. Due to the process of knowledge diffusion, the earliest individual labor time is socially necessary, since social necessity includes the time consumed in repeated experiments with inevitable losses.

Most outcomes of S&T labor are intangibles like knowledge or concepts. In common with public goods they are characterized by non-exclusivity. According to the economic theory of property rights, these are generally provided by government, because this is the only way to avoid unwanted transaction costs and to prevent damage from monopolization. However, under capitalist production, because the means of production are in private hands, the results are owned by individuals. S&T products created by workers in private enterprises are no exception. Exclusion therefore takes place: those who own the results get the benefits. This is protected by law. The person who first produces an S&T outcome is recognized by society, so their labor is effective. However, other workers engaged in the same labor are not recognized and their labor becomes invalid, because they were not the first to produce the result.

If we accept that individual labor time determines the value magnitudes of S&T products, will the producers waste labor, or become lazy or inefficient? This is not the case; in order to secure social recognition for their labor, laborers will strive to produce a result first. For material products, the decisive factor is prime cost; for S&T products, it is whether the labor is effective or invalid. Because of this institution, it is individual labor time that determines the value of products, and this brings about no decrease in efficiency or waste of labor.

Forms of realization of S&T labor

The value of S&T labor may be realized directly, through market exchange, or indirectly.

Direct realization through market exchange

Some outcomes of S&T labor, such as patents, technical know-how, and new materials, are directly exchanged on the market. Theoretically speaking, their value is determined by the individual labor time that produced them for the first time. In practice the issue is more complex. Among factors to be taken into consideration are R&D input costs, technical maturity, the technology update cycle, technology transfer, and the benefits to the purchasing industry. The actual transaction price generally understates the value contribution of S&T laborers, because of way new technology gets recognized in the market. As the market for S&T products extends, it becomes possible to estimate the value of some outcomes.

Indirect realization

As noted, the constant capital of research has two components: physical products such as machines or paper whose cost is easily calculated, and the "spiritual means of production" (Marx and Engels 1972a, p. 52), which comprise the knowledge and experience of previous generations whose contribution to value is harder to estimate. Lags in time and space prevent their value contribution from being realized directly.

The creation and realization of value are different concepts. When S&T outcomes are embodied in machinery engaged in production, though the "theoretical labor" is not counted as a cost, it is transferred to the final product. The products made with this machinery will contain this abstract labor even if it is not accounted for in the cost. If all other conditions remain unchanged, this is the origin of "additional surplus value" (Yang 2001, p. 294).

226

Marx held that capital incorporates science and social advances in productivity arising from cooperation and the division of labor "without any cost," appropriating the benefits privately.

Practical evaluation of S&T outcomes

The final outcomes of S&T labor are those reflecting the creativity of S&T activities and the experimental verification of natural phenomena and objective laws. They are acknowledged socially through expert appraisal or by other means, and possess definite academic, social, or economic value. These outcomes constitute a kind of knowledge formation; they may be intangible products embodied in theses, design drawings, reports, technological processes, formulae, or standards; or they may be physical products such as new materials or machinery.

These outcomes differ from normal commodities. Their special features included the following.

Diversity: science, society and the economy all benefit, and different S&T activities deliver these benefits in different proportions.

Lags: it always takes new technology several years to demonstrate its economic benefits, and these also vary according to the environment. For example, nylon was invented in 1935 but its industrial production began four years later.

Uncertainty: S&T labor is exploratory and creative, so the value of some theoretical results is difficult to measure in advance and may deviate from what was expected.

For these reasons, the value contribution of much S&T labor is reflected only indirectly in the market, and is in general always underestimated.

S&T labor as noted can be divided into basic research, applied research, and development. Generally speaking, the first two kinds do not figure in market exchange, but the third may. In the next section we develop a system for evaluating the value magnitudes of each of these. Currently, we employ the following three methods to evaluate the outcomes of S&T.[1]

---

1   There are also other evaluative methods, which however constitute variants of one or more of the three methods given below. See Zhu (1998).

The cost approach

The cost approach is also called the replacement cost approach. Under the assumption that assets are used continually, we can get an index of value by subtracting accrued losses from the estimated current cost of replacing or updating assets. The formula is

Value of an asset = replacement cost – cumulative accrued loss

The crux of this approach is the determination of replacement cost and accumulated accrued loss. Replacement cost may be estimated on two bases: the cost of recovery, which supposes the same materials, standards, and skills would be applied as originally; and the cost of updating, which supposes new materials, skills, and standards. In both cases, the cost is what it would take to rebuild the assets with the same functions at current market prices.

Updating cost is most commonly adopted and so is more comparable. A variety of measures are in use: replacement accounting, the functional coefficient method, the price index method, or statistical analysis. We can only decide which measure to adopt on the basis of the special characteristics of the asset.

Accumulated accrued loss can be further divided into tangible loss, functional loss, and economic loss. Tangible loss refers to the effect of natural forces on the asset, and can be calculated in two ways: by observation or using service life. Functional loss means the intangible loss of assets, and refers to the depreciation arising from obsolescence caused by technical advance.

Economic loss is an intangible loss caused by the elements other than capital, for example environmental damage. In the past, there was no standard for sewage discharge, but the limits are strict now; either stopping production or meeting the standard incurs a cost.

Since the outcomes of S&T labor are generally intangible, they lack many features of material assets, making these losses hard to grasp. In particular there is no real equivalent of replacement cost. This method is therefore not applicable. Nowadays, this method is rarely used in evaluating the results of S&T labor.

The market approach

The market approach, also termed the market comparison approach, estimates value from the current market price of similar assets. The method requires a vigorous and open market, ad that the transaction costs are comparable. Real estate is a good example.

Theoretically speaking, market price is a negotiated price in an assumed open and competitive market, representing the consensus of buyers and sellers at a certain point in time. For S&T labor, the adjustments required depend on the degree of marketization. The formula is:

Asset value = current market price of similar assets × adjustment coefficient

This adjustment covers time, function, region, and other elements. The evaluative method calculates the income ratio of price to sale price (PS). Its formula is:

Asset value = asset income × PS

PS could be evaluated through regression analysis using market statuses. Taking into consideration such elements as risk, earnings growth, dividend payout ratio, and net profit margin yields the following regression formula:

$$PS = a + b \times R_p + c \times \beta + d \times EGR + e \times PM$$

where
R_p = the dividend payout ratio
β = risk coefficient
PM = net profit margin
EGR = the anticipated earnings growth ratio in the coming five years.

In practice outcomes can be evaluated by substituting the relevant variables in this formula.

The income approach

The income approach is also named the net present value (NPV) or present earning value method. It measures asset values by estimating the anticipated future income of these assets and converting it into a current price. Since the results of S&T labor can yield quite large future cash flows, this approach is a key method for estimating their value. The basic formula is:

$$PV = \sum_{i=1}^{n} \frac{Y_i}{(1-r)^i}$$

where PV = present value, Y_i = income in period i, r = discount rate, and n = number of periods

Once the S&T outcomes have been applied to production, there is always a period of rapid cash returns, followed by a period of steady development, so the formula is often amended to provide for two sums representing the income expected from these two stages. The amended formula is:

$$PV = \sum_{i=1}^{n} \frac{FCFF_i}{(1+WACC)^i} + \frac{FCFF_{n+1}}{(1+WACC)^n(WACC-g_n)}$$

where
$FCFF_i$ = cash flow of the ith year
g_n = growth rate of the steady period
n = anticipated length of the high-speed stage
WACC = weighted average cost of capital.

The crucial requirements of this approach are measuring the income and determining the discount rate. Since the income is anticipated, it is uncertain, but can be calculated by statistical means. Likewise, the discount rate calls for careful consideration of relevant factors.

Of the three methods, the income approach is the mostly widely adopted. However, none of these methods accurately reflect the value contribution of S&T labor because of the lack of historical data and the immaturity of the market. We shall therefore look into more efficient and accurate approaches.

230

The options pricing model: a new evaluative approach

As noted, S&T outcomes are uncertain but can yield great value for enterprises. However, possible cash flow is not the same as present cash flow, being imbued with uncertainties and risks. What is important is that S&T provides opportunities for value realization, which is characteristic of an *option*. Therefore, an option pricing model can better reflect the value of an S&T output.

Theories of options

An option is a compensated use of right; it is a contract to the effect that the payment of a premium to the seller entitles the buyer to buy or sell a certain quantity of assets at the agreed price (the striking price or exercise price) within the specified time period. It is a right, not an obligation.

There are two fundamental types of option: call and put. A call option entitles the buyer to buy or not to buy a predetermined amount at the exercise price before the expiration date; a put option entitles the buyer to sell or not sell this predetermined amount before the expiration date. The elements of the contract in an option transaction are:

The *option buyer* is the party which pays the option fees and obtains the right. They have the power to perform or give up this right.

The *option seller* is the party that receives the fees and undertakes the obligation to fulfill the contract within the specified period.

The *agreement price*, also called the striking price or exercising price, is the transaction price of the objects determined by the seller and buyer in advance.

The *option premium* is the fee that is paid by the buyer to the option seller for obtaining the right to which the contract entitles them.

The *notice day* is based on the conventions of futures trading and the provisions of each futures exchange. It is generally the first trading day of the contract delivery month.

The *expiration date* is the performance date of the option contract.

According to the above option theories, the option value of futures (PV) equals the sum of intrinsic value (IV) and time value (TV). The option value refs to the market price of the option contract. The intrinsic value indicates that portion of the gain that the option buyer can buy at a better price than the current market price: that is, the gains from selling the underlying securities at higher than the current market price. The time value is equal to the premium, so

$$PV = IV + TV$$

From a dynamic perspective, the time value of the option decreases as the period of validity of the contract decreases, and becomes zero at the expiration date, so the premium is totally constituted by the intrinsic value.

The changing relationship between the premium, the embedded value and time value of the call option is shown in Figure 10.1.

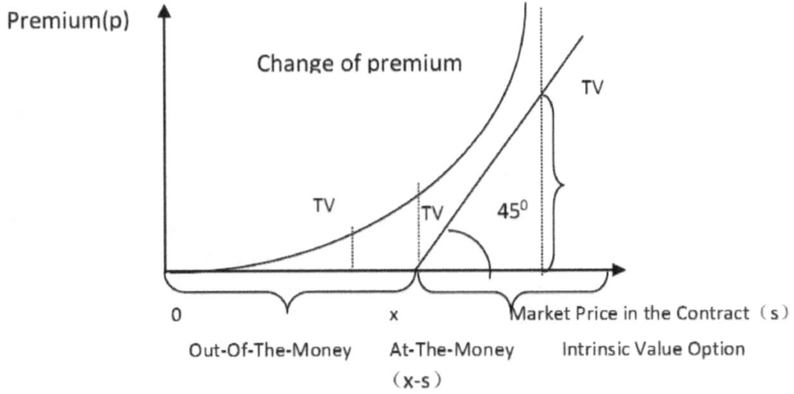

Figure 10.1 The changing relationship between the premium, the embedded value and the time value of a call option

The Black–Scholes model

Since there is no appropriate way to account for the fluctuations in the prices of option objects and their effect on option prices, Professors Fisher Black and Myron Scholes of the University of Chicago published "The pricing of options and corporate liabilities" in 1973. They were the first to propose the options pricing model, which had strong repercussions and was widely used in both theory and practice.

The Black–Scholes (B–S) model estimates the premium with a mathematical model governing the object price, its range of fluctuation, the exercise price, the time left to the due date, the risk-free rate, and other variables. The formula makes seven assumptions:

The option is a European option.

There is no option to pay off the object asset before the due date.

The variation of profit rate and the risk-free rate are constant during the period of validity of the option.

No outside elements, such as transaction cost, affect the profit.

The object price conforms to "Brownian motion."

There are no restrictions on short-selling and the capital can be used freely by investors.

The object of the contract is a capital with risks associated, and its current price is S.

Under the above assumptions, the expected value of the European call option is:

$$X[max(Ut–E),0]$$

where Ut is the object price at time t and E is exercise price.

The application of the B–S model to S&T labor

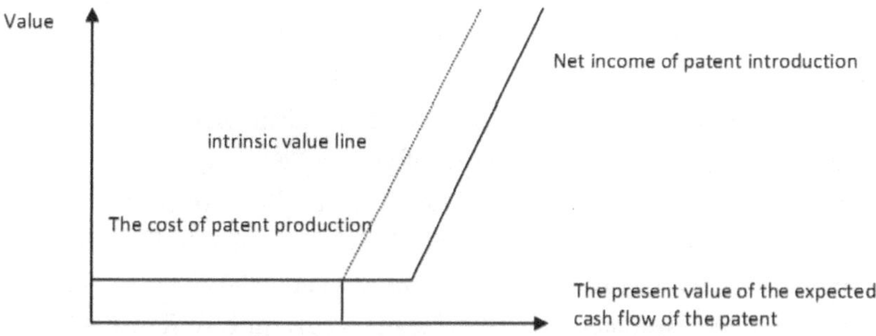

Figure 10.2 The break-even chart for a patent

One condition for the application of the B–S model is a capital transaction with a definite market maturity. The outcomes of S&T labor, being intangible assets, exhibit relatively similar features to the objects of the B–S model, such as big changes in price, uncertainty, and the potential for a large future yield. We shall take patent rights, one of the outcomes of S&T labor, as an example to show how the B–S model may be used to evaluate the value of S&T outcomes.

We treat a patent as a call option. If the present value of the expected cash flow is higher than that of the cost of buying or developing the patent, we suppose that a buyer would consider investing in developing or buying the patent. The break-even point of the patent is similar to the buyer's call option, which is shown in Chart 10.2.

The input variables are:

The value of the object patent: its current value is the sum of present value of the expected cash flow brought by the patent.

The variance of the object patent's value. The price fluctuation of the income brought by the patent could be evaluated by other methods: generally speaking, the greater the variance, the higher the patent value.

The exercise price: the cost of investment and development.

The time limit and risk-free rate: the time limit is the protection period of the patent. According to Chinese patent law, this is 20 years, and 10 years for utility model and design patents. The risk-free rate should apply during this time limit, and is generally replaced by national interest rate.

The dividend yield: since the patent is invalid after the specified date, delaying its practical application means losing a cash flow. Assuming the time limit to be n years, with the cash flow evenly distributed, the cost of delay is $1/n$. This rate can replace the indicator of the dividend yield.

As an example, let us suppose that after years of study, an S&T laborer invents a new production tool which can dramatically increase productivity, and has applied for a patent with a time limit of 20 years. If the purchasing party wants to exercise this patent, they need to add ¥50,000 to the original investment. The estimated present value of its current cash flow is ¥35,000. Then suppose the variance of the cash flow of this patent is 0.05, and the free-risk rate is 7%. Let us now assign values to the variables in the B–S formula as follows:

Present value U = ¥35,000

Exercise price E = ¥50,000

Time limit t = 20 years

Risk-free rate r = 7%

Variance σ = 0.05

Dividend yield: g = 1/20 = 0.05.

This yields a patent value of 0.5102, showing that though currently there is a negative cash flow, because of the changing character of the market, the patent has value. If we use the income approach, the net present value is 3.5 − 5 = −1.5, which means the patent has no value, but using the B–S model, we get the opposite result. So, the options pricing model reflects the contribution of the outcomes of S&T labor better because it allows us to factor in the relatively large potential cash flow in the future.

Empirical studies of value creation by S&T labor

Having discussed the theoretical framework for value creation by S&T labor, we now turn to empirical studies, focusing on the science park Zhongguancun of Beijing as an example. We then consider value creation by scientific labor in business establishments.

Zhongguancun's development has seen three important phases. The first falls between the early 1980s and 1988. China's first private high-tech enterprise was formed and was called Modern Technological Services. Over several years it evolved into the "electronic products and services street" of Beijing. By the end of 1988, about 148 high-tech enterprises had settled in the science park and more than 3,800 people were employed. Among these, as many as 46% of the workforce were S&T personnel. The total output of Zhongguancun was valued at ¥220 million.

Between 1988 and 1998 Zhongguancun underwent rapid development. By the end of 1988, about 6,057 high-tech firms had settled, and its industrial output came to ¥24.55 billion, comprising 14.3% of Beijing's total industrial output.

The third period covers June 1999 to the present. In June 1996, the State Council of China finally approved a proposal entitled "Application for Implementing the Strategy for Reinvigorating China with Science and Technology and Speeding up the Construction of Zhongguancun Science Park," submitted by the Municipal Government of Beijing and the Ministry of Science and Technology of China. The experimental zone, which was the prototype of Zhongguancun Science Park, expanded in size significantly, evolving into a belt circling Haidian District, Fengtai District, Changping District, the Digital Park, and Yizhuang S&T Park, along the Fourth Ring Road of Beijing. The Municipal Government of Beijing and the Ministry of Science and Technology were determined to make Zhongguancun Science Park a world-class science park.

Contribution of S&T labor to value creation i n Zhongguancun's   high-tech firms

After 20 years' development, Zhongguancun's achievements are an impressive testimony to the role played by S&T labor in Zhongguancun, and constitute a prime example of value creation by scientific labor.

The vast majority of Zhongguancun's enterprises were high-tech firms. Their number grew significantly after 2000 when the "electronic products and services street" of Beijing was first organized, reaching 8,186 in 2000, about 55 times of the number of 1988. Table 10.3 provides more detailed information.

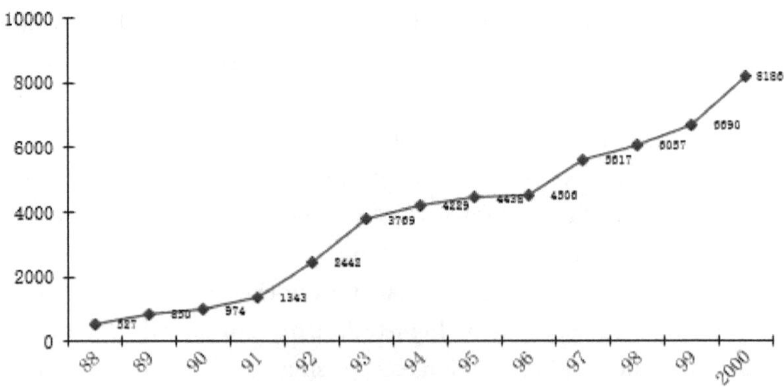

Figure 10.3 Number of high-tech firms each year in Zhongguancun

Source: Li et al. (2003).

236

The output from Zhongguancun firms totaled ¥25.8 billion in 1996, of which about one-third came from the Science Park. By 1999, the output of Zhongguancun high-tech firms made up about 70% of Beijing's added industrial value. This was obviously an important contribution to Beijing's economic growth (*Report of S&T Development of China (2001)*, p. 66). S&T labor also speeded up value creation. In 2000, the added value realized by Zhongguancun high-tech firms totaled ¥32.6 billion, 44.2% greater than the year before. Earnings from trade in the products of the technology industry were ¥167.9 billion, an increase of about 60.1%. These two indexes grew to ¥45.57 billion and ¥215.1 million, an increase of 39.8% and 28.1% respectively (Li et al. 2003, p. 261).

The above data shows that S&T labor not only creates value, but can create much more value than material production. It is expected that in future economic development, the ratio of value created by S&T labor to the total value created by a country will be greater. Its place in economic development is clearly increasing.

Value creation by scientific labor in business establishments

Business establishments are undeniably the most important social organizations engaged in production, creating social wealth as well as value. As S&T develops and labor productivity rises, we should expect the modes of production to also experience dramatic change. It is therefore reasonable to suppose that S&T labor will play an increasingly important role in business establishments. Since the end of the Second World War, many multinational companies have been working hard to allocate their resources efficiently on a worldwide scale. They poured huge amounts into R&D by recruiting qualified personnel: that is, they became more and more dependent on S&T superiority to make a profit. Table 10.2 compares the returns on assets of listed high-tech enterprises and all listed enterprises in China.

Table 10.1 Returns on technology stocks
issued by high-tech industries in 1999

	Shanghai stock market		Shenzhen stock market		Shanghai and Shenzhen stock markets	
	Tech stocks issued by high-tech industries	All listed enterprises	Tech stocks issued by high-tech industries	All listed enterprises	Tech stocks issued by high-tech industries	All listed enterprises
Average returns on stock (¥)	0.229	0.204	0.283	0.214	0.254	0.199
Average net rate of return on assets (%)	7.94	8.17	10.67	8.6	9.13	7.99

Table 10.2 Returns on each technology stock
issued by 10 high-tech enterprises

Code	Enterprise	Returns on each tech stock (¥)
600854	Chunlan Limited Liability Company	0.865
600135	China Lucky Film Corporation	0.843
600779	Quanxing Limited Liability Company	0.841
400	Xuji Group Corporation	0.82
537	The Great Wall PC	0.793
730	Huanbao Limited Liability Company	0.778
636	Fenghua High-Tech Group	0.71
583	Qingdao Haier	0.66
66	Oriental Electronics	0.6525
600100	Tongfang PC	0.62

**Table 10.3 Top 10 listed high-tech enterprises
in terms of net rate of return on assets**

Code	Enterprise	Net rate of return on assets %
600779	Quanxing Limited Liability Company	41.66
730	Huanbao Limited Liability Company	34.41
636	Fenghua High-Tech Group	32.98
600862	Gaotong Machine Tools	32.24
633	Hejin Holding Co, Ltd	30.67
682	Oriental Electronics	27.41
66	The Great Wall PC	25.86
537	Naikai Guard	24.63
583	Sichuan Topsoft Investment Co., Ltd CITIC Guoan	24.45
839	Information Industry Co., Ltd	21.75

Source: Report of S&T Development of China (2000, pp. 149–50).

Table 10.1 shows that the weighted average earnings of each tech stock issued by high-tech firms listed in Shanghai and Shenzhen stock markets was ¥0.254, and the weighted average rate of return was 9.13%, 27.64% and 14.27% higher than the average level of listed companies at Shanghai and Shenzhen stock markets respectively.

Among the top 10 listed high-tech firms, the earnings of each tech stock issued by Tongfang PC were ¥0.62, about 3.1 times of the weighted average of the Shenzhen and Shanghai stock markets. The earnings of each tech stock issued by Chunlan Limited Liability Company were 4.35 times the average.

Among the top 10 listed high-tech enterprises in terms of net rate of return on assets, Guoan Information Industry Co., Ltd was ranked last. However, the net rate of return on assets of Guoan Information was 21.75%, 2.72 times the weighted average of the Shenzhen and Shanghai stock markets. By contrast, the net rate of return on assets of Quanxing Limited Liability Company was 5.21 times the average. The contribution of S&T labor to value creation is clear.

We now present a cross-sectional study on value creation by S&T labor by business establishments. As noted earlier in this chapter, the bulk of S&T labor in business establishments consists of R&D. This always requires a certain amount of funding; by studying financial input into R&D we hope to find ways to measure the contributions of S&T labor to value creation.

Table 10.4 Structure of sources of R&D funds for major countries and regions

Country	Year	Total	Government sources		Private sources		Others	
			Total	%	Total	%	Total	%
USA	1988	124,915	59,200	47.40%	60,530	48.50%	5,185	4.20%
Japan	1987	9,836,640	2,111,840	21.50%	6,716,615	68.30%	1,008,175	10.40%
UK	1986	8,778	3,382	38.50%	4,348	49.50%	205	11.90%
India	1986	26,675	23,494	88.10%	3,183	11.90%		
South Korea	1986	1,523	289	19.00%	1,233	80.90%	1	0.10%
Brazil	1982	305,500	204,300	66.90%	60,500	19.80%	40,700	13.40%
Taiwan	1986	28,702	14,638	51.00%	14,064	49.00%		
China	1988	6,967	3,943	56.60%	3,024	43.40%		

Unit: millions, domestic currency; percent where designated

Source of data: Statistical Abstracts on Science and Technology of China in 1989 (1989).

Table 10.4 shows the sources of R&D funds in a number of countries. The primary source of R&D funds in the major developed countries was industries, which implies that business establishments were making a large contribution to scientific R&D. By contrast, countries like India and China relied primarily on governments for R&D funding, which suggests the R&D that took place was weakly related to economic development.

<h2 style="text-align:center">Table 10.5 Distribution of R&D funds</h2>

Country	Year	Total	Research institutions		Industries		Colleges and universities	
			Total	%	Total	%	Total	%
USA	1988	124,915	22,515	18.0	89,400	71.7	13,000	10.4
Japan	1987	9,836,640	1,384,452	14.1	6,494,268	66.0	1,957,921	19.9
UK	1986	8,778	1,681	19.2	6,075	69.2	1,021	11.6
India	1986	26,675	20,843	78.1	5,552	20.8	280	1.0
Korea	1986	1,523	337	22.1	1,022	67.1	164	10.8
Brazil	1982	5,390	937	17.4	3,602	66.8	850	15.8
China	1988	6,967	3,850	55.2	2,066	29.7	1,051	15.1

Unit: millions, domestic currency

Source: Statistical Abstracts on Science and Technology of China in 1989 (1989).

Table 10.5 suggests that apart from India and China, industry also used more R&D funds, making up 60–70% of the R&D usages of these countries. In the USA, as much as 71.7% of R&D funds were consumed by industry, while in China the proportion was only 29.7%, less than one-third of the total funding. This percentage was even lower in India at one-fifth of total R&D funding.

We would expect businesses to create value, so S&T labor should figure prominently in this process. And in fact, the value created by this type of labor in business establishments is large. Their competitiveness has been proven to be positively related to their ability to increase earnings. By contrast, the S&T labor input into industries of China and India was low. R&D funds devoted to business establishments comprised less than one-third of all R&D uses of funds. One of the most important consequences was that China's R&D capacities were underdeveloped and the competitiveness of China's business establishments was rather low. The value created by business establishments was small, showing that research institutions supported by large amounts of R&D funds failed to commercialize their findings. As a result, the potential value created by scientific labor could not be realized, which was a waste of social resources and scientific labor, and not conducive to scientific progress and socioeconomic development.

Comparative studies at international level on value creation by S&T labor

We have proven theoretically that S&T labor can create more value than non-S&T labor. A consequence is that value and welfare creation are becoming more dependent on S&T advances, which are a key factor not only in building the overall strength of a country, but also in raising living standards, in economic development, and in deciding the position of a country in the world.

First, let us take a look at the indexes of China's GDP and per capita income, and their growth rate compared with the world, since the modern era began.

Table 10.6 Growth rate of GDP

Year	1820–1952	1952–1978	1979–2000
China	0.22%	4.40%	About 9%
World	1.60%	4.52%	About 3%

Source: All tables and data from Deng and Wang (2002).

Table 10.7 China: percentages of world GDP and world per capita GDP

Year	1820	1890	1919	1952	1978
Percentage of world GDP	32.4	13.2	9.1	5.2	5.0
Percent of world per capita GDP	89.0	50.0	36.7	23.7	22.3

Table 10.7 suggests that before 1978, China's GDP level, per capita GDP, and growth rate continued to decline. After 1978, with China's reform and improvements in S&T, the trend started to reverse. China's per capita GDP had been far below the world's average level since 1840. The reason was that since the Opium War in 1840, China had been reduced to a semi-feudal and semi-colonial society, and the development of its S&T was brought to a standstill. Meanwhile, the major Western powers had evolved from capitalism

characterized by free competition to monopoly capitalism. During this period, S&T witnessed the second and the third technological revolutions, and the S&T gap between China and the Western powers widened. Table 10.8 provides more information. We assume the national strength of USA in 2000 is 100, and dividing the national strength of the other countries by the strength of the USA, we arrive at an index of S&T strength.

Table 10.8 Overall and S&T national strengths compared

Country	USA	Japan	France	UK	Germany	Russia	China
Overall national strength	100	60	50	50	50	40	25
S&T strength	100	80	75	75	75	30	15

Note: The data related to China do not include Hong Kong, Macao, and Taiwan.

Table 10.8 suggests that compared with six other major powers, China took last place in terms of overall national strength and S&T innovation. Its overall national strength was only a quarter that of the USA, while the gap in S&T was even wider. S&T strength was also positively related to overall national strength. We believe that the more powerful a country's S&T, the greater its overall national strength.

The three major indexes best adapted to study the S&T labor of a country are the number of scientists and engineers, the time use efficiency of scientists, and the funds available for R&D activities. We will consider them in order.

The number of scientists and engineers

S&T human resources refers to scientists and engineers with a certain amount of knowledge of science in a particular organization, region, or country at any given time. This can be subclassified into three groups. The first includes professionally qualified scientists and engineers, both in-service and retired. The second refers to technicians and those who provide technical services. The third refers to scientists specialized in R&D. We argue that the more abundant its S&T human resources, the more value the country is likely to create.

Table 10.9 Human S&T resources

Country	USA	Japan	France	Former Soviet Union	Brazil	Korea	India	Egypt	China
Scientists and engineers per million	147,777	59,636	23,747	53,487	11,231	2,426	3,374	13,196	5,627
GNP per capita (US$ current)	17,560	12,840	10,720	3,064	1,820	2,370	290	650	299
Labor productivity (US$ per person per year)	38,712	26,652	27,871	6,561	4,809	6,519	992	2,728	600

Source: *China Statistical Yearbook on Science and Technology, 1992 (1993).*

Note: *The reference year is 1985 for France and India, 1982 for Brazil, and 1989 for China. For the remainder it is 1986.*

As Table 10.9 suggests, the number of scientists and engineers in a country is closely related to its per capita GNP and labor productivity. The more scientists and engineers a country has, the higher its per capita GNP and labor productivity will be. A simple linear regression analysis yields a correlation coefficient of 0.84 between the number of scientists and engineers, and per capita GNP.

Time use efficiency of scientists and engineers

In addition to the sheer number of scientists and engineers, their time use efficiency is also important. S&T labor is highly complex, and its creative thoughts may occur at any time, at which time they need to be noted. So, this work does not begin and end at fixed times. Once they have given undivided attention to scientific research, more often than not they completely ignore their surroundings. In addition to normal scientific research, most of China's scientists and engineers have to devote additional time to social activities, which may even exceed the time spent on research. According to a survey conducted by the Chinese Academy of Science and Technology (CAST) in October 1990, the average time Chinese scientists and engineers spent on scientific research was 7.5 hours per day, while the average time spent on other activities was 4 hours. Clearly, the time spent on social activities equaled 57% of the time spent on scientific research. The data could well suggest that the time the Chinese scientists spent on scientific research was really less than for their counterparts in the developed countries.

**Table 10.10 Time use efficiency of R&D
personnel in China's colleges and universities**

	1988	1989	1990	1991	1992
R&D Personnel	189683.0	196781.0	213188.0	217344.0	226087.0
Full-time R&D personnel	117595.0	122599.0	126041.0	126873.0	132010.0
Time use efficiency (%)	62.0	62.3	59.1	58.4	58.4

Source: China Statistical Yearbook on Science and Technology (1993).

Table 10.10 could suggest that time use efficiency by scientists and engineers in China's colleges and universities between 1988 and 1992 was decreasing gradually. Since we know that value created depends on the time worked, the less labor time is devoted to any activity, the smaller the value created. With the deepening integration of the world economy, socially average necessary labor time devoted to products has evolved to form a world average. Consequently, the less labor time a country devotes to any activity, the less value it will create.

R&D spending

R&D requires funds. Theoretically, these should include funds for R&D, for technological services, and for education and training. However, UNESCO defines S&T more strictly, to cover only funds related to R&D. To facilitate the comparisons, we use R&D spending as a proxy for S&T funding as a whole, and use GDP as an index of total annual value.

246

Table 10.11 R&D spending and GDP

Year	1991			1992			1993		
	R&D	GDP	R&D/GDP	R&D	GDP	R&D/GDP	R&D	GDP	R&D/GDP
China	151.34	21.62	0.7	159.84	26.64	0.6	207.78	34.63	0.6
USA	1621.92	57.11	2.84	1675.78	60.28	2.78	1685.97	63.42	2.66
UK	125.13	5.74	2.18	131.34	5.97	2.2	137.75	6.29	2.19
Germany	744.89	28.54	2.61	763.59	30.79	2.48	768.85	31.64	2.43
France	1633.02	67.76	2.41	1694	70	2.42	1733.86	70.77	2.45
Japan	131162.2	4300.4	3.05	137489.7	4582.99	3.0	138480.17	4710.21	2.94
Russia	0.143	0.01	1.43	1.4	0.19	0.74	13.24	1.72	0.77
Korea	40128.27	2157.43	1.86	50001.54	2403.92	2.08	61443.58	2671.46	2.3
Singapore	7.6	0.76	1.0	9.48	0.81	1.17	10.15	0.94	1.08
India	524.28	61.68	0.85	585.89	70.59	0.83	697.2	81.07	0.86
Italy	173006.99	13106.59	1.32	187011.8	14275.71	1.31	189314.12	15024.93	1.26
Canada	101.62	6.73	1.51	106.49	6.87	1.55	113.37	7.13	1.59

Year	1997			1998			1999		
	R&D	GDP	R&D/GDP	R&D	GDP	R&D/GDP	R&D	GDP	R&D/GDP
China	509.16	74.46	0.64	551.12	78.35	0.69	678.91	82.07	0.83
USA	2123.01	78.34	2.71	2427.02	86.99	2.79	2587.53	92.74	2.79
UK	146.98	7.86	1.87	153.36	8.52	1.8	171.47	9.03	1.9
Germany	836.07	36.28	2.31	881.67	37.84	2.33	748.82	19.79	2.42
France	1893.82	81.28	2.23	1860.85	85.36	2.18	1902.09	87.65	2.17
Japan	141460.66	4998.61	2.83	141075.21	4984.99	2.83	158979.35	5095.49	3.12
Russia	243.08	25.86	0.94	250.73	26.96	0.93	504.26	47.57	1.06
Korea	121665.24	4209.87	2.89	120867.82	4443.67	2.72	136616.6	4827.44	2.83
Singapore	21.02	1.43	1.47	25.02	1.39	1.8	27.19	1.43	1.9
India	1176.86	141.79	0.83	1427.71	176.26	0.81	1617.36	188.07	0.86
Italy	202244.58	18726.35	1.08	229514.7	20677	1.11	226459.07	21567.53	1.05
Canada	134.59	8.41	1.6	142.81	8.87	1.61	157.86	9.81	1.61

Year	1994			1995			1996		
	R&D	GDP	R&D/GDP	R&D	GDP	R&D/GDP	R&D	GDP	R&D/GDP
China	233.8	46.76	0.5	348.68	58.48	0.49	404.48	67.88	0.64
USA	1707.64	67.23	2.54	1856.98	70.34	2.64	1973.39	73.91	2.67
UK	140.53	6.66	2.11	141.6	7.01	2.02	144.11	7.39	1.95
Germany	752.12	33.28	2.33	785.42	34.6	2.27	814.66	35.42	2.3
France	1758.82	37.9	2.38	1792.91	76.62	2.34	1823.75	78.61	2.32
Japan	129779.01	4753.81	2.73	132755.02	4792.6	2.77	138200.92	4832.2	2.86
Russia	51.32	6.11	0.84	118.87	15.85	0.75	189.2	22	0.86
Korea	79246.23	3059.7	2.59	94329.3	3519.75	2.68	108757.83	3898.13	2.79
Singapore	12.09	1.08	1.12	13.67	1.21	1.13	17.95	1.31	1.37
India	780.43	96.35	0.86	928.77	111.9	0.83	1072.68	127.7	0.84
Italy	184485.22	15502.96	1.19	185169.26	16386.66	1.13	198492.45	17722.54	1.12
Canada	117.75	7.5	1.57	125.13	7.87	1.59	129.28	8.08	1.6

It can be seen that R & D spending in major developed countries like the United Kingdom, the USA, Germany, Japan, and France was more than 2% of GDP, while that of Italy and Canada, as well as Singapore and South Korea, exceeded 1%. Moreover, this percentage has been increasing. Only China and India spent less than 1% of GDP on R&D. India's level has remained at 0.8% while China was below 1% until 1999. In 2000 China's R&D input started to grow, and it has remained over 1% since then. In conclusion those countries that spend more on S&T are likely to create more value.

Business establishments are the basic value-creating organizations in society, and their S&T labor is the most important source of higher than average surplus value, and a key factor for survival and development in competition. Multinational corporations are willing to hire first-class scientists and engineers, and purchase sophisticated equipment to develop state-of-the-art products. By comparing the ratio of their R&D funding with the overall R&D input of a country, we can gauge their contribution to overall value.

R&D spending by business establishments in the major developed countries has taken up more than 60% of total R&D input. In the Republic of Korea, one of Asia's "four little dragons," it is more than 70% of the whole country's R&D spending. This has propelled large and medium-sized enterprises to a leading position in S&T, and consequently helped their products secure monopolies on the world market. In contrast some business establishments, handicapped by the lack of infusion of R&D funds, have failed to improve their S&T competitiveness. For example, the percentage of R&D spending by business establishments in China, India, and Canada is less than 50%, and it is even lower in India at around 25%. R&D spending by business establishments is positively related to value creation in general.

248

Table 10.12 R&D funding of business establishments compared with total national R&D funding

Year	1990	1991	1992	1993	1994	1995	1996	1997
China	27.4			22.7		31.9	36.8	42.9
USA			68.5	52.0	59.0	61.4	61.6	64.3
UK	40.2			52.1	50.7	48.0		49.5
Germany		69.3	68.6	66.9	66.3	66.4	66.3	67.5
France			61.1		61.6		51.2	50.3
Japan		72.7			68.2	67.1		72.7
Russia								66.0
Korea			24.0	76.2	73.0	70.5		72.7
Singapore	54.0			61.0	62.7			
India	23.2		25.7					
Italy			51.5			48.9		44.3
Canada			41.3	42.3		45.7		48.9

Source: Deng and Wang (2002, pp. 214–15).

11
Value creation by management labor

History keeps up with human development. As soon as human beings appeared on earth, their history began. In order to maintain the species in the struggle against a harsh natural environment, humans must work together. Thus the concept of "group" gradually came into being. As human knowledge advanced and productivity improved, groups developed into tribes. After tens of thousands of years' evolution, a huge organization – the nation – was formed. During the long course from a group to a nation, the group leader gradually evolved into a director with the power to make decisions. Whether in groups, tribes, or nations, management activities exist. We conclude that management activities, as old as human history, are concomitants of human civilization.

Since the formation of the advanced organization called the nation, human management activities have reached a higher stage, and attain different levels of development in different fields. In early history of nation formation, military management and administrative activities developed greatly while the management of production remained relatively underdeveloped, corresponding to low levels of productivity. However, productivity is the most active factor. In a certain sense, the development of human society is a history of understanding nature, transforming it, and so raising productivity. Changes in management activities are associated with the level of understanding, the use of tools, and the organization of the means of production. A change in any of these three factors promotes the development of human management activities. Conversely, expanding the depth and breadth of management activities contributes to improvements in productivity, making it a fundamental driving force for the development of human society.

Although management has a long history, the labor of management in the economic sense is not so-called public administration or military management. It has a unique range of applicability: economic entities' concern with production leads to the use of certain management methods to mobilize resources and achieve their objectives.

Contents and characteristics of management labor activities

The historical development of management activities

The content of management activities depends on the historical period and on organizational structures. Since changes in objective circumstances have a significant impact on the way the goals of an organization are realized, management activities also vary. In general, changes in management practices arise from environmental changes inside and outside the organization. Historically they have evolved from classical to contemporary management, their content changing from general supervision to the management of transactions and transformation.

The two main external factors that determine the nature of management activities are markets and competition. The first is obvious. When production was underdeveloped and demand was low, the market had less need of corporate management. As the supply of products exceeds the demand, the market becomes a primary consideration. Competition also increases the demand for management activities.

Two internal factors should be considered. *Scale* determines the range, efficiency, and difficulty of management. A large-scale enterprise needs more management. *Technology* requires corporate management to adapt to new modes of production in a timely way.

External and internal factors have brought about a transition from classical to modern management, which can be divided into four periods.

The phase of classical management lasted from the mid-18th century to the 1920s. During this period, capitalist production underwent a transition from handicraft workshop to machine production. The main problems facing enterprises were low efficiency, the cruel exploitation of workers, labor alienation, low enthusiasm for production, and constant labor conflicts. The focus of management was on improving efficiency and reducing labor conflicts.

This led to the emergence of scientific management theories, including Taylorism, Fayol's general management theory, and Weber's theory of bureaucracy. These still exert great influence on the practice of corporate management in all countries, and have played a positive role in promoting labor productivity in enterprises.

This was followed by a transition phase. In the classical management stage, managers treated workers as general "production tools" without taking into account their needs and behavior. From 1920 to 1950, as economic ties between capitalist countries deepened while demand on the world market rose, managers became preoccupied with getting workers to play a better role in production. Corporate management focused on workers' needs, motivation, mutual relations, and the social environment, and on changing production conditions to eliminate dissatisfaction and thus raise productivity.

Modern management lasted from the 1950s to the 1970s. After the Second World War, the massive production capacity that the capitalist countries had accumulated in wartime had to be transferred into sales in the world market to maintain capitalist reproduction. After the 1960s, the high-volume low-variety model improved, resulting in intensified market competition. With the oil crisis and social and political unrest, business operations came under serious threat and the uncertainty of the corporate environment increased. The simple management of production gave way to strategic and contingency management.

From the 1980s to the present a new phase emerged. By the 1970s, many countries had accumulated a wealth of management theories and practice, leading to improvements in labor productivity and rapid economic development. With the rise in the scale of the individual enterprise, a series of questions arose, such as how to coordinate the staff of diverse cultural backgrounds to form a unified corporate culture, and how to manage a huge bureaucracy with slow response, low efficiency, high cost, and serious waste. Old management methods having failed to solve these problems, new methods arose. Their focus was corporate culture, construction, and business process reengineering, and a mutation from transaction management to the management of change.

Thus, a survey of managers in a medium-sized Honeywell subsidiary showed that in 1970, about 75–80% of the plant manager's time was spent maintaining the normal operation of the plant, while by 1985, launching and leading change took up 35–60% of this time (Wang and Li 2003, p. 307). Modern enterprise managers thus face a more complex internal and external environment with greater uncertainty, demanding that they capture favorable opportunities, avoid risk, and seize opportunity arising from changing circumstances, to keep the enterprise intact and provide for its long-term development.

The main content of management activities

Depending on the circumstances, management comprises planning, organizing, leading, and controlling resources to accomplish the established goals of an organization. The process is composed of a series of interrelated and continuous activities or functions. Fayol, who first put forward the concept of management function (activities and behavior), thinks that management has five functions: planning, organizing, commanding, coordinating, and controlling. There are a number of different views of management's functions; generally, its activities consist of planning, organizing, leading, and controlling (Wu 2002, p. 7).

Planning is the primary work of management. It consists of researching the organization's environment and conditions so as to achieve its purpose, and on this basis making decisions and devising action plans, and so on. Organizing consists of making systematic arrangements for supplying and scheduling the organization's resources, and includes organizational design, staffing, organizational change and development, and so on. Leading means exerting influence on members of the organization, enabling them to strive for the organization's goals with enthusiasm and high morale. Specifically this includes guidance, communication, incentives, and the like. Controlling consists of checking the organization's activities for deviations from its program, identifying the reason, and taking measures to rectify things or adjust the original plan to adapt it to operational requirements. This includes setting control standards, measuring performance, checking deviations, and correcting them.

Characteristics of management labor

Management labor has a number of distinct characteristics compared with general production activities. First, it is based on mental work. Enterprise personnel can be divided into production-line operators, auxiliary personnel in production, S&T personnel, management personnel, and so on. Regardless of their level, managerial work consists of nothing more than planning, coordinating, controlling, and organizing. In distinction from that of production-line operators, this labor is mental. In plain words, managers work in offices and work with their pens or their mouths.

Second, the basic functions of management are quite similar in different types of organization as regards their principles and methods. Management in different types of organizations has similarities and commonality. Managers can therefore work in both production-oriented enterprises and service-oriented enterprises with only small differences.

Third, the object of management activities is people rather than things. For example, the leadership function is to exert influence on staff, directing them to achieve the goals of the organization. Whether achieved through guidance, communication, or incentives, the object of management is people.

Finally, managers have an innovation function. Since both external and internal factors are constantly changing, management must devise appropriate strategies based on circumstances. If a manager disregards changes and simply copies other people's management experience and methods, they will fail: not, however, because of incorrect principles or methods but because the conditions in which these principles and methods apply have changed. This explains why different management methods can produce equally good results while the same management method can lead to different results. This suggests that management labor is not mechanical and repetitive, but innovative.

The nature and requirements of management labor

The twofold nature of management labor

Because of the twofold nature of the production process, which reproduces both the material conditions and social relations of production, management also has a twofold nature. As Marx noted, "The labor of supervision and management is naturally required wherever the direct process of production assumes the form of a combined social process, and not of the isolated labor of independent producers" (Marx and Engels 1998, p. 381). The distinction between supervision and management indicates the twofold nature of the labor involved. This labor arises from general characteristics of human social activity, which include all kinds of management functions that do not change with different social systems, culture, or historical stage, but are affected mainly by the development of productivity.

The material function of management reflects the requirement to apply advanced scientific methods to productivity development. Without it, not even social production can be carried out smoothly, let alone development. This aspect of management is objective and independent of people's will, and will not change with different social systems and ideologies.

Management activities are however naturally constrained by relations of production. Management is conducted in the service of the ruling class, the possessors of the means of production, and reflects certain social relations of production. This is management's social function, which reflects the requirements of the ruling class and is influenced and restricted by relations of production or the economic base. It adapts the relationship between people according to the will of the ruling class, to maintain and develop the relations of production.

Understanding this twofold nature of management has important practical significance. On one hand, we need to be aware of management's material, or natural, function. There is succession and continuity in the functions of management in different social formations, with common laws governing the management of large-scale social production. Therefore, we should actively and boldly absorb scientific management experience from abroad in line with the law of large-scale social production, digesting and applying this experience in our specific national conditions. On the other hand, we must grasp management's social function. In the management of capitalist enterprises, workers are exploited to serve the reproduction of capitalist production relations. But in China, corporate management has to coordinate the opposed interests of the workers, and serve the reproduction of socialist production relations.

Classification of managerial staff

"Managerial staff" is the general term for people engaged in management activities. In modern corporate organizations, bureaucracy is a general fact. Managerial staff at different levels have different functions. Managerial staff fall into three categories depending on their level.

Senior managers, such as the chair or president of the enterprise, take full responsibility for its activities, managing and taking integrated command of the entire organization. They represent the organization externally; internally, they have decision-making power on major issues. They have chief responsibility for defining the organization's goals and policies, and evaluating its performance as a whole.

Middle management consists of people between senior and operational management, such as department managers and workshop directors. They play a connecting role in the management of the organization. Their main responsibilities are to carry out the decisions of senior management, and to supervise and coordinate the organization's primary activities so as to implement the goals set by senior management.

Operational managers, also known as front-line managers, take charge of daily primary activities. For instance, they include operation team leaders. Their duty is to organize, command, and engage in line with the arrangements made by middle management.

Managerial staff at different levels focus on different management functions, as shown in the Figure 11.1.

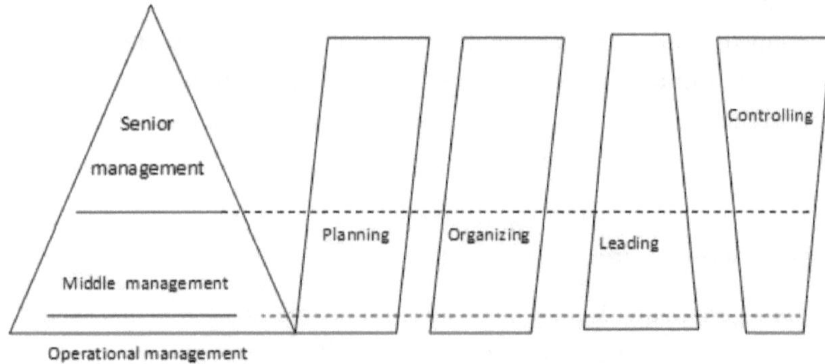

**Figure 11.1 Managers of different levels
focus on different jobs in management**

Capability requirements of managers

Certain technical capabilities are required of managerial staff at different levels. First, they need to conceptualize: to analyze, judge, and make decisions. Since internal and external environments vary, they need to penetrate to the essence of things, to understand their correlation, coordinate conflicts, and control the situation. They must also deal with relationships, interacting with all kinds of people and dealing with their relationship to each other. This calls for the ability to identify, appoint, unite, and organize people, and to generate the enthusiasm to achieve goals. Manager also need technical capabilities: they must grasp the professional techniques and methods required at the operational level. They do not need to become technical experts, but they have to know and master the basic technical knowledge in the field they manage, or they will not be able to communicate with the technicians, or give them guidance.

Managerial staff of different levels needs different management skills, as shown in Figure 11.2.

First-line manager	Middle-level manager	Senior manager
Technical skills	Human skills	Concept skills

Figure 11.2 Managers at different levels need different management skills

258

The logical investigation of value creation by management labor

As social production and technology have developed, management has become more important, especially for large and medium-sized state-owned enterprises that are in transition from the traditional planning system to a market economy system. This is generally acknowledged. However, some argue that enterprise management creates no specific use value and is therefore unproductive.

Is it in fact productive, and if so, then how does it create and realize value? Most of this section deals with this and related questions.

Differences in the connotation of management labor

Where there are people, there are management problems. But management has changed much with the socialization of production and the advances of S&T. Consequently, so have its techniques, methods, and connotation. In the mid-19th century, British industry had completed a transition from manual workshops to large-scale machine industry, leading to the modern factory. At that time, factories used steam as the main motive power: technically, they exhibit a typical layout in which raw materials pass through various processes until the final manufactured product emerges, defining the characteristics of production management in which the owner or partner takes both ownership and control of the factory, employing only a small number of supervisors.

The corporate management of this era is still in capitalism's early stages. Basic functions, such as marketing, production, finance, and procurement, are coordinated through market transactions between different corporate enterprises, or given to different partners to achieve a division of labor. The unified management of the modern enterprise does not exist (Shi 2002, pp. 3–6). The focus of management labor is the coordination of production and the external relations of the enterprise. There is no purely technical management except for modern double-entry accounting. However, management in classical enterprises begins to manifest some of the general roles that emerge later. Having studied Britain's textile factories, Marx abstracted from the specific features of management as follows:

All combined labour on a large scale requires, more or less, a directing authority, in order to secure the harmonious working of the individual activities, and to perform the general functions that have their origin in the action of the combined organism, as distinguished from the action of its separate organs. A single violin player is his own conductor; an orchestra requires a separate one. (Marx and Engels 1996, p. 336)

He further says,

A greater number of labourers working together, at the same time, in one place (or, if you will, in the same field of labour), in order to produce the same sort of commodity under the mastership of one capitalist, constitutes, both historically and logically, the starting point of capitalist production. (Marx and Engels 1996, p. 327)

A major change took place in the Managerial Revolution of the 1920s and 1930s, characterized by the separation of ownership and management. Corporate management became more professional, managers became more numerous, and management labor became more complex, evolving from the owners' paternalistic leadership to a system of bureaucracy. By the 1950s, most leading industrial companies had basically completed this historic change. Since then, the world economy has become more integrated; technology has developed into the intelligence era; competition has become increasingly fierce, mergers and acquisitions happen frequently and giant multinational companies emerge; corporate management has faced an unprecedentedly complex environment, making its tasks extremely difficult.

Contemporary corporate management no longer relies on one person; it has developed into a systematic activity which has its own structure, function, and life. The American mega-company GE is an example: it has a big management system, a lot of personnel (GE's finance staff amounts to more than 4,000, while the workers in a typical Manchester textile mill numbered several hundred), and a strict and complex control program, unequalled by the enterprises of Marx's time (Shi 2002, p. 52). We cannot overlook these changes in our studies of the labor theory of value.

How management labor creates value

To understand how and why management labor creates value, we need to grasp the following points.

First, managerial staff are part of the overall workforce, and their labor is part of the enterprise's overall labor. In the early stage of capitalism, the main content of management activities is production management, with few specific techniques, simple management technology, and a small number of managerial staff. Modern corporate management in contrast is divided into strategic management and operational management; in depth and breadth its activities are quite different from those of classical enterprises. Even in the era of large-scale machine industry, management was also indispensable. Marx once said:

> *As the co-operative character of the labor-process becomes more and more marked, so, as a necessary consequence, does our notion of productive labor, and of its agent the productive laborer, become extended. In order to labor productively, it is no longer necessary for you to do manual work yourself; enough, if you are an organ of the collective laborer, and perform one of its subordinate functions. (Marx and Engels 1996, p. 510)*

In modern capitalist enterprises, there are three types of laborer: front-line operators, managerial staff, and S&T personnel. However, their labor is very different: the work of managerial staff and S&T personnel is mainly mental, while that of front-line operators is mainly physical. Each of these three types is indispensable, and their cooperative labor, which constitutes a community of production, creates the products.

Their abstract labor creates value, and their concrete labor creates use value. Managerial staff and scientific and technical personnel:

> *all together, as a workshop ... are the living production machine of these products ... . All these persons are not only directly engaged in the production of material wealth, but they exchange their labor directly for money as capital, and consequently directly reproduce, in addition to their wages, a surplus-value for the capitalist. Their labor*

consists of paid labor plus unpaid surplus-labor. (Marx and Engels 1972c, p. 444)

So managerial staff are part of the overall workforce, and their labor is part of the enterprise's collective labor in production. Their labor creates not only value, but also surplus value.

Second, management labor is mentally based complex labor. The management requirements of classical enterprises are relatively low. Usually people with some experience can handle them, and there are few managers. With the increasing uncertainty of the enterprise's external and internal environment, its growing scale, and intensified competition between enterprises, there is stronger need for scientific organization and management, and mere personal experience is far from enough. This generates higher requirements for managerial staff, especially when developed S&T is involved. Management labor is not ordinary mental and physical labor, but more advanced and mentally based complex labor. Modern managers not only need appropriate professional skills, but also are required to master modern management theory, techniques and methods, which requires education and training. The modern enterprise stands or falls on a knowledge of scientific management. So modern management labor is not normal labor, but advanced and complex labor.

Complex labor is a multiple of simple labor. Modern management labor, being mentally based, is complex labor, and thus creates more value. To take IBM as an example: in 1991 and 1992 it had huge losses; in 1993, the company's share price dropped from $175 to less than $40, the lowest for 17 years. The company appointed Louis Gerstner as CEO. He adopted scientific management methods which were in line with IBM's reality, and soon reversed the losses. In 1994, the company's share price rebounded to $73.5, in 1995, $91.4 and further to $158.5 in 1996 (Zhao 2002, p. 139). Modern and scientific management can indeed create greater value, bringing major economic benefits for enterprises and society.

Third, management labor is innovative complex labor. Before the managerial revolution, the main problem was to increase labor productivity, reduce costs, and create low-priced, high-quality material products for the market. With the progress of S&T, production has undergone tremendous changes, and the internal and external environments of enterprises are constantly changing. Only by breaking the traditional management model and innovating can the enterprise adapt. Managerial staff and leaders of modern enterprises need to apply S&T innovation, system innovation, and management innovation. Innovation is required throughout management, becoming its essence. Innovative management activities create more value.

Finally, since the value of managerial staff's labor power is relatively high, they can materialize more value at the same time. According to Marx, the value of labor power is determined by labor time necessary for the production and reproduction of this unique commodity. In terms of labor power representing value, labor power itself only represents a certain amount of average labor which has been objectified.

The labor time necessary for the production of labor power can be attributed to labor time necessary for the production of the means of subsistence. In other words, the value of labor power is the value that can acquire the means of subsistence that the possessor of labor power needs. It usually includes three parts: the means of subsistence needed to survive, the necessary cost of education and training, and the cost of raising children. Modern enterprise management requires staff to accept higher education and continuous on-the-job training. This is expensive and requires much labor time. Therefore, the labor-power of modern managers is of higher value. For example, the tuition fees for contemporary MBA and EMBA degrees are tens or even hundreds of thousands of yuan, not including time, effort, and opportunity cost.

The quality of managerial staff is related to the scale of the enterprise and the complexity of management. The larger the enterprise, the higher the educational level required. According to a survey by the National Bureau of Statistics, in 1994 the average academic qualifications of managerial staff in large enterprises took 14.8 years (tertiary education level), in medium-sized enterprises 12.2 years (high school graduation level), and in small enterprises 11.3 years. Managerial staff with lower educational levels cannot adapt to what is required by modern enterprises (Wang 1996, p. 324).

Moreover, since managerial work is complex mental work, it requires better nutrition, increasing its value accordingly. Modern medical research shows that the oxygen consumption of an ordinary worker of 60 kg typically accounts for 20–25% of the body's total, while the brain's oxygen consumption of a mental worker accounts for about 32% of the total (Wang 1996, p. 248). During the same labor time, mental workers' oxygen consumption is higher than that of manual workers. To recuperate mentally and physically, protein and various vitamins, especially phosphorus compounds and amino acids, are required, a further reason that the labor power of managers is more valuable. Therefore, this is more advanced labor which can create more value:

> *All labor of a higher or more complicated character than average labor is expenditure of labor-power of a more costly kind, labor-power whose production has cost more time and labor, and which therefore has a higher value than unskilled or simple labor-power. This power being higher-value, its consumption is labor of a higher class, labor that creates in equal times proportionally higher values than unskilled labor does. (Marx and Engels 1996, p. 208)*

Path analysis of value creation by management labor

The above analysis shows that management labor creates value. How does it do so? There are four major ways.

Improving cooperation through the division of labor

Classical economist Adam Smith first analyzed the impact of the division of labor on labor productivity, further pointing out that division of labor is limited by the scope of the market. But with the development of world economic integration, the scope of the market expands, further promoting the social division of labor. This results in cooperation, creating a kind of productivity increase. However, this is only a potential, calling for management to organize it and make it work.

Enterprise constitutes a complicated combination of resources. The simple factors of production are capital (C), labor (L), technology (T), environment (E), and so on. These only create wealth when combined according to certain technical standards. Without proper management, they cannot play

264

their proper role and may even cause business failure. Formulaically we can write

$$M = f(L, C, T, E, ...)\qquad\qquad 11.1$$

where M stands for Management. Its function is to allocate corporate resources in order to maximize performance and benefits. Marx says:

> *The effect of the combined labor could either not be produced at all by isolated individual labor, or it could only be produced by a great expenditure of time, or on a very dwarfed scale. Not only have we here an increase in the productive power of the individual, by means of co-operation, but the creation of a new power, namely, the collective power of masses. (Marx and Engels 1996, p. 331)*

The increased productivity due to management coordination is social. In summary, management labor creates value by improving cooperation through the division of labor.

Saving labor time by allocating resources

The basic functions of management are planning, organizing, leading, and controlling. Each of the functions requires resources in the enterprise. A basic task of management is to reduce production costs through the efficient use of materialized and living labor. The value thus created arises from the difference between the individual labor time required in the enterprise where the managers work, and socially necessary labor time.

In enterprises where managerial labor is appropriately deployed, the individual labor time required will be lower than the social average, resulting in excess profits. However, these will not exist for a long time. Other enterprises will imitate the enterprise that first introduces productivity improvements arising from enhanced management input, and labor time will be saved in the entire department, while the excess profits of the leading enterprise will disappear. This both concludes the current round of competition and begins the next. Management competition among enterprises thus leads to improvements in the overall level of enterprise management and the reduction of the commodity's value.

Creating value by innovation

Contemporary enterprises face a constantly changing environment with growing uncertainty. If management sticks to convention, the enterprise cannot adapt to market competition and will be eliminated. The end result is to reinforce management's role in innovation. S&T are primary productive forces whose the core lies in innovation.

To achieve innovation, managers must learn constantly, which requires strenuous labor. The labor intensity of innovative management is consequently higher than that of general repetitive management, which consequently materializes more value in the same labor time than general complex labor. However innovative management always appears in a few enterprises, which others cannot imitate. It thus creates more value than ordinary enterprise management. This also produces a kind of excess profits, but since innovative management is difficult to imitate, such enterprises can produce more surplus value, which lasts a long time and ends with the disappearance of the innovation.

Contribution of management labor to the realization of value

In a product economy, producers do not need to exchange their products. However, in a commodity economy, especially the modern market economy, most products have become social products through exchange. Without successful exchange or realization of the full product value, the producers' labor is partly or wholly invalid. Marx once described the exchange of products to obtain a currency equivalent as a "breathtaking leap."

In fact, after the managerial revolution, management's focus was no longer on production management, but on R&D and marketing strategies. The reason is simple: to become social labor, private labor's products must be social: accepted by consumers and society. Otherwise, they will be overstocked and enterprises will go bankrupt. The essence of the capitalist system is the production of surplus value whose prerequisite is the transformation of individual into social labor. Marketing thus becomes a key aspect of modern management. The value of manager's labor achieves social recognition only when commodities complete their exchange in the market. The market thus evaluates the value created by management labor. The present economic system in China is a socialist market economic system, so managers must manage marketing effectively to realize the value created by all the workers in the enterprise and carry out reproduction smoothly.

Practice has proved that a high-quality manager can make a state-owned enterprise return to profitability, unite workers to be constantly innovative, expand market share, and improve economic benefits to both enterprises and the country, while a low-quality manager can run a good state-owned enterprise into the ground. Competent managers can ensure that products create more value in the market than that created by the remaining workers; conversely, incompetent managers can lead to these products creating less value in the market, or even fail to realize their value because they are unwanted (Wei 2001, p. 124).

This shows that realizing the commodity value produced by modern enterprises is a key function of management labor. It therefore plays an important role in value realization.

How to understand the labor of capitalists

Origin of the problem

In the primary stage of socialism in China, the country is practicing a socialist market economy, with the basic economic system of public ownership as the pillar, and all forms of ownership developing together. Because of this, in addition to state-owned enterprises, there is a growing development of mixed joint-stock enterprises, foreign enterprises, and private enterprises. The latter include enterprises of three types: private companies limited by shares, partnerships, and individual-owned enterprises.

In general, business owners are involved in managing enterprises. Private business owners are thus both capitalists – the possessors of capital – and managers. What, then, is the nature of their labor? Is it productive? Is there exploitation in the private sector? These are aspects of the general problem: how to understand capitalist labor.

Capitalists in the classical enterprise system

In Marx's day, since the factory scale was generally small, there was little need for venture capital, and the production process was relatively simple, so capitalists usually had to be personally involved in management. These typically sole proprietor enterprises formed a system which gathers investment capital, forms businesses, and manages them. Without middle-level management, supervisory relations between capitalists and workers are clear at a glance, as are the economic conditions and contradictions of the two classes. Marx studied the role of capitalists and management in this light. Capitalists are engaged in that aspect of enterprise management – the labor of "supervision and commanding" – which gives management the character of capital management. It should be pointed out that Marx strictly distinguished between capitalists and managers. He thought that managers who are "different from capitalists" "belong to the scope of production workers," while capitalists are naturally excluded. Unlike the professional manager, capitalists become managers because they are capitalists. Of course, since capitalists are involved in management, "in this sense, capitalists play an active role in the labor process itself. ... Combined with exploitation, this labor ... like the labor of workers, is a labor which the product value has added to" (Marx and Engels 1972d, pp. 550–1). However, the wages of management were small in relation to surplus value.

In modern enterprises, capital owners have been separated from managers. Managers contribute a definite labor value, and are entrusted with the management of enterprises. Managers, S&T personnel, and production workers together create value and surplus value. In addition to these operators' pay, a lot of surplus value is appropriated by capitalists outside the production process. Capitalist exploitation still exists. History shows that the development of capitalism makes the capitalists supernumeraries, just as the capitalists thought of landlords as supernumeraries.

Capitalist and socialist management are different. As noted above, the twofold nature of social production determines a twofold nature of capitalist management: on the one hand, it has the functions associated with productivity and social production; on the other, the antagonism between capital and labor gives it an obvious social function. In sole proprietorships, the choice of managers is subject to capital, and meets the requirement of helping the enterprise to grow. Appearing as spokespeople of capital, managers are in contradiction with production workers. Their central purpose is to freely appropriate the surplus value created by workers, by virtue of the ownership of the means of production, which is exploitative.

In the primary stage of socialism, management labor also has a twofold nature. It must organize social production; however, public ownership is the pillar of a system with many other kinds of ownership. Management in state-owned or controlled enterprises reflects socialist relations of production, and thus has social functions associated with an advanced social system. Management labor's essence is to maintain and improve socialist production relations, improve labor productivity and economic benefits through a rational allocation of resources, and create wealth to meet the growing needs of material and cultural life. Managers are paid in accordance with the principle of distribution according to work.

How the value of management labor is determined: dependency theory

A problem remains: how is the value of labor in management determined? We propose a theoretical basis, the dependency theory of management labor.

Some argue that management does not act on the means of production, but by allocating resources and commanding workers. Since managers are not directly engaged in production, it is claimed, their work does not create value. But as we have noted, although managers may not act directly on the object of labor, managers do contribute a certain quantity of undifferentiated human labor. They work together with S&T personnel and production workers to produce social products and create value; thus, theoretically, there is a problem of how to measure the value they contribute. Although it is difficult for us to clarify the specific proportion of this value that each part of the labor force contributes, this does not stop us theoretically investigating it.

We have established that management is a general feature of human societies, and we have accumulated rich experience of it in history. We also know that economic and especially corporate management was underdeveloped before the industrial revolution, and that in recent times this has changed.

Abstractly, an enterprise is a production unit which uses and rationally allocates various resources to produce the best economic results. Its problems are no more than the problem of organizing resources and combining factors to raise labor productivity and reduce costs. This shapes the content of management theories and techniques which serve to inform management in any economic organization, whether industrial, commercial high-tech, or a general productive enterprise.

Of course, management techniques vary corresponding to what is produced and how. But the technical differences are not the most important: what matters is the management concept. This differs from the natural sciences where, for example, a chemist cannot practice physics professionally.

According to the labor theory of value, the magnitude of value is determined by socially necessary labor time. However, in each specific enterprise, this has a different form. In general material production, value is determined by socially necessary labor time, and Marx's theory is still applicable. However, the scope of modern labor has greatly expanded, and with the development of S&T, mental labor is becoming the main mode of labor. The magnitude of the value of S&T goods is no longer determined by average socially necessary labor time, but by the individual labor time that first produces the products.[1] For other commodity types, the magnitude of value is determined in various ways, depending on the particular labor involved (mental or physical) and the particular products (personal belongings or "public goods").

Finally, since managers do not undertake production work alone, but jointly with S&T personnel and workers, and since their function is to allocate productive resources, the characteristics of labor in each particular area of production determine the nature of management. For instance, a high-tech enterprise engaged in new drug research and development shapes what its management does; a material production enterprise making color televisions brings about a different variant of management labor. Management labor depends on the specific production process and product. It can create value only when abstracted, together with scientific, technological, and productive labor, to become general human labor.

---

1   If we take into consideration the social distribution of labor, individual labor time is still socially necessary in this sense.

Therefore, the magnitude of value in each specific field of production establishes the rule for determining the value contribution of management. In production sectors where value is determined by socially necessary labor time, so is the contribution of management; where value is determined by individual labor time, the value contribution of management is likewise determined by individual labor time. Management labor is thus in essence a dependent form of labor.

An econometric model of value creation by management labor

A manager not only gives orders from top to bottom according to the rules of bureaucracy, but also provides feedback from bottom to top based on practical implementation. In a well-managed enterprise, the manager coordinates the activities of every subordinate department as well as directing coordination between departments to achieve vertical and horizontal interactive communication.

To this extent, management activity is a kind of information-processing activity. Value creation by the enterprise calls for the coordination of the whole organization. While it is true that every department and all personnel including management conduct value creation, they are only one part of the value-creation activities of the entire enterprise. Moreover, value creation by each department depends on coordination with the others.

We can divide value-creation activities into vertical and horizontal information networks. Each subject collects information and processes it according to certain criteria. The simple model is shown in Figure 11.3.

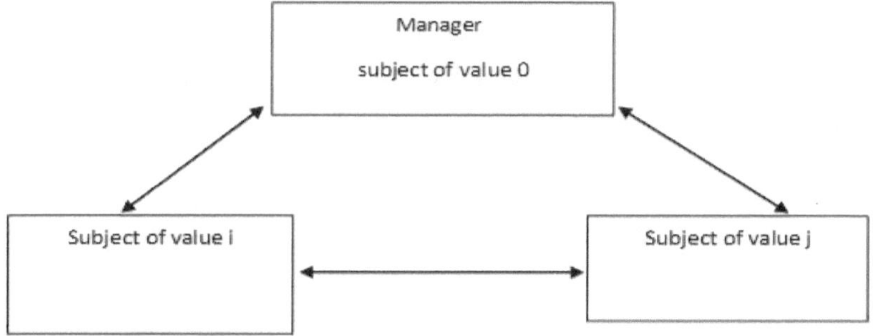

Figure 11.3 Information network model

This network creates cost advantages which benefit coordination. In consequence, the network has the potential to create value. Visser points out that sequential decision based on hierarchical and multipolar structure creates value (2000, pp. 231–52).

How management activities can lead to cost advantages and the creation of value can be investigated using a standard quadratic cost model (Li et al., 2002, pp. 78–9).

The model assumes that, except for the highest-value subject level, value subjects accept information $\alpha + e_{\alpha}$ with probability P, and that the value subject at a higher level either processes information that is difficult to process for value subjects at the lower levels, or deals with activities that it cannot itself coordinate (with a probability 1–P), sending information to the ith value subject.

It turns out that if and only if management tries to make the information-processing capability of all value subjects positive, then:

(I) The stronger the information-processing capability of all the subjects of value is, the more obvious the cost advantage will be, and the more value will be created.

(II) The cost-minimizing input of management labor is a decreasing or increasing function of p, depending on the variance of the information-processing capacity of the subjects. The quadratic cost model thus identifies, mathematically, conditions under which the activities of the manager can indeed create leading cost advantage, so as to create value.

Empirical research into value creation by management labor

The first section of this chapter discussed the meaning of management labor. It is a process which, under certain conditions, effectively plans, organizes, leads, and controls the organization's resources to achieve a definite goal.

In studying this definition further, we find that management labor has a twofold nature. First, management activities form a result reflecting some kind of purpose or action plan. For example, given some fixed problems or constraints, a manager may make a judgment or formulate a strategic plan, an annual working program or decision-making opinion which can be used in the next phase of management. There is thus an external outcome of the management process.

This kind of management activity is important in enterprise management, especially for large-scale enterprises. Such institutionalized management practices are a precondition for enterprises to operate. Without them there will be poor coordination, inefficiency, and even corrupt practices. An action plan is management's first step; the next step is to follow up with implementation and examination. Divided up thus by function, planning and controlling are management activities.

A second kind of management activity arises without such external action plans, such as the functions of organizing and leading. Since activities are already in process, once the process is over, this type of management labor ends. Its characteristic is that once it has been provided, it disappears, unlike the first kind which is materialized in an external object.

These two types of management labor cannot completely be separated. On the contrary, they are combined in the enterprise to provide unified management activities. Such comprehensive management labor, along with other forms of management labor, together form abstracts and create value. But since the first kind of management labor can be materialized in external objects, it can appear in the form of management consultancy outside the enterprise. Management consultancy has thus formed an independent branch of the division of labor, and has a market value. It can thus be observed and studied separately. The second kind of management labor is in contrast just a kind of specialism in organizing and leading activities, without any reference market value,   so the value it creates cannot be measured.

This section uses two types of empirical research: first a comprehensive study of value creation by management labor, and second, a study of market value creation by the first type of management labor. Both are elaborated in what follows.

The empirical analysis of value creation by labor in comprehensive management

China has many enterprises with high energy consumption, low labor productivity, high costs and poor economic benefits. A very important reason for this is backward corporate management. Enterprises lack not only outstanding managerial staff, but also effective management techniques and methods. Strengthening enterprise management is of great significance to raise labor productivity, reduce costs, and increase economic benefits. The saying "30% technique, 70% management" indicates the importance now attached to management labor.

As an example, we consider the Hebei Hangang Iron & Steel Group Co., Ltd (hereinafter referred to as "Hangang"). Hangang is an oversized provincial iron and steel joint enterprise established in 1958 in Handan, Hebei. The company consists of 30 plant units, more than 30 offices and 40,000 employees. Its total assets are ¥21 billion. In 1999 its profits and taxes were ¥1.12 billion. In the 40 years from 1958 to 1998, this enterprise had 17 years of losses, its accumulated losses amounting to ¥172 million. Taking 1990 as a turning point, Hangang's development history changed, indicating the important role of management labor in the creation of enterprise value.

In 1990, Hangang's steel production was only 1.1 million tons, its sales income was ¥1.02 billion, profits plus taxes were ¥210 million, profits were ¥1 million, total assets were ¥2.2 billion, net assets were ¥580 million, the debt ratio was 70%, and there was a single product variety. By 1999 steel production had jumped to 3.52 million tons, sales income was ¥8.12 billion, profits and taxes were ¥820 million, profits were ¥780 million, total assets were ¥19.9 billion, net assets were ¥9.6 billion, and the debt ratio dropped to 49.5%.

In 1991, Hangang adopted Deng Xiaoping theory, putting into practice a series of principles and policies issued by the Party Central Committee and State Council on building good state-owned enterprises, adapted to the objective requirements of the socialist market economy. The company implemented an economic operation mechanism which it termed "simulating market accounting, executing cost veto," and achieved remarkable economic and social benefits. Hangang used to be a medium-sized steel enterprise with backward equipment and causing serious pollution, which could only produce ordinary construction-grade steel and was on the verge of collapse. It has become a modern large-scale enterprise with first-class equipment and a beautiful environment, producing mainly sheet and plate steel, whose economic results place it among the top firms in the national metallurgical industry.

The company has been a shining example on the industrial front. In January 1996, the state council issued a circular calling for the Hangang experience to be learned and promoted all over the country, leading to an upsurge in learning from Hangang and provoking state-owned enterprises to change their operational mechanisms and strengthen enterprise management.

Hangang's management experience includes four aspects: first, a reform of the enterprise internal price system; second, the calculation of target costs by studying market prices; third, the decomposition of cost indicators and their assignment to individuals; four, rigorous cost assessments combined with the imposition of a cost veto. This can be summed up in four key phrases: market, backward calculating, veto, and the whole.

The reform of the internal price system and replacement of state-allocated prices with market prices

Previous accounting practices in Hangang established the corporate headquarters as the accounting center. Accounting in secondary plants was based on an internally allocated price without reflecting changes in the market. When there were major changes in market prices, headquarters rapidly came under pressure from the market while secondary plants did not feel this pressure since they were affected by the distorted information of planned price. This led to the abnormal phenomenon that the branches would report earnings while the company reported losses.

Based on this situation, Hangang's managerial staff first reformed the internal price system. They abandoned the original internal planned price for transferring intermediate and semi-finished products among secondary plants, and replaced it with an internal settlement price, calculated in accordance with the prevailing market price, for settling accounts for labor supply and material acquisition. They built a "stimulating market" within the enterprise linked to the external market, to reflect the pressure of price fluctuations in raw materials. Management labor is thus used to study the market price of raw materials and labor, devise a reasonable internal settlement price system, and dynamically adjust the system over certain periods to reflect changes in market price.

"Backward calculating" to determine target costs

Previous cost accounting adhered to the "sequential calculation" method; product cost was calculated in accordance with the process sequence from front to back, the cumulative cost being the target cost of a product. This target cost only reflected actual consumption in the internal production process, which differed substantially from the cost index of the market. Hangang managers adopted a new method, which defined product price based on the prices accepted by the market, and calculated the target cost of each process from back to front following the process sequence in reverse, so as to recover potential cost savings and provide for the realization of target costs with well-defined profits. The formula is thus:

Product target cost = accepted product market price
– product expenses for the period
– target profit.

The cost forecast of Hangang's φ14mm round steel is an example. The accepted product market was determined to be ¥2,200/ton; the expenses of the period were calculated at ¥238/ton; and the product's target profit margin was fixed at ¥389 /ton. This leads to a target cost of 200– 238–389 = ¥1,573/ ton. Then the difference between the actual cost and target cost is calculated, that is, ¥1,627/ton (actual cost) – ¥1,573/ton (target cost) = ¥54/ton. Finally, the cost is reduced by ¥54/ton in every process. The function of management labor here is to analyze the technical indicators of each process, identify practical and feasible ways to reduce costs, and implement savings to reach the target cost.

Delegation combined with responsibility in cost control

After determining target costs, the next task was delegation and implementation. On the basis of the target cost determined by head office, secondary plants further delegated work to specific locations in accordance with the cost components. This method was described by the phrase "vertically to the bottom and horizontally to the edge," as a way of delegating target cost.

Rigorous assessment and cost veto

Rigorous assessment is required to establish an effective incentive and restraint system, by ensuring that the labor contribution of persons in charge is ascertained. Rigorous assessment is based on a veto, reflected in the "four don'ts": don't compromise, don't practice favoritism, don't focus on objectivity, and don't engage in "just this once."

Many economic and technical indicators figure in assessment, such as product quality, output, consumption quotas, and cost. The veto is only implemented in relation to cost indicators. If cost targets are not achieved, all bonuses are removed. Management's function is to realize costs below target and honor labor contributions to cost reduction.

Summary

Hangang's changes constitute a comprehensive management system in which cost management is the core which drives other management functions, including planning, organizing, leading, and controlling. It is applied not only in overall enterprise management, but to every management activity. For example, the work of making clear responsibilities and delegating implementation includes these four functions. Without planning, delegated indicator targets cannot be met on time with high quality; without organizing, indicators cannot be delegated systematically; without leading, departments do not coordinate; without controlling, indicators cannot be delegated smoothly and reasonable adjustments cannot be put into effect when new situations are encountered. The consequences are described below.

First, economic and technical indicators are rising. Cost indicators have declined year on year. In the first year they fell by 6.36% and from 1995 to 1998 by 5% per year. Profit indicators have risen qualitatively. Profit in 1990 was ¥1 million; in 1998 it was ¥503 million. From 1991 to 1998, total profits were ¥3.853 billion, accounting for 85% of the total profit over 41 years. Energy consumption and quality indicators are improving. In 1998, Hangang reached the top three enterprises for 26 of the 40 indicators used by the metallurgical industry. Comprehensive energy consumption in the production of one ton of steel is 805 kg/ton, about 270 kg/ton less than the average in this industry; the stable coefficient of product quality was 100%.

Labor productivity indicators have also risen qualitatively. Unit labor productivity rose from ¥20,473/year to ¥100,752/year, and per capita output labor productivity from 41 ton/year to 121 ton/year.

Promoting the Hangang experience caused steel costs in the metallurgical industry to greatly reduce, leading to steel price reductions. The whole industry has improved, and cheap and good-quality steel is being provided for the national economy.

Second, a solid foundation has been laid for management work in the enterprise. The delegation of targets and indicators has led to higher and stricter requirements from enterprise management. After several years of experience, fruitful work has been done in calculating, environmental protection, information dissemination, setting quotas, and on-site management, laying a solid foundation for basic management work.

Third, the cohesion of enterprise workers has been strengthened. Eight years of strict management activities have greatly raised the enthusiasm of workers. Under the principle of more pay for more work, cohesion has improved, and with it the cultural and professional quality of the workers. Furthermore, the work effectiveness of the staff and workers has also been strengthened, and the coordination of people in different departments has been enhanced, which is good for value creation by labor.

Empirical analysis of value creation by management labor with market value as reference

We have pointed out that there are two functions of management labor, one of which can form definite materialized external objects. Although they are the output of intangible intellectual work, realized in varying media, such outputs, for example decisions and action plans, have a definite use value. Their successful deployment depends on implementation by other managers, but the value thus created can be measured. The criterion is the market value provided by independent management consultancy companies.

In principle, such decision-making schemes or plans should be produced inside enterprises. Since they exist in a social environment which is constantly changing, their managers should be able to respond quickly to changes, develop action plans, and put them into effect. However, some enterprises have limited resources, so their managers' qualities and talents are insufficient for these purposes. They look for remedies outside the enterprise. Once such demand arises, a market supply also emerges, and specialized external management consultancy companies come into being.

Management consultancy means the diagnosis and assessment of operational and management problems in the enterprise, with the aim of improving the enterprise's operation and enhancing profits. Its content includes making development plans and policies; evaluating aims and strategies; producing medium and long-term plans and marketing strategies; production management, financial management, budget control, personnel management, training, and selection; economic information, research into the operational environment, and environmental protection.

Generally speaking, management consultancy involves two work processes: analysis and diagnosis, and program formation and report submission. The final outcome is thus the consultancy report; implementation remains with the enterprises. Sometimes the consultant provides helpful suggestions for implementation.

Consultancy involves the same kind of labor as management within the enterprise. So it is practical to use its market value to approximate the value created by management. If specialized management consultancy companies are taken as a benchmark, the value created by management labor in the enterprise is quite dramatic. In 2000, the annual revenue of McKinsey & Company was $3.4 billion and of Accenture, $10.3 billion (Li 2003, pp. 51–2). The value of the global consultancy market is estimated to have reached £116 billion in 1999, which included £50 billion in the American market, £36 billion in Europe, and £30 billion in the remainder (Sadler 2003, p. 36). In mainland China, it is estimated that the revenue of classical management consultancy companies may reach ¥3.2–5.9 billion annually; IT management consultancy companies may attain ¥9.7–17.9 billion. Currently, no classical management consultancy company has an annual revenue greater than ¥100 million (Li 2003, p. 53).

Let us assume that in the enterprise as a whole, the two kinds of management each account for 50%, and that the outsourced part of the first kind of management is one-third that produced inside the enterprise. Taking the

United States in 1999 as an example, the value of its consultancy market was £50 billion, or $80.9 billion at 1999 exchange rates. US gross domestic product (GDP) was $9,237 billion, while gross consultancy market value accounted for 0.875% of GDP. Since this gross consultancy market value is one-sixth of the value created by management as a whole, we can estimate total value created by management at $323.6 billion, or 3.5% of GDP.

References

Note: the authors of this book cited many Chinese translations of Western titles. The convention that we have tried to follow is to cite the original Western versions where they are the source of quotes or where they are standard works, especially Marxist works, but to cite the Chinese versions where it is important to recognize that the authors consulted these in translation. In some cases, these two requirements conflict. Therefore, whilst we have taken every precaution, on some occasions the page numbers cited in the text may not correspond to those in the English editions.

Aglietta, M. 1979. *A Theory of Capitalist Regulation: The US experience.* London: New Left Books.

Aquinas, St Thomas. 2017. *Summa Theologica*, ed. J. E. Stief. Privately published.

Aristotle, 2003. the *Nicomachean Ethics.* [In Chinese.] Beijing: The Commercial Press.

Aristotle, 2007. the *Politics.* [In Chinese.] Beijing: The Commercial Press.

Bade, O. 1985. *An Introduction to Marxist Political Economy.* London: Zed Books.

Bai, B. 1999. *Value and Price Theory.* [In Chinese.] Beijing: China Economic Press.

Bai, B. 2001. "The duality of the category of labor and production in Marxist philosophy and its unification." [In Chinese.] *Contemporary Economic Studies*, no. 5, pp. 5–11.

Bai, B. 2002. *Hot Issues in Value of Labor.* [In Chinese.] Beijing: Economic Science Press.

Bai, B. 2003. *Labor and Value of Wealth.* [In Chinese.] Beijing: China Economic Press.

Bastiat, F. [1850]/1996. *Economic Harmonies.* trans. W. Hayden Boyers, ed. G. B. de Huszar, intro. by Dean Russell Irvington-on-Hudson, N.Y.: Foundation for Economic Education. http://oll.libertyfund.org/titles/bastiat-economic-harmonies-boyers-trans1995 (Accessed September 14, 2018).

Baumol, W. 1967. "Performing arts: the permanent crisis." *Business Horizons*, vol. 10, issue 3, pp. 47–50.

Baumol, W. 1974. "The transformation of value: what Marx 'really' meant – an interpretation." *Journal of Economic Literature*, vol. 12, no. 1, pp. 51–62.

Böhm-Bawerk, E. 1936. *Karl Marx and the Close of His System.* [In Chinese.] Beijing: The Commercial Press.

Böhm-Bawerk, E. 1959. *Capital and Interest: A critical history of economic theory.* [In Chinese.] Beijing: The Commercial Press.

Black, F., and Scholes, M. 1973. "The pricing of options and corporate liabilities." Journal of Political Economy, vol. 81, no. 3, pp. 637–54.

Blaug, M. 1979. *Economic Theory in Retrospect*, 3rd edn. Cambridge: Cambridge University Press.

Campbell, A. 1997. "The transformation problem : a simple presentation of the 'new solution.'" *Review of Radical Political Economics*, vol. 29, no. 3.

Cao, P. 1999. *Studies on China's Newspaper Group Development.* [In Chinese.] Beijing: Xinhua Press.

Chen, C., and Liang, C. 2003. "On the value creation in management and value distribution," pp. 318–30 in Cheng Enfu (ed.), *Labor, Value and Distribution.* [In Chinese.] Hefei: Anhui University Press.

Chen, D. 2002. "Labor theory of value and income distribution," pp. 263–74 in H. Jun and F. Jianxin (eds.), *Deepening Understanding of the Labor Theory of Value.* [In Chinese.] Beijing: Economic Science Press.

Chen, M. 2003. *A Coursebook on the History of Economics.* [In Chinese.] Beijing: Renmin University Press.

Chen, X. (ed.) 2000. *World Service Trade – Principles, Policies and Industries.* [In Chinese.] Shanghai: Lixin Accounting Press.

Chen, X., et al. (eds). 2002. *New Developments in Management Science.* [In Chinese.] Beijing: Science Press.

Chen, Y. 2003. "Science and technology, S & T labor and value creation, "
pp. 330–45 in E. Cheng (ed.), *Labor, Value and Distribution*. [In Chinese.]
Hefei: Anhui University Press.

Chen, Z. 2002. "Do not abandon Marx's value transformation theory," pp.
151–65 in J. Hu and J. Fan (eds.), *Deepening Understanding of Labor Theory
of Value*. [In Chinese.] Beijing: Economic Science Press.

Cheng, E. 1995. "Productive Management Activities are Productive Labor
that Creates Value." [In Chinese.] *Journal of Social Sciences*, no. 7: 20-22.

Cheng, E. 1997. *A Review of Western Property Theory*. [In Chinese.]
Beijing: Contemporary China Press.

Cheng, E. 1999. *An Introduction to Cultural Economics*. [In Chinese.]
Shanghai: Shanghai Finance and Economics University Press.

Cheng, E. 2000. "Establishing the monism on the new living labor value,"
pp. 177–85 in J. Hu and J. Fan (eds.), *Deepening Understanding of Labor
Theory of Value*. [In Chinese.] Beijing: Economic Science Press.

Cheng, E. 2001 "The Scientific Recognition and Development of the
Theory of Labor Value--On Establishing 'the New Labor Theory of Value.'"
[In Chinese.] *The Study of Finance and Economics, no*.11: 3-9.

Cheng, E. 2001. "Establishing a "new labor theory of value," in J. Hu
and J. Fan (eds.), *Deepening Understanding of Labor Theory of Value*. [In
Chinese.] Beijing: Economic Science Press.

Cheng, E., and G. Wang. 2002. "Review of the theory and reality of
exploitation." [In Chinese.] *Journal of Beijing Normal University*, vol. 6.

Cheng, E., and G. Wang. 2003. "Comments on Current Exploitation
Theory and Reality." [In Chinese.] *Research on Mao Zedong and Deng
Xiaoping's Theory*, no. 6: 118-22.

Cheng, E., and Gu, Y. 2001 "Monism on living labor creating value." [In
Chinese.] *Contemporary Economic Research*, no. 1, pp. 16–21.

Cheng, E., and L.Hu (eds.) 2002. *Methodology in Economics*. [In Chinese.]
Shanghai Finance and Economics University Press.

Cheng, E., and Wang, G. 2002. "Review of the theory and reality of
exploitation." [In Chinese.] *Journal of Beijing Normal University*, vol. 6.

Cheng, E., and Wang, G. 2003. "Comments on current exploitation theory and reality." [In Chinese.] *Research on Mao Zedong and Deng Xiaoping's Theory*, no. 6, pp. 118–22. Shanghai: Shanghai Finance and Economics University Press.

Cheng, E., and Y. Gu. 2001 "Monism on Living Labor Creating Value." [In Chinese.] *Contemporary Economic Research, no.*1: 16-21.

China Labor Statistical Yearbook. 2002. [In Chinese.] Beijing: China Statistics Press.

China Statistical Yearbook on Science and Technology, 1992. 1993. China Statistical Press,

China's Cultural Industry between 2001-2002. [In Chinese.] Beijing: Social Science.

China's Cultural Industry between 2001–2002. [In Chinese.] Beijing: Social Science Literature Press.

China's Cultural Industry in 2003. [In Chinese.] Beijing: Social Science Literature Press.

Cihai. 1980. [In Chinese.] Shanghai Lexicographical Publishing House.

Clark, C. 1940. 'Conditions of Economic Progress'. [In Chinese] *Theory Monthly,* No.9,7.

Cutler, A., Hindess, B., Hirst, P., and Hussain, A. (1977) *Marx's "Capital" and Capitalism Today.* London: Routledge & Kegan Paul.

Солодков,м.1985.*Non-productive Economics.* [In Chinese.] Shanghai Translation Press.

Darwin, F. (ed.) 1887. *The life and letters of Charles Darwin, including an autobiographical chapter.* London: John Murray.

Deng, X. 1993. *Selected Works of Deng Xiaoping,* Vol. 3. [In Chinese.] Beijing: People's Publishing House.

Deng, X., and Wang, S. 2002. *Modern Management on Science and Technology.* [In Chinese.] Economy and Management Publishing House.

Desai, M. 1974. *Marxian Economic Theory.* London: Gray-Mills.

Desai, R., and Freeman, A. 2011. "Value and crisis theory in the 'Great Recession.'" World Review of Political Economy, vol. 2, no. 1, pp. 35–47. ideas.repec.org/p/pra/mprapa/48645.html

Dickinson, H. D. 1956. A comment on Meek's "Note on the transformation problem." *Economic Journal*, Dec, pp. 740–1.

Ding, B. 1995. "Was Marx only halfway?" [In Chinese.] *Beijing Social Sciences*, no. 1, pp. 35–48.

Ding, B. 1999 "Studies on the transformation problem." [In Chinese.] *Social Science in China*, no. 5, pp. 21–36.

Ding, B. 2000. "Defending Marx's labor theory of value, " pp. 238–49 in J. Hu and J. Fan (eds), *Deepening Understanding of Labor Theory of Value.* [In Chinese.] Beijing: Economic Science Press.

Ding, B. 2001. "A review of Sraffa's price theory." [In Chinese.] *Contemporary Economic Studies*, no. 1, pp. 19–22.

Ding, B. 2002. "On broadening the scope of application of the labor theory of value," in J. Hu. and J. Fan (eds.), *Issues in Deepening the Cognition of the Labor Theory of Value.* [In Chinese.] Publishing House of Economic Science.

Dobb, M. 1955. "A note on the transformation problem," in *Economic Theory and Socialism.* London: Routledge & Kegan Paul.

Dobb, M. 1973. *Theories of Value and Distribution Since Adam Smith.* London: Cambridge University Press.

Dongfang, Y. 2002. *Management of Southern Cosmopolis.* China Finance and Economic Press.

Duan, Y. 2003. *Incentivism, Model and Practical Guide to Stock Right.* [In Chinese.] Beijing: Economic Management Press.

Duménil, G. 1980. *Valeur aux Prix de Production.* Paris: Economica.

Duménil, G. 1983. "Beyond the transformation riddle : a labor theory of value." *Science and Society*, vol. 4, pp. 427–34.

Feng, W.1997. "Marx's theory of value determination and its practical significance." [In Chinese.] *Marxism and reality,* no.2:15-19.

Fine, B. 1986. *The Value Dimension.* London: Routledge & Kegan Paul.

Fitzsimmonds, J. A. , and Fitzsimmonds, M J. 2006. *Service Management. Operations, strategy, and information technology,* 5th edn. New York: McGraw Hill/Irwin.

Foley, D. 1982. "The value of money, the value of labor power and the Marxian transformation problem." *Review of Radical Political Economics,* vol. 4, no. 2.

Franz, D. 1957. *Darwin's Life and Letters.* Translated by D. Ye, and G. Meng. Beijing : The Joint Publishing Company, Ltd.

Freeman, A. 1995. "Marx without equilibrium." *Capital and Class,* vol. 19, issue 2.

Freeman, A. 2014a. "The new driver of economic and human growth: the scientific basis for the DCMS's new Creative Economy employment and output data," 14 January. https://www.academia.edu/5712049/The_new_driver_of_economic_and_human_growth_the_scientific_basis_for_the_DCMS_s_new_Creative_Economy_employment_and_output_data (accessed September 19, 2018).

Freeman, A. 2014b. [2014d]"Twilight of the machinocrats: creative industries, design, and the new future of human labour," in K. Van Der Pijl (ed.), *The International Political Economy of Production.* Cheltenham: Edward Elgar.

Freeman, A. 2014c. 'What causes booms," in A. K. Bagchi and A. C. Chaterjee (eds.), *Marxism: With and beyond Marx.* London: Routledge.

Freeman, A. 2015. "Introduction to Chris Freeman's 'Schumpeter's 'business cycles' revisited.'" *European Journal of the Social Sciences,* vol. 27, no 1–2. https://ideas.repec.org/a/ris/ejessy/0003.html (accessed September 19, 2018).

Bakhshi, H., A. Freeman and Peter Higgs *A Dynamic Mapping of the UK's Creative Industries,* NESTA, January 2013.nesta.org.uk/publications/dynamic-mapping-uks-creative-industries

Freeman, A., Pratt, A., and Naylor, R. 2008. [2008c] London: *A cultural audit.* London: London Development Agency, March. ideas.repec.org/p/pra/mprapa/9008.html (accessed September 19, 2018).

Freeman, A. and G. Carchedi. 1996. *Marx and Non-Equilibrium Economics.* Aldershot and London: Edward Elgar

Fu, J. 1995. "Summary of the symposia on labor theory of value in China." [In Chinese.] *Social Science of China,* no.5, pp. 35–44.

Fuchs, V. R. 1968. *The Service Economy*. New York: National Bureau of Economic Research.

Fuchs. R, 1968. "Productivity trends by sector and major industry group productivity differences within the service sector: a statistical analysis productivity in services: three case studies," pp. 301–3 in R. Fuchs (ed.), *Production and Productivity in the Service Industries*. New York: Columbia University Press.

Gu, S. 2001. "From distribution of commodities to labor theory of value." [In Chinese.] *Nankai Economic Review*, no.5, pp. 20–1.

Gu, S., and Liu, X. 1993. "New explanation of labor theory of value." [In Chinese.] *China Social Science,* no. 6, pp. 83–94.

Gu, Y. 1996. "Re-discussion on Living Labor is the Only Source of New Value." [In Chinese.] *Academic Monthly,* no. 11: 71-73.

Guo, G. 2001. "A rethink of the inner connections between value and price of production." [In Chinese.] *Journal of College of Shandong Management and Official Training*, no. 4, p. 53.

Guo, X. 2001. "Does service labor produce value?" [In Chinese.] *Jianghan Forum*, no. 1, pp. 35–7.

Guo, X. 2002. *History of Thoughts on Western Management*, 2nd edn. [In Chinese.] Beijing: Economic Management Press.

Han, Z., and Fu, J. (eds). 2000. *Generalized Economics: Theory of value*. [In Chinese.] Guangzhou: Guangdong Economic Press.

Harry, 2011. *History of Economic Thought (4th edition)*. [In Chinese.] Beijing: Post &Telecom Press.

He, B. (ed.) 2003. *A New Treatise on the Labor Theory of Value*. [In Chinese.] Beijing: Social Science Literature Press.

He, G. 2000. *Basic Thoughts and Theoretical Logic of the Capital Theory*. [In Chinese.] Beijing: China Economic Press.

He, X. 2000. "Talents strategy, the key factor in newspaper management and development." [In Chinese.] *Journalistic Front*, no. 8, pp. 24–7.

He, Y. 1999. *Knowledge is Power: The knowledge economies going to the frontier*. [In Chinese.] Guangdong: Guangdong Tourism Publishing House.

He, Y. et al. (eds). 2002. *Critique and Transcendence : Commentaries on western radical economics*. [In Chinese.] Beijing: Contemporary China Press.

He, Y., and Liu, L. 2002. "Evaluating time of labor by money: elaboration and comment." [In Chinese.] *Teaching and Research*, no. 5, pp. 33–36.

Hill, T. 1997. "On goods and services." *Reviewer of Income and Wealth*, vol. 23, no. 4, pp. 315–38.

Hittvail, eds.1996. *The New Palgrave Dictionary of Economics, vol. 2*. [In Chinese.] Economic Science Press.

Hodgson, G. 1982. *Capitalism: Value and exploitation – a radical theory*. Oxford: Blackwell.

Hong, Y. 1985. *Probing into Difficult Issues in "Capital"*. [In Chinese.] Jinan: Shandong Press.

Hong, Y., and Ma, Y. 2002. "Ten viewpoints on labor theory of value." [In Chinese.] *Journal of Fudan University (Social Science Edition)*, no. 2, pp. 1–5.

Howard, B. 1982. *Classical Political Economics and Marxist Political Economics*. Basingstoke, UK: Macmillan.

Howard, M., and King, J. 1985. *The Political Economy of Marx*. London: Longman.

Hu, D. (ed.). 1990. *Studies on Marx's Capital Theory by Contemporary Western Scholars*. [In Chinese.] Beijing: China Economic Press.

Hu, D. 1988. *Review of Western Economic Theories and Econometrics*. [In Chinese.] Beijing: Economic Science Press.

Hu, J. 2001. "Understanding Marx's labor theory of value." [In Chinese.] *Internal Circulation*, no. 9, pp. 5–7.

Hu, J., and Fan, J. (eds.). 2001. *Deepening the Understanding of Labor and Theory of Labor and Value*. [In Chinese.] Beijing: Economic Science Press.

Hu, J., and Fan, J. (eds.). 2002. *Some Key Issues during the Process in Deepening the Understanding of Labor Theory of Value*. [In Chinese.] Beijing: Economic Science Press.

Hu, Z. 2002. *A Practical Guide to Copyright Economics*. [In Chinese.] Beijing: China Economic Press.

Huang, B. 2003. *Studies on Risk Management of Stock Options and Corporate Finance.* [In Chinese.] Beijing: China Finance and Economics Press.

Huang, S. 2000. *Service Sector and Economic Growth.* [In Chinese.] Beijing: Economic Science Press.

Hunt, E. K., and Schwartz, J. G. (eds). 1973. A Critique of Economic Theory: Selected readings. London: Penguin.

James, A. , and J. Mona. 2003. Service Management. [In Chinese.] China Mechanical Industry Press.

Japanese Data Compiler Center of the Chinese Research Association. 1983. *On Das Capital: Materials on Capital in Japanese,* issue 3. [In Chinese.]

Jiang, L., Xie., S. et al. (eds). 2002. *Report on the Development of China's Cultural Industry between 2001–2002.* [In Chinese.] Beijing: Social Science Literature Press.

Jiang, L., Xie., S. et al. (eds). 2003. *Report on the Development of China's Cultural Industry in 2003.* [In Chinese.] Beijing: Social Science Literature Press.

Jiang, X. 1996. "How to adhere to and develop labor theory of value in the context of modern market economy." [In Chinese.] *Development of Economics,* no. 4, pp. 4–12.

Jin, B. 2002. *Newspaper Economics.* [In Chinese.] Beijing: Economic Management Press.

Jones, G. R., George, J. M., Barrett, M., and Honig. B. 2003. *Contemporary Management,* 4th edn. Melbourne, Vic.: McGraw-Hill Australia.

Junankar, P. N. 1982. *Marx's Economics.* Oxford: Philip Allan.

Kliman, A. 2007. *Reclaiming Marx's "Capital": A refutation of the myth of inconsistency.* Lanham, MD: Lexington Books.

Kliman, A., and McGlone, T. 1999. "A temporal single-system interpretation of Marx's value theory." *Review of Political Economy,* vol. 11, no. 1.

Kotler, P. 2007. *Marketing Management.* London: Pearson Education.

Kühne, K. 1979. *Economics and Marxism.* Basingstoke, UK: Macmillan.

Kuznets , S.1999. *Economic Growth in Countries: Gross Output Value and Production Structure.* [In Chinese.] Beijing: The Commercial Press.

Lenin, V. I.]1896]. *The Collected Works of Lenin,* vol. 41. https://www. marxists.org/archive/lenin/works/cw/volume41.htm (accessed September 14, 2018).

Li, B., Wang, J., et al. (eds.). 2003. *Theory on the Appreciation of Intelligence Capital in High-Tech Enterprises.* [In Chinese.] Beijing: Enterprise Management Press.

Li, C. 2003. *Incentivism of Senior Management Staff.* [In Chinese.] Shanghai: Shanghai Finance and Economics University Press.

Li, D. 1994. "On Advanced technology creating value." [In Chinese.] *Economist.* no. 9:100-107.

Li, G. 2002. *Analysis of Input and Output in Service Industry.* [In Chinese.] Beijing: China Price Press.

Li, H., et al. 2002. "Internal management mechanism of value network based on value creation," in X. Chen (ed.), *Development of Management Science: Research Collects of Young Scholars on Management.* [In Chinese.] Beijing: New Science Press.

Li, J. 1990. *The Service Industry Economics.* [In Chinese.] Guangdong: Guangdong People's Press.

Li, J. 1998. *Knowledge Economy: A new economic form in the 21st century.* [In Chinese.] Beijing: Social Sciences Academic Press.

Li, J. 2001. "Some Problems in the Tertiary Industry and China's Modernization Construction." [In Chinese.] *Macroeconomics.* no. 10:45-49.

Li, Q. 2001. "Marxist labor theory of value and China's distribution system." [In Chinese.] *Vista of Theory,* issue 4, pp. 14–16.

Li, R. 2002a. "Commentaries on three perspectives on the debate over the transformation issue." [In Chinese.] *Studies on Socialism with Chinese Characteristics,* no. 1, pp. 59–62.

Li, R. 2002b. "Theoretical premise on the evolution from value to price of production." [In Chinese.] *Essays of Northern China,* issue 2, pp. 73–6.

290

Li, S., and Xiao, Y. 2002. "Rethinking the fallacy of 'materialized labor creating value.'" pp. 193–208 in H. Jun and F. Jianxin (eds.), *Deepening Understanding of the Labor Theory of Value.* [In Chinese.] Beijing: Economic Science Press.

Li, X. 2003*a*. *Salary Management in Enterprises.* [In Chinese.] Tianjin: Nankai University Press.

Li, X. 2003*b*. *The Truth of Consultation.* [In Chinese.] China Machine Press.

Lipietz, A. 1982. "The so-called 'transformation problem' revisited." *Journal of Economic Theory*, vol. 26, no. 1, pp. 59–88.

Liu, S. 1994. "Value transformation theory and balanced allocation of resources." [In Chinese.] *Journal of Sichuan Teachers' College* (Social Science Edition), no. 1, pp. 85–90.

Liu, X. 1994. *The Capital Theory: Value, distribution and increment.* [In Chinese.] Taijuan: Shanxi People's Press.

Lu, C. 2001. "Deepening the understanding of labor theory of value and China's distribution of income." [In Chinese.] *Contemporary Economic Studies*, no. 6, pp. 3–7.

Lu, J. 1985. "Theoretical commentary on S&T results of economic circle in Soviet Union." [In Chinese.] *Economics Information*, no. 7.

Lu, X. 2002. *S&T is the Great Source of New Value Creation.* [In Chinese.] Publishing House of Economic Science.

Luo, G. 1990. *Marxist Theory on Production and Labor.* [In Chinese.] Beijing: Economic Science Press.

Luo, J., Youxin, W., and Deqiong, L. 2002. "A theoretical reflection on value transformation." *Journal of Chongqing Institute of Commerce*, no. 2, pp. 9–11.

Ma, Y., and Cheng, E. 2002. "New research on the change rules of the quantity of value and labor productivity in Marxism." [In Chinese.] *Journal of Finance and Economics*, no. 10, pp. 43–8.

Macmillan (eds). 1996. *The New Palgrave Dictionary of Economics*, vol. 2. Basingstoke, UK: Palgrave Macmillan.

Makoto, I. 1980. *Value and Crisis.* London: Pluto Press.

Malthus, 1962. *Principles of Political Economy.* [In Chinese.] Beijing: The Commercial Press.

Mandel, E. 1974. *An Introduction to Marxist Economic Theory*, 2nd edn. London: Pathfinder.

Marshall, 1964. *Principles of Economics.* [In Chinese.] Beijing: The Commercial Press.

Marx, K. 1962. *Poverty of Philosophy.* [In Chinese.] People's Publishing House.

Marx, K. 1965. *Capital,* vol. 1. Moscow: Progress Publishers.

Marx, K. 1979. *Economics and Marxism*, Macmillan, vol. 1.

Marx, K. 1979. *Economics and Marxism*, vol. 1. Basingstoke, UK: Macmillan.

Marx, K., and Engels, F. 1974. *Karl Marx and Frederick Engels*, vol. 26(Ⅲ). [In Chinese.] People's Publishing House.

Marx, K., and Engels, F. 1972b. *Karl Marx and Frederick Engels*, vol. 4. [In Chinese.] People's Publishing House.

Marx, K., and Engels, F. 1972d. *Karl Marx and Frederick Engels*, vol. 26(III). [In Chinese.] People's Publishing House.

Marx, K., and Engels, F. 1972a. *Selection of Karl Marx and Frederick Engels*, vol. 2. [In Chinese.] People's Publishing House.

Marx, K., and Engels, F. 1972c. *Karl Marx and Frederick Engels*, vol. 26(I). [In Chinese.] People's Publishing House.

Marx, K., and F. Engels. 1972. *Karl Marx and Frederick Engels*, vol. 23. [In Chinese.] People's Publishing House.

Marx, K., and Engels, F. 1965. *Karl Marx and Frederick Engels*, vol. 3. [In Chinese.] People's Publishing House.

Marx, K., and Engels, F. 1988. *Karl Marx and Frederick Engels*, vol. 30. New York: International Publishers.

Marx, K., and Engels, F. 1994. *Karl Marx and Frederick Engels*, vol. 34. New York: International Publishers.

Marx, K., and Engels, F. 1996. *Karl Marx and Frederick Engels*, vol. 35. New York: International Publishers.

Marx, K., and Engels, F. 1998. *Karl Marx and Frederick Engels*, vol. 37. New York: International Publishers.

Marx, K., and Engels, F. 2012. *Selection of Karl Marx and Frederick Engels*, vol. 3. [In Chinese.] People's Publishing House.

Marx, K., and Engels, F. 1962. *Karl Marx and Frederick Engels*, vol. 12. [In Chinese.] People's Publishing House.

Marx, K., and Engels, F. 1979a. *Karl Marx and Frederick Engels*, vol. 46(II). [In Chinese.] People's Publishing House.

Marx, K., and Engels, F. 1979b. *Karl Marx and Frederick Engels*, vol. 46(I). [In Chinese.] People's Publishing House.

Marx, K., and Engels, F. 1984. *Karl Marx and Frederick Engels*, vol. 6. [In Chinese.] People's Publishing House.

Marx, K., and F. Engels. 2012. *Selection of Karl Marx and Frederick Engels*, vol. 3. [In Chinese.] People's Publishing House.

Marxist-Leninist Institute of Chinese Academy of Social Sciences. 1982. Materials on Marxist philosophy studies.

May, K. 1948. "Value and production price: a note on Winternitz' solution." *Economic Journal*, vol. 58, no. 232, pp. 596–9.

Meek, R. 1956a. "Some notes on the transformation problem." *Economic Journal*, vol. 66 (March), pp. 94–107.

Meek, R. 1956b. *Studies in the Labor Theory of Value*. New York: Monthly Review Press.

Meek, R. 1967. *Economics and Ideology and Other Essays: Studies in the development of economic thought.* London: Chapman & Hall.

Meek, R. 1977. *Marx and After.* London: Chapman & Hall.

Meek, R. 1982a. "From values to prices: was Marx's journey really necessary?" pp. 12033 in *Smith, Marx, and After: Ten essays in the development of economic thought.* New York: Springer.

Meek, R. 1982b. *Smith, Marx, and After: Ten essays in the development of economic thought.* New York: Springer.

Mendel, E. 1979. *An Introduction to Marxist Economic Theory.* [In Chinese.] Beijing: Commercial Press.

Meng, Y. 1999. *On the Society Field of Economics.* [In Chinese.] Beijing : China Renmin University Press.

Mill, 1991. *The Principles of Political Economy: with some of their applications to social philosophy.* [In Chinese.] Beijing: China Social Sciences Press.

Moretti, E. 2012. *The New Geography of Jobs.* New York: Mariner.

Morishima, M. 1973. *"Marx's Economics: A dual theory of value and growth."* Cambridge: Cambridge University Press.

Morishima, M., and George, C. 1978. *Value Exploitation and Growth.* New York: McGraw-Hill.

Pack, S. J. 1985. *Reconstructing Marxian Economics: Marx based upon a Sraffian commodity theory of value.* New York: Praeger.

Pei, X. 2003. *History of Western Economic Thoughts.* [In Chinese.] Beijing: China Finance and Economics Press.

Peng, B. 2001. "The contributions of Marx to the reinterpretation of labor and criticism he received." *Economic Review*, issue 1, pp. 20–23.

Philip, S. 2003. *Management Consultancy: A Handbook for Best Practice.* 2nd. Translated by S. Duan. China Labor and Social Security Publishing House.

Piketty, T. 2014. *Capital in the Twenty-First Century*, trans. A. Goldhammer. Cambridge, Mass.: Belknap Press.

Plato, 1986. *The Republic.* [In Chinese.] Beijing: The Commercial Press.

Plato, 2001. *The Laws.* [In Chinese.] Shanghai: Shanghai People's Publishing House.

Qi, G., and Cai, Z. (eds.) 2002. *History of Foreign Economic Thoughts.* [In Chinese.] Shanghai: Shanghai Finance and Economics University Press.

Qian, B. 1995. "On the duality of materialized labor. " [In Chinese.] *Academic Monthly*, no.7: 21-26.

Qian, B. 2001. "Theoretical Considerations on a Deeper Understanding of Labour Value. " [In Chinese.] *Journal of Xiamen University(A Quarterly for Studies in Arts & Social Sciences*, no.2: 30-35.

Qian, B., and Wang, L. 1999. "Denying the value created by materialized labor equates denying Marx's labor theory of value." [In Chinese.] *Economic Review*, no.2: 8–12.

Qian, J. 2001. *Theory of Value.* [In Chinese.] Beijing: Social Science Literature Press.

Ramos-Martínez, A. and Rodríguez-Herrera, A. 1996. 'The Transformation of Values into Prices of Production: A different reading of Marx's text', in Freeman and Carchedi (1996).

Report of S & T Development of China (2001). 2000. Beijing: Social Sciences Academic Press.

Research Team of "Research Study on China's Scientific and Technological Development". 2000. *Research Study on China's Scientific and Technological Development 2000: Globalization of S & T and Challenges China Is Facing.* Beijing: Social Science Literature Press.

Research Team of the Institute of Economics at CASS. 2001. "Probing into the issues concerning socialist labor and labor theory of value." [In Chinese.] *Economic Studies*, no. 12: 33–41.

Review of Western Economic Thoughts. Issue 1. 1984. Commercial Press.

Ricardo, D. [1817] 2004. *On the Principles of Political Economy, and Taxation.* Carmel, Ind.: Liberty Fund.

Robert, S. 1991. *Analysis on Economic Growth Factors.* [In Chinese.] Beijing: Commercial Press.

Robinson, J. 1950. "Review on Karl Marx and the Close of His System by Eugen von Böhm-Bawerk and Böhm-Bawerk's Criticism of Marx by Rudolf Hilferding." *The Economic Journal*, June.

Roemer, J. 1981. *Analytical Foundations of Marxian Economic Theory.* Cambridge: Mass.: Cambridge University Press.

Rowthorn, Bob.1980. *Capitalism, Conflict and Inflation.* London: Lawrence and Wishart.

Sadler, P. 2003. *Management Consultancy: A handbook for best practice*, 2nd edn. London: Kogan Page.

Samuelson, P. 1957. Wages and interest: a modern dissection of Marxian economic models." *American Economic Review*, vol. 47, no. 6, pp. 884–912.

Samuelson, P. 1971. 'Understanding the Marxian Notion of Exploitation: A Summary of the So-Called 'Transformation Problem' Between Marxian Values and Competitive Prices', *Journal of Economic Literature*, 9(2), 399-431.

Samuelson, P. 1987. *Economics*, 2nd edn. New York: McGraw-Hill.

Samuelson. 1957. "Wage and Interest: A Modern Analysis of Marxian Economic Model." [In Chinese.] *The American Economic Review*, no. 12: 888.

Say, J.-B. [1821] 2001. *A Treatise on Political Economy*, trans. and intro. M. Quddus and S. Rashid. New York: Transaction.

Senior, 1997. *An Outline of the Science of Political Economy*. [In Chinese.] Beijing: The Commercial Press.

Seton, F. 1982. "Issues of value transformation." *Review of Economic Studies*, vol. 24, pp. 149–60.

Shaikh, A. 1977. "Marx's theory of value and the 'transformation problem.'" www.anwarshaikhecon.org/sortable/images/docs/publications/political_ economy/1977/1-Marx%27s%20Theory%20of%20Value%20and%20 the%20%27transformation%20Problem%27.pdf (accessed September 14, 2018).

Shaikh, A. 1984. "Transformation from Marx to Sraffa,, in E. Mandel and A. Freeman (eds.), *Ricardo, Marx, Sraffa*. New York: Verso. https:// marxismocritico.com/2013/09/30/ricardo-marx-sraffa/ (accessed September 14, 2018).

Shi, K. 1999. "Discussions on the exploitation standards." [In Chinese.] *Economic Perspectives*, no. 8, pp. 14–17.

Shi, Z. 2002. *Labor and Value in Modern Enterprise: Modern expansion of Marx Value Theory*. [In Chinese.] Shanghai: Shanghai People's Press.

Smith, A. [1776] 2007. *An Inquiry into the Nature and Causes of the Wealth of Nations*, ed. S. M. Soares. Metalibri online edition. www.ibiblio.org/ml/ libri/s/SmithA_WealthNations_p.pdf (accessed September 14, 2018).

Society of S & T of Hubei Province and Association of Social Science
at Hubei. (eds). 1984. *The Value and Characteristics of S & T Labor.* [In
Chinese.] Wuhan: Wuhan University Press.

Sholokhov, M. 1985. *Non-Productive Economics.* [In Chinese.] Shanghai:
Shanghai Translation Press.

Song, C. 1997. *Contemporary Western Economics: Micro-economics.* [In
Chinese.] Shanghai: Fudan University Press.

Song, H. 1998. "A Note on the International Division of People's Daily." [In
Chinese.] *International Journal of Communication,* no. 1, pp. 42–5.

Song, T. 2002. "A Note on the International Division of People's Daily." [In
Chinese.] *Contemporary Economic Research,* no. 11:11-15.

Song, Z. 1997. *A Revisit to Marxist Economic Theory.* [In Chinese.] Beijing:
Economic Science Press.

Spencer, P. 1985. *An Introduction to Marxian Economics.* New York:
Praeger.

Sraffa, P. 1979. *Production of Commodities by Means of Commodities:
Prelude to a critique of economic theory.* Cambridge: Cambridge University
Press.

Statistical Abstracts on Science and Technology of China in 1989. 1989.
China Statistical Press.

Steedman, I. (ed.) 1981. *The Value Controversy.* New York: Verso.

Steedman, I. 1977. *Marx after Sraffa.* London: NLB and Verso.

Steven, D., and B. Lawrence. 1996 *The New Palgrave Dictionary of
Economics.* [In Chinese.] Economic Science Press.

Su, X. 1995. "Debate about the monism on labor theory of value: response
to Gu Shutang and Liu Xin." [In Chinese.] *Economic Universe,* no. 7, pp.
14–18.

Sun, X., et al. (eds). 1995. *Analyses and Comments on S & T Development.*
[In Chinese.] Beijing: Petroleum Industry Press.

Sun, Y., et al. (eds). 2003. *Management.* [In Chinese.] Beijing: Tsinghua
University Press.

Sweezy, P. [1942]1993. *The Theory of Capitalism Development: Principles of Marxian political economy.* New York: Monthly Review Press.

Sweezy, P. ed. 1949. *Karl Marx and the Close of His System by Eugen von Bohm-Bawerk and Bohm-Bawerk' Criticism of Marx by Rudolf Hilferding.* Augustus M Kelly.

Sweezy, P. M., Böhm-Bawerk, E. von, and Hilferding, R. 1984. *Karl Marx and the Close of His System & Böhm-Bawerk's Criticism of Marx.* New York: Orion.

Tang, G. 2001. "Marx's Labor Theory of Value and Contemporary Era." *Academic Journal of Hebei university of economics and business,* no. 3: 9-14.

Tang, M. 2003. "On the measurement of the value of complex labor and the realization of value." *Consumer Economics,* no. 3, pp. 61–4.

The Japanese dada Compiler Center of the Chinese Research Association. 1983. *On Das Capital: Materials on Capital in Japanese.* [In Chinese.] Issue 3.

The New Palgrave Dictionary of Economics. 1996. [In Chinese.] Economic Science Press.

Thomas, A., 2013. *The Summa Theologica.* [In Chinese.] Beijing: Commercial Press.

Visser, B. "Organizational Communication Structure and Performance." *Journal of Economic Behavior and Organization*(42): 231-52.

Visser, B. 2000. "Organizational communication structure and performance." *Journal of Economic Behavior and Organization,* vol. 42, pp. 231–52.

Wang, D. 2001. "Rethinking the role of exploitation theory and practice." *Journal of Northeast Normal University,* issue 4.

Wang, F., and D. Li.2003. *Management.* [In Chinese.] China Renmin University Press.

Wang, F., and Li, D. 2003. *Management.* [In Chinese.] Beijing, China Renmin University Press.

Wang, J., and Deng, E. (eds). 2003. *A Coursebook on Management.* [In Chinese.] Beijing: Tsinghua University Press.

Wang, P. (ed.) 2003. *Doing Management Consulting in China.* [In Chinese.] Beijing: China Mechanical Engineering Press.

Wang, S. 1996. *Leading Industry of 21st Century: The fourth industry.* [In Chinese.] Jinghua Press.

Wang, S. 2001. *Appraisal of the Value of High-Tech Industries.* [In Chinese.] Beijing: CITIC Press.

Wei, X. 2001. "On deepening the understanding of labor and labor theory of value." [In Chinese.] *Macro-Economic Review*, no.3, pp. 3–8.

Wei, X. 2002. "Exploitation under Marxist writers and China's situations," in H. Jun and F. Jianxin (eds.), *Deepening Understanding of the Labor Theory of Value.* [In Chinese.] Beijing: Economic Science Press.

Wei, Z. 2002. *Investment in Stock Options.* [In Chinese.] Beijing: China Finance and Economics Press.

Winternitz, J. 1948. "Value and prices: a solution of the so-called transformation problem." *Economics Journal*, vol. 58, no. 230, pp. 276–80.

Wolff, D. 1984. "Antonino Callari and Bruce Roberts : a Marxian alternative to the traditional "transformation problem." *Review of Radical Political Economics*, vol. 16, nos. 2/3, pp. 118–26.

Wright, E. O. 1979. "The value controversy and social research." *New Left Review*, vol. 1, no. 116.

Wu, X. 1998. "Materialized labor cannot create value and surplus value." [In Chinese.] *Economic Review*, no. 3, pp. 6–12.

Wu, Y. 2001. "Adhering to and developing labor theory of value." [In Chinese.] *Forum*, no. 2, pp. 13–15.

Wu, Z. 2001. "Dialectics of Marx's Capital theory and joint labor theory of value." [In Chinese.] *Contemporary Economic Studies*, issue 6, pp. 7–11.

Wu, Z. 2002. *Management*, 4th edn [In Chinese.] Beijing: Economic Management Press.

Wu, Zhao., et al., eds. 2002. *Management.* 4th ed. [In Chinese.] Beijing: Economic Management Press.

Xenophon, 2014. *Economics* and *De Vectigalibus.* [In Chinese.] Beijing: The Commercial Press.

Xi, Z. 2002. "On value creation by materialized labor and living labor." [In Chinese.] *Economic Review*, issue 1, pp. 3–9.

Xiang, Q. 2001. "Marxist Economy and Modern Situation." [In Chinese.] *Theoretical Front in Higher Education.* Issue 9:42-50.

Xie, F. 2000. "Commentaries on Marx's value transformation theory by Western scholars." [In Chinese.] *Teaching and Research*, no. 10, pp. 19–26.

Xu, D. (ed.) 1983. *Studies on the Capital Theory.* [In Chinese.] Jiangsu People's Press.

Xu, X. 2002. "A Historical Survey of Labor Value." [In Chinese.] *Journal of Henan University(Social Science)* . Issue 1:45-49.

Yan, P. 2002. "A review and reflection on the debate about labor theory of value," In *Deepening Understanding of Labor Theory of Value*, edited by J. Hu., and J. Fan.

Yan, P. 2002. "How to understand labor and labor theory of value: pros and cons and reconstruction," in H. Jun and F. Jianxin (eds), *Deepening Understanding of the Labor Theory of Value.* [In Chinese.] Beijing: Economic Science Press.

Yan. Z. 2001. "Revisit to Marx's labor theory of value." [In Chinese.] *Developments of Economics*, no. 3, pp. 18–22.

Yang, C. 2002. *Macro-Income Distribution in Transitional Economy.* [In Chinese.] Beijing: China Labor and Social Security Press.

Yang, G. 2001. "The role of S & T in creating value." [In Chinese.] *People's Daily*, August 21.

Yang, G. 2002. "Deepening research into labor theory of value needs understand the sources of value correctly."*China Economic Issues*, no. 2, pp. 3–7.

Yang, J. 2001. "On the role of knowledge and technology in forming value." [In Chinese.] *Developments of Economics*, no. 7, pp. 36–7.

Yang, Q. 2000. "On the productive quality of management." [In Chinese.] *Qilu Journal*, no. 2, pp. 92–6.

You, L. 2000. "Some thoughts on the controversial issues of labor theory of value," in H. Jun and F. Jianxin (eds.), *Deepening Understanding of the Labor Theory of Value.* [In Chinese.] Beijing: Economic Science Press.

You, L. 2002. "The living labor is the only source of value creation," in H. Jun and F. Jianxin (eds), *Deepening Understanding of the Labor Theory of Value.* [In Chinese.] Beijing: Economic Science Press.

Yue, H. 2002. "A restudy on the transformation issue." [In Chinese.] *Contemporary Economic Studies*, no. 10, pp. 41–5.

Zhang, F., and Yang, J. 2003. *Philosophy of Management*. [In Chinese.] Beijing: Economic Management Press.

Zhang, G., and Zhang, L. 2001. *The Western Marxist Economics*. [In Chinese.] Beijing: Economic Science Press.

Zhang, L. 1988. *The General Theories on Political Economics*. [In Chinese.] Sichuan Social Science Press.

Zhang, L. 2001. "Labor creating value cannot be the basis of creating an income distribution system." *Introduction to Teaching Thoughts and Theory*, issue 7, pp. 34–6.

Zhang, L. 2002. "Understanding and developing labor theory of value," in H. Jun and F. Jianxin (eds.), *Deepening Understanding of the Labor Theory of Value*. [In Chinese.] Beijing: Economic Science Press.

Zhang, M. 1987. *Technology Marketing*. [In Chinese.] Shanghai: People's Publishing House.

Zhang, S. 2003. *Explorations into Market Economic Theory*. [In Chinese.] Chengdu: Sichuan People's Press.

Zhang, W. 2002. "the Allocation Problem in Labor Theory of Value." *Contemporary Economic Research*. Issue 2:3-6.

Zhang, X. 1999. *A Thumbnail Sketch of "Capital"*. [In Chinese.] Shanghai: Fudan University Press.

Zhang, Y. (ed.) 2003. *A Coursebook on Derivative Instruments*. [In Chinese.] Beijing: Capital Economic and Trade University Press.

Zhang, Y. 2002. "A preliminary exploration of the transformation of value in Marxism." [In Chinese.] *Theory Monthly*, no. 3, pp. 16–8.

Zhang, Y., J. Yu. and X. Zhang., ed. 2003. *A Coursebook on Derivative Instruments*. [In Chinese.] Beijing: Capital Economic and Trade University Press.

Zhao, S., et al. (eds). 2002. *Analysis of Well-Known Cases in Media Economics of China*. [In Chinese.] Beijing: Xinhua Press.

Zhao, Z. 2001. "Reflections on whether or not the management of knowledge and S&T could create value."*Developments of Theory*, no. 2, pp. 18–20.

Zheng, Z. 2000. *Exploring Value Appreciation: A study dedicated to the new century.* [In Chinese.] Beijing: Economic Science Press.

Zheng, Z. 2002. *Studies on the Validity and Development of the Labor Theory of Value.* Beijing: People's Press.

Zhou, T. 2002 "Intellectualized hi-tech means of labor also create and form value." [In Chinese.] *Research on Financial and Economic Issues*, no. 1, pp. 13–15.

Zhou, X. 2002. "Questions needing to be clarified in the debate about labor theory of value," in H. Jun and F. Jianxin (eds.), *Deepening Understanding of the Labor Theory of Value.* [In Chinese.] Beijing: Economic Science Press.

Zhu, F. 2001. "A paradox in the labor theory of value and its explanations." [In Chinese.] *Jiangsu Social Sciences*, no. 4, pp. 1–6.

Zhu, P. 1998. *A Course in Assets Evaluation.* [In Chinese] Shanghai: University of Finance and Economy Press.

Zhu, S. 2000. *Classic Economics and Modern Economics.* [In Chinese.] Beijing: Beijing University Press.

Zhu, Z. 1989. "A Problem Not Fully Addressed: How to Restore Complex Labor to Simple Labor." [In Chinese.] *The Study of Finance and Economics*, no. 4: 25-29.

Zhu, Z. 1991. *Studies on Marxist Economic Theories by Western Scholars.* [In Chinese.] Shanghai: Shanghai People's Press.

Zong, H. 1986. "How the Value and Price of Intellectual Products Determined? " [In Chinese.] *The Flag*, no. 7.